CARS OF THE FABULOUS '50s

A DECADE OF HIGH STYLE AND GOOD TIMES

Publications International, Ltd.

Louis Weber, CEO
Publications International, Ltd.
7373 North Cicero Avenue
Lincolnwood, Illinois 60712

Manufactured in China.

8 7 6 5 4 3 2 1

ISBN: 0-7853-6901-5

Library of Congress Catalog Card Number: 95-69021

Acknowledgements

Chapter-Introduction Paintings: Mitch Frumkin

PHOTOGRAPHY
The editors gratefully acknowledge the cooperation of the following people who supplied photography to help make this book possible.

Dan Lyons; Bud Davis, **Sunoco;** John M. Weir and Art Kistler, **Illinois Dept. of Transportation;** Dan Erickson, **Ford Photographic Services;** Leo Larkin, **Chicago Auto Trade Association;** Chan Bush; Bud Juneau; Ron McQueeney, **Indy 500 Photos;** Hampton Smith, **Minnesota Historical Society;** Barbara Fronczak and Brandt Rosenbush, **Chrysler Historical Society;** Helen Early and James R. Walkinshaw, **Oldsmobile History Center;** Milton Gene Kieft; Vince Mannochi; Linda Ziemer, **Chicago Historical Society;** Joseph Wherry; Richard Langworth; Sam Griffith; Brooks Stevens; Hub Willson; Debra Gust, **Curt Teich Postcard Archives, Lake County (IL) Museum;** Mike Mueller; Richard Quinn; Nicky Wright; Christopher Raab, **A&W Restaurants, Inc.;** Rick Blodgett; Christine J. Baker, **Pennsylvania Turnpike Commission;** Jack Markley and Mark McDonald **Illinois State Police;** Thomas Glatch; Steve Statham; Christina M. Purcell, **Cadillac Public Relations;** Lt. C. Gross, **Cicero Police Department;** John A. Conde Collection; Pat Witry, **Skokie Historical Society;** Mary M. Belen, **Michigan State Police;** Laura Toole, **Chevrolet Public Relations;** Daniel F. Kirchner and Peggy Dusman, **American Automobile Manufacturers Association;** Mary Keane, **Mobil Oil Corp.;** Bill Watkins; H. Russ Garrett; Rick Lenz; Joseph H. Wherry Collection; John Blake; Richard Spiegelman; Doug Mitchel; Bert Johnson; Lloyd Koening; **Houston Police Dept;** Laurel H. Kenney; Thomas A. Suszka, **New Jersey Turnpike Authority; Cinema Collectors;** Art Kistler, Kim Bartley, **White Castle System, Inc.;** Jim Frenak; Debbie Mason, **JM Family Enterprises;** Richard M. Langworth; Jean Denham, **Studebaker Museum;** Jim Thompson; David Gooley; Gary D.Smith; Fay Meek, **California Dept. of Transportation;** C. Thomas; Larry Gustin and David Roman, **Buick Public Relations;** Bill Kilborn; Jim Frenak; Jack C. Miller Collection; Jim Benjaminson; Terrell Photography; Bill Nichols and David G. Shirley, **Mitchell Corporation;** Joe Bohovic; Michael Brown; Eddie Goldberger; Jerry Heasley; Tom Storm, **Hawaii State Archives;** Robert Waggener; Peter McNicholl; Ron Moorhead; Linda Fontana, **McDonalds Corporation;** Scott Baxter; Tom Ernst; Elaine Richner, **Denny's Inc.;** Ted Clow; Steve Statham; D. Randy Riggs; Thomas Photos; Ross Tse; Scott Brandt; Charles Sullivan, **Cambridge Historical Commission;** William Cornelia; S. Scott Hutchinson; Richard Lucas; Mitch Frumkin; Ilene Shaw, Gary Rovenska and Adrienne Ross, **J.C. Whitney/Warshawsky;** Jay Peck; Phil Toy; Hub Willson; Tony Eboli; Tim Kerwin; Phillips Camera House; Michael Brown; Frank Lipo, **Historical Society of Oak Park and River Forest, IL;** Mike Moya; Gene's Studio; Al Ferreira; David Jensen; Lou Puckelis, **Chicago Motor Club; University of Akron Archives;** Mike McKernan, **Superior Coaches;** Steve Tracey, **P&S Group;** Tom McPherson, **Specialty Vehicle Press;** Barbara Dunn, **Hawaiian Historical Society;** Charlene Noyes, Harry Sweet, and Nikki Pahl, **Sacramento Archives and Museum Collection Center;** Dr. John W. Little; Joe Rodrigus, **Hanna Sherman, International;** Kim Bartley, **White Castle System, Inc.**

OWNERS
Special thanks to the owners of the cars featured in this book for their enthusiastic cooperation.

1950: Paul A. Leinbohm; Dr. Tom Eganhouse; Edward Giacobrazzi; Danny L. Steine; Loren E. Miller; Frank C. Guzzo; Dan and Barb Baltic; Roy E. Schneckloth; Wayne Laska; John Pollack; Paul and Peg Mather; Dix Helland; Ray Tomb; Clarence Becker; Joseph C. Ezell; Larry K. Landis; Roy Yost; Robert G. Seals; Donald L. Muchmore; Philomena Ronco Kohan; Arthur J. Sabin; Robert Heimstra.

1951: Tom Andrews; Jeff Walther/Jeff Walther Dodge; Rich and Norma Felschow; David Doyle; Donald W. Peters; Dells Auto Museum; Jim Stewart; Anthony J. Gullatta; Cal and Nancy L. Beauregard; Bob Ward; Earl Heintz; Edward George Allen; Earl J. Carpenter; Bill Goodsene; Bill Burgun; Bonnie and Dennis Statz; William D. Albright; Doug Burnell; William Tresize; Brook Stevens; John Keck; Chuck and Charlotte Watson; Keith Zimmerman; Jack Mueller; Victor Jacoellis; Gary McClaine; Steve Carey; Henry Smith; Jerry Jaragosky; Bonnie Carey; Henry Smith; Chuck Rizzo; Ken Netwig; Greg Pagano; James L. Dowdy; Jack Karleskind; James C. Pardo; Bobby Wiggins; Robert Rocchio; Bob Hassinger; William G. Burgun; Doug Burnell; Rosemary and Duane Sell; Steve Carey; Hudson D. Firestone; Henry Smith; Verne Leyendecker/Classical Gas; George S. Jewell.

1952: Robert Frumkin; Keith Cullen; Jerry Tranberger; John L. Murray; Alvin Buechele; Charles O. Sharpe; Bob Adams Collectibles, Ltd.; Jerry Ferguson; John R. Vorval; Richard Clements; John Sanders; Bill Burgun; Harrah National Auto Museum; Jerry Johnson; Lowell Johnson; Brooks Stevens Museum; George A. Buchinger; Phil and Louella Crus; Alan and Wilma Jordan; Steve Megyes; Lewis E. Retzer; Douglas J. Smith; Tom Mcdowell; George Pitts; Glen and Vera Reints; Edward J. Ostrowski; John J. and Minnie G. Keys; Chuck Bernecker; Bob and Brad Chandler; Homer Jay Sanders, Sr.; Robert Gernhofer; Bill Burgun; Bobby Wiggins; Carl and Mary Allen; Henry Patrick; Jerry Johnson.

1953: Bob Brannon; Bill Knudsen and John White; Briggs Cunningham Museum; Tim Graves; Stanley and Phyllis Dumes; Mitchell Corporation of Owosso; H.H. Wheeler, Jr.; William R. Lindsey; Kurt Fredricks; Gary Gettleman; F. James Garbe; Carl Noll; Norman Plogge; Dr. Ernie Hendry; John Rikert; Dorothy Clemmer; Hank Roeters; Dale and Marily Dutoni; Paul and Nancy Vlcek Jr.; Dick Choler; Bortz Auto Collection; William D. Albright; Bob Hill; Jerry Johnson; John E. Parker; Dale Osten; James Saicheck; Gerald Newton; Steve LeFevre; J. Saicheck; Dr. Douglas L. Bruinsma; Richard Presson; Deer Park Car Museum; Wayne R. Graefen; Bob and Wendi Walker.

1954: Frederick J. Roth; David Emery; Frank and Gene Sitarz; Everett Michaels; Robert Hetzel; Forrest D. Howell; Richard and Janice Plastino; Ray Ostrander; Suburban Motors, Tucson, Arizona; Ed Oberhaus; Erville Murphy; Eugene Vaughn; Thomas Armstrong; Thomas H. Peterson; Robert Babcock; Bill and Dorothy Harris; James and John Sharp; Virgil and Dorothy Meyer; Dwight Cervin; Cal and Lori Middleton; Bob Shapiro; Joe Bortz; James A. Milemak; Roger Clements; George Lucie; Jim Mueller; Ted Freeman; Norman Kirchner; Roy Umberger; Norman W. Prien; Bob Webber; Robert C. Fox; Rachel Markos; David L. Stanilla; Howard Johnson; Fritz Hugo; Jim Clark.

1955: Tom Griffith; Warren P. Lubich; George P. Valiukas; Gary Richards; Ed Tolhurst; Gary L. Walker; Greg Gustafson; Kennedith Turner; Charles M. Havelka; David L. Ferguson; Carl Herren; Nolan Adams; Bob and Frances Shaner; Vern Burkitt; Dennis Flint; Albie Albershardt; Bill Barbee; Richard Matson; William Lauer; R. McAtee; Jerry Avard; Myron Davis; Otto T. Rosenbush; Jeff and Aleta Wells; Lester Schnepen; Bob and Janet Nitz; Arthur and Suzanne Dalby; Harry Demenge; Leonard Quinlin; O'Ceola Sloan; Stuart Echols; Mervin Afflerbach; Bob Strous; Dan and Karen Bilyeu; Peter McNicholl; Alan C. Parker; Don and Sue Fennig; Tom Franks; Fred and Diane Ives; Warren P. Lubich; John Riordon; Bill and Lanee Proctor; Leroy Janisch; Mac Horst; Kennedith and Wayne Turner; Bill Groves; Joe Malta; Richard Kalinowski; Jim Cahill; Bill Curran; Gene R. Deblasio Jr.; Paul Eggerling; Ron Welch; Norb Kopchinski; Terry McElfresh; Jack Gratzianna; Clayton E. Bone; June Trombley; Tom Null; Kenneth G. Lindsey; Raymond and Marylin Benoy; Jim Wickel; Harold Gibson; Joseph R. Bua.

1956: Edmund L. Gibes; Ed Wassmann; Glendon and Betty Kierstead; Bob Adams; Burt Carlson; Robert W. Paige; Richard Brinker; A. La Rue Plotts, Jr.; B. Stevens and J. Wolfe; James C. Lipka; Roger and Connie Graeber; Jack E. Moore; Stan and Betty Hankins; Dick Rosynek; Kathy Barber; Dick Roynek; Bill Stone; Paul Hem; Art and Vicky Hoock; John and Peggy Clinton; Brian Long; Alan Wendland; Ray and Nancy Deitke; Edward R. Keshen; Dennis Hauke; M. Randall Mytar; David Barry; David Senholz; Edwin C. Kirstatter; Mary Jaeger; John V. Cavanugh; Michael Vacik; Allen Spethman; Orville Dopps; James R. Cunningham; Ron Pittman; Gary Johns; Sherry Echols; Eugene Sinda, Jr.; Jeff Dranson; Edward S. Kuziel; Dave Higby; Charles and Veronica Wurm, Jr.; Kenneth Regnier; Jim Bombard; Robert J. Matteoli; Charlene H. Arora; John Krempasky; Dr. Art Burrichter; Henry T. Heinz; Steve Williams; Jerry Kill; Dave Hill; Jay Harrigan; Chicago Car Exchange; Studebaker National Museum; Bob Peiler; David Hill; Lester H. Hooley; Donald L. Waite; Donald G. Elder; Robert Sexton; Ken Carmack; Jim Scarpitti; Wayne Davis Restoration; Hank Kubicki; Don Simpkin; William B. Edwards; Robb Petty; Don Wendel; Ross Gibaldi; Paul A. Buscemi; Russell and Shirley Dawson; Michael Vacik; Eli Lader; Sheldon Grover; Kenneth Geiger; Joseph Minnetto; Edward Ballenger II; Kenneth Ugolini; Robert Sexton.

1957: Monte McElroy; Frank R. Magyar; Eldon Anson; Robb Petty; Charles G. Roveran; Paul F. Northam; William R. Lindsey; James and Susan Verhasselt; Bob Rose; David and Ann Kurtz; Tom and Karen Barnes; Joe Bortz; Alan C. Hoff; Frank R. Bobek; Richard Zeiger, MD; Wayne Rife; Noel Blanc; Bill Ulrich; Larry Hill; Dennis McNamara; Dave Higby; Bernie and Ann Buller; Glenn R. Bappe; David L. Goetz; Dennis M. Statz; John Krempasky; Dick Hoyt; Michael Wehling; Tim and Sharon Hacker; Bernard Powell; Herbert Wehling; Donald R. Lawson; Harry E. Downing; Neil S. Black; Bob Aaron; Bud Hiler; Dr. William H. Lenharth; Terry Davies; Dale and Roxanne Carrington; Richard E. Bilter; David L. Griebling; Ken Block; Richard Carpenter; Jim D. Gregorio; Jess Ruffalo; Tom Devers; John and Susan Gray; Charles Phoenix; David Rosenfield; Vito S. Ranks; Bill Warren; Neil Vetter; John J. Oakes, Jr.; Ralph M. Hartsock; Jess Ruffalo; David Lawrence; Tom Devers; Sherwood Kahlenberg; Bob Schmidt; Ross Gibaldi; Amos Minter; Jerry Capizzi; J.W. Silveira; Fraser Dante Limited; Jim Ferrero; Julie M. Braritz; Denis Beauregard; George Swartz; Gordon Christl; John W. Petras/Classic Chrome; Brian L. Kelly; Jerry L. Keller; Glyn and Jan Rawley.

1958: Dean Ullman; George Berg; S. Holloran; J. Alexander; Maurice B. Hawa; Vern Hunt; Jack Sawyer; William Amos; Charles Hilbert; Art Gravatt; Dr. Gerrard DePersio; John P. Fitzgerald; John Scopelite; Jerry Cinotti; Barry and Barb Bales, Mario Gutierrez; Jim DiGregorio; Richard Daly; Thomas L. Karkiewicz; Bob Mongomery; Gary Mills; Wayne Essary; Marvin Wallace; Andrew Alphonso; Michael J. Morelli; Gene Povinelli; Neil W. Sugg; Christopher Antal; Jeff Ruffalo; Jim Crossen; Tim Fagan; Bob and Brad Chandler; Jim Mueller; Virgil Hudkins; Andrew Krizwan; Joel Twainten; Aaron Kahlenberg; Christopher Antal; Dennis L. Huff; Ted Maupin; Jerry Capizzi; Michael L. Berzenye; Ruth Dulik; Robert P. Hallada; Bruce Sansone; John Sobers; Michael D. McCloskey; Dean Ullman; Buddy Pepp; Darryl Salisbury; Douglas Suter; Frank Wrenick.

1959: T.L. Ary; Ted Hinkle; Bob and Roni Sue Shapiro; Dennis B. Miracky; Mervin M. Afflerbach; Bill Lauer; Richard Carpenter c/o Yesterday Once More; Jon Hardy; Bill Henefelt; Robert and Diane Adams; Wendi Walker; Charles A. Rublaitus; David Frieday; Dr. John W. Little; Dennis Huff; Edsel Ford; William R. Kipp; Steve and Dawn Cizmas; Classic Car Center; Eric Hopman; Walter J. Smith; Don R. Kreider; Harrah National Auto Museum; Glen and Fay Erb; Elmer and Shirley Hungate; J. Franklin; S. Halloran; Harold Stabe; Ray Geschke; Orville Dopps; Christine and Robert Waldock; Bob Moore; Bill Schwelitz; Joe Wenzlich; Al Schaefer; Bill Stearns; Barry and Barb Bales; Don and Bonnie Snipes.

Table of Contents

As the decade begins, automakers are still striving to meet the pent-up demand for cars that was created when the industry shut down during World War II. Studebaker debuts new "bullet-nose" models, and nearly all manufacturers prosper—but not for long.

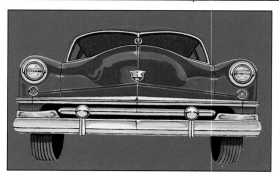

Independents Kaiser and Packard offer new designs, but most manufacturers serve up only facelifts. That's all that is needed: With the war in Korea looming, buyers fearing another shut-down keep demand high.

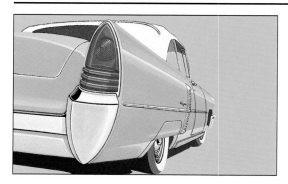

Ford, Lincoln, and Mercury all boast new styling, but their industry rankings don't improve. Despite production cutbacks by almost all automakers in the face of the Korean War, sales begin to slump, and cars start to pile up on dealers' lots.

Highlights include Chevrolet's legendary Corvette, a trio of "custom" GM ragtops, and Studebaker's classic "Loewy" coupes, but a turnaround in the seller's market causes Ford and Chevy to duke it out in a sales blitz—to the detriment of the independents.

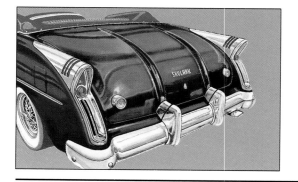

Buick and Cadillac tone down their specialty convertibles (Olds drops its version), and the public tones down its desire for Detroit's wares. In a slow-down year for the industry, Ford beats Chevrolet in the production race for the first time since '49.

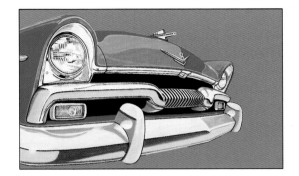

1955 .... page two-ten

A great year for the Big Three turns into a dismal year for the independents. Chrysler Corporation and GM bring out exciting new designs wrapped around powerful V-8 engines, while the independents wither—and some die.

Despite modern styling and brilliant engineering, the proud Packard nameplate graces its last luxury automobile. After record-shattering '55 sales, the industry generally coasts on the styling front, but engines get bigger and brawnier.

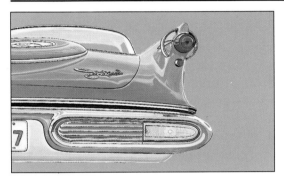

No doubt about it, the horsepower race is in full swing, and tailfins reach new heights—particularly at Chrysler Corporation, which advances its "Forward Look." Sales rebound, but the industry faces some dark days ahead.

Detroit unleashes bigger, flashier cars—just as the economy unleashes a recession. This spells trouble for most mid-priced makes, but spells *disaster* for Ford's new entry. It isn't just the "horse-collar" grille that dooms the Edsel....

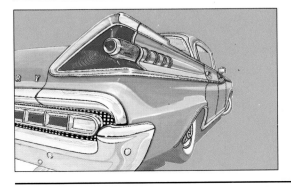

In deference to a sudden interest in economy, compacts rise in popularity and the horsepower race momentarily slows to a near standstill. But tailfins gain in prominence, even on normally conservative Ford Motor Company products.

Foreword

Looking back, the Fifties are remembered as a decade of vitality, of prosperity, of unabashed promise. Americans saw the economy zooming, babies booming—and the Cold War looming.

In our collective memories, at least, it was a time of innocence: of simple pleasures and basic values, linked with boundless enthusiasm. This was also a decade of conformity, as families scurried for security. But more than most Americans realized, these were also years of profound change. Television overtook radio as the foremost influence on popular culture. Rock 'n' roll, unheard of as the decade opened, developed into a major force. McDonald's made the scene.

Labor-saving devices filled the ranch-style homes of the growing suburbs. The Depression mentality finally was fading, elbowed aside by a "buy now, pay later" philosophy. Jobs were plentiful—until a recessionary downturn in 1958 took millions of upward-strivers by surprise.

In the friendlier Fifties, even the celebrity scandals were mild. Politicians weren't yet reviled. And the local filling station was staffed by attendants eager to wash your windshield, check your oil, fill your tank *and* your tires, and oftentimes award you a "free gift with every fill-up."

Looking deeper, we find that the decade wasn't quite so simple as people like to believe. *Ozzie and Harriet* might have served as role models for America, but not all citizens led TV-style lives. Teens were just as confused and misunderstood as in later years. Back-seat romances flourished, if unacknowledged by parents—though any suitor arriving in a Nash, with its famous "mobile motel" fold-down seats, was sure to get the cold shoulder from his date's father. Respect for authority reigned, but stirrings of rebellion began to emerge.

For those smitten with automotive fever, though, this was a singularly glorious epoch. Only Detroit had the cure, and its prescription was doled out every fall to great fanfare.

TV sets broadcast the latest shapes, radios blared the car companies' catchy jingles. Young car buffs scanned magazine pages for pictures of the spanking-new mechanical attractions. Errands demanded an end run past dealers' row, just to see if the

paper coverings had yet been torn down from the showroom windows to reveal the splendor of next year's models.

As the Fifties began, 40 million automobiles roamed American roads. Three out of five families owned one. Automakers still were trying to satiate pent-up demand for new cars. Several independent makes had sprouted, notably Kaiser and Frazer. Others had been around since before World War II: Crosley, Hudson, Nash, Packard, Studebaker, Willys. Imports trickled into American ports.

As manufacturers met—then exceeded—the nation's automotive appetite, sales began to sag. Ford and Chevrolet waged a price war in 1953 that injured the independents far more than the "Big Three" (General Motors, Ford Motor Company, and Chrysler Corporation).

Crosley, discovering that Americans weren't yet ready for sub-compacts, dropped out after 1952. Kaiser sighed its last gasp in '55. Hudson and Packard soon followed. Nash diminished to its compact Rambler spinoff. Studebaker gained a temporary reprieve only by virtue of its well-timed '59 Lark compact.

Meanwhile, the horsepower race that had begun with Rocket Oldsmobiles in '49, then escalated to Chrysler "Hemis" and Chevrolet V-8s, progressed into a leapfrogging bout. Cars, too, grew bigger—and presumably better, in a culture that tended to equate the two. Chrome oozed from every panel. Tailfins, having started small, sprouted beyond belief. The Edsel quickly came and went: a noble hope for 1958, a synonym for failure by '60.

Styling took over from engineering as the driving force behind sales. Automatic transmissions began to edge aside traditional stickshifts. Power gadgetry blossomed, climaxing with Ford's elaborate retractable hardtops.

Pillarless four-doors joined their two-door mates. Three-tone paint jobs appeared. Station wagons emerged as the vehicle of choice in growing suburbia.

This book presents it all. While automobiles serve as its hub, *Cars of the Fabulous '50s* is more than a mere "car book." Instead, it's a spirited romp through a period that's filled with fond memories for those who lived it, and inspires awe—and even disbelief—in the generations that came after.

American cars exemplified the spirit of those times: brawny and proud, hopeful and boastful, strong and special. We hope you find this tribute to the '50s as colorful and stirring as the decade itself.

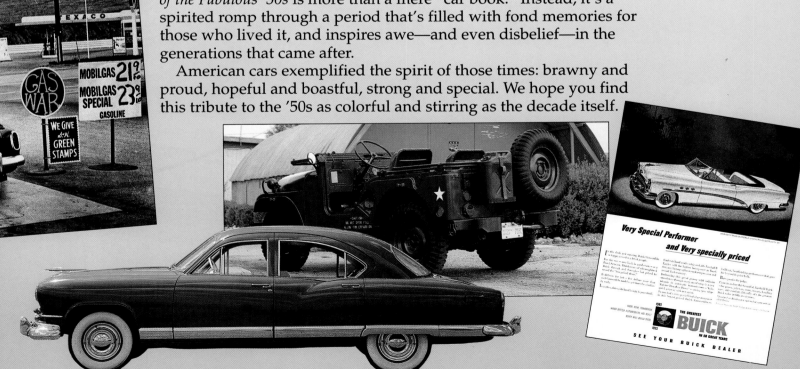

1950

America was changing rapidly as the 1950s began—and the pace was about to pick up. World War II had been over for half a decade. Memories of the Great Depression grew blurred. Families began their migration to the suburbs, which sprouted like tentacles around the nation's cities.

Kids watched Howdy Doody on 12-inch black-and-white TV sets, and spent Saturdays at 15-cartoon matinees. Rock 'n' roll hadn't yet been heard—though an occasional burst of jazz or rhythm and blues might jar the air. Sex was a private matter, violence rare. People knew their neighbors.

Veterans and civilians who'd endured privation in the past now faced a cornucopia of consumer goods—and were determined to enjoy the bounty. Women who'd toiled in factories and offices during the war resumed their roles as housewives, making

Dad—more often than not—the sole breadwinner. Even with a single salary, though, most folks had money to spend.

Incomes had risen steadily, despite a wave of strikes. Median family income topped $3300 a year. Manufacturing workers earned an average $56.20 per week—a new high. A loaf of bread cost 14 cents, pork chops ran 75 cents a pound, and a half-gallon of milk sold for 41 cents—delivered to your door.

Not every sign was positive. Unemployment hit 7 percent in January—up from 4.5 percent a year earlier, setting a postwar record. Still, the American Dream was simple enough: a good job, well-behaved family, pleasant home. Oh, and one more thing—an impressive automobile.

In the hardest of times, Americans of modest means had struggled to maintain an automobile, even if it was a jalopy. Now, men who'd once taken a streetcar to their jobs not only wanted, but *needed* a reliable car. Before long, their wives and children would be wanting one of their own.

By 1950, some 39.6 million passenger cars traveled American roads—40-percent more than in 1941. Three fifths of American families owned one, but the average car was 7.8 years old.

When World War II ended, automakers had nothing fresh to offer car-hungry Americans; they simply issued mildly revised prewar models. Studebaker was first with a completely new design, which debuted for 1947. By then, Henry Kaiser and Joe Frazer had joined forces, producing cars under both names. A year later, Hudson launched its low-slung "Step-down" design, and the new Cadillac body displayed the first tailfins.

Most automakers waited until 1949 to release redesigned models. Meanwhile, some new manufacturers tried their hand. Best known is the Tucker, of which 51 were built before legal troubles ended its day in the limelight. There was also a Davis three-wheeler, a Bobbi-Kar—even a couple of flying cars.

Chevrolet and Pontiac launched curvy new bodies for 1949. Ford chose a boxier (but tasteful) shape, while companions Lincoln and Mercury showed more roundness. Chrysler products stood steadfastly upright. Nash went wild, with an aerodynamic form that many said resembled an "upside-down bathtub."

One new body style emerged, this from GM. Called the "hardtop convertible," it melded the vitality of a convertible with the practicality of a closed coupe.

Through the late '40s, demand was stronger than automakers could hope to fulfill. By 1950, though, nearly all designs were at least a year old, and the seller's market was subsiding. Manufacturers had to deliver something fresh, something exciting, if they hoped to continue the strong sales totals.

But not yet. With only a few exceptions, facelifts were the order of the year. Most 1950 models— Chevrolet and Plymouth to Hudson and Nash— showed little more than touch-ups. Studebaker's innovative "bullet nose," for instance, led a body that differed little from its 1947-49 predecessor.

Several more automakers introduced automatic transmissions. Available in Oldsmobiles since 1940, automatics took their time in gaining converts. Chrysler products and Hudsons had *semi*-automatics, which retained a clutch but changed gears as the driver's foot let up on the gas pedal.

One-piece curved windshields appeared on more makes, such as Cadillac and Oldsmobile, joining those from '49 or before. Buick announced low-glare glass.

Because truth in advertising was not yet an issue, automakers could claim their products were the handsomest, the most frugal—or simply the best, period. Pontiac, for instance, declared its dashboard "the most beautiful in the industry." Hudson called its cars "safest" (not without validity, in view of their rigid construction).

Without quite realizing it, Oldsmobile managed to set off a "horsepower race" that would overtake the industry. All the engineers did was create a short-stroke, overhead-valve V-8: the '49 Rocket engine. Far more efficient than inline and L-head engines that powered most cars, the ohv V-8 would become the engine of choice for a new breed of driver—the hot rodder—and for millions of ordinary Americans.

Chevrolet and Ford had pondered a *small* American car, but only Powel Crosley enjoyed some triumph in that realm. After a strong 1948, however, Crosley's star began to fade, reaching the sick list by 1950. Americans liked *big* cars—a craving destined to flourish. Yet Nash took another tack, launching the first successful compact: Rambler.

Quite a few automakers cut prices on 1950 models. As a result, a whopping 6,663,461 cars (8,004,242 total vehicles) were built—an all-time record, 30 percent above the '49 total. Meanwhile, the Federal Reserve Board placed stricter limits on credit—an issue destined to rise again as incomes trailed the public's urge for automobiles.

Americans finally were managing to forget war. Then, on June 25, President Truman ordered U.S. troops to Korea in a "police action" that would last for several years. Fear of wartime shortages triggered a car-buying frenzy. In December, a "state of emergency" was proclaimed.

Auto production never halted, as it had during World War II, but certain raw materials wound up in short supply, and makers faced output limits. No matter. As 150 million Americans thirsted for private transport, Detroit was eager to provide.

1950 Chrysler

Chrysler Corporation

Chrysler products earn mild facelift of "box-on-box" shape

Company marks 25th anniversary

Longer rear fenders hold flush-mounted taillights, and back windows grow in size . . . flat two-piece windshields remain

Hardtop coupes arrive late in model year, from Chrysler, DeSoto, and Dodge

Chrysler's posh Imperial and Town & Country hardtop adopt four-wheel disc brakes

Ignition-key starter switches replace former pushbuttons

Chryslers carry six-cylinder or straight-eight engines; DeSoto, Dodge, and Plymouth have sixes only

Chrysler, DeSoto, and Dodge use semi-automatic transmissions; Plymouth sticks with plain three-speed column shift

Final "woody" station wagons go on sale

Strike begins January 25, lasts 14½ weeks—yet record 1.27 million cars are built

DeSoto's output jumps 42 percent, but market share sinks

Plymouth builds 610,954 cars, yet dips to fourth—behind Buick

Long-time president K.T. Keller is named chairman . . . "Tex" Colbert takes the presidency

1. Chrysler immodestly declared its "distinguished" New Yorker and Saratoga the "finest in the fine car field." Their 135-bhp Spitfire straight eight had "the speed of the wind." 2. Formerly a wood-structure convertible, the Town & Country became a Newport hardtop, with white-ash framing attached to steel body panels. Just 700 were built, this year only. 3. Cars wearing a Chrysler badge included the eight-cylinder New Yorker, Saratoga, T&C, and Imperial, plus Royal and Windsor sixes. 4. Leather topped foam rubber on the Safety-Cushion dashboard. At 13 mph or more, Prestomatic slipped into high gear as the driver let up on the gas.

The Beautiful 1950
CHRYSLER Town & Country
NEWPORT

TODAY'S NEW STYLE CLASSIC . . . .

> "The public likes a car that is designed primarily to ride in, with its appearance governed by its functions."
>
> *Chrysler Division general sales manager* **Joseph A. O'Malley**; *January 1950*

1. Far cheaper than an eight, the six-cylinder Windsor promised "breathtaking beauty." 2. A Newport hardtop mixed a convertible's "low-swept road-hugging lines" with steel-roofed protection. Clearbac rear windows used three sections of curved glass. 3. In addition to summer fun, a Windsor convertible promised to be "the sweetest running car in America." 4. Back when service stations made house calls, the "chaser" motorcycle was towed behind the customer's car, here a Chrysler Highlander. 5. Except up front, can you tell that this stripped "movie car" is a New Yorker?
6. Station wagons came only in the Royal series, with an all-steel or "woody" body. 7. With rear seat folded, a wagon's loading platform measured nearly 10 feet long.

1950 DeSoto

1. All DeSotos had 112-horsepower six-cylinder engines, including this $2174 Custom four-door sedan, pictured in the sales brochure. The make had been named for Spanish explorer Hernando de Soto. In addition to regular and eight-passenger sedans, DeSoto's Custom line included a wagon, hardtop coupe, club coupe, and convertible, but the sedan accounted for nearly two-thirds of production. 2. Interiors of a Custom DeSoto sedan were better appointed than those of the more utilitarian DeLuxe series. DeSoto promoted its cars' plentiful "hat room," as well as "big, wide doors [that] let you walk in . . . not wiggle in!" 3. Dashboards were recessed to allow more leg room, and the ignition key operated the starter switch. Instrument faces displayed a new metallic gold sheen. Tip-Toe hydraulic shift and Fluid Drive, standard on the Custom series, required use of the clutch only to shift into Reverse or Low gear. 4. Easy-to-operate radio and heater controls were placed "within instant reach." 5. Most Custom (shown) and DeLuxe DeSotos rode a 125.5-inch wheelbase. Minor styling revisions included a wider grille and new flush-mounted tail-lights that included the stoplight; formerly, DeSotos had a separate center-mounted stoplight.

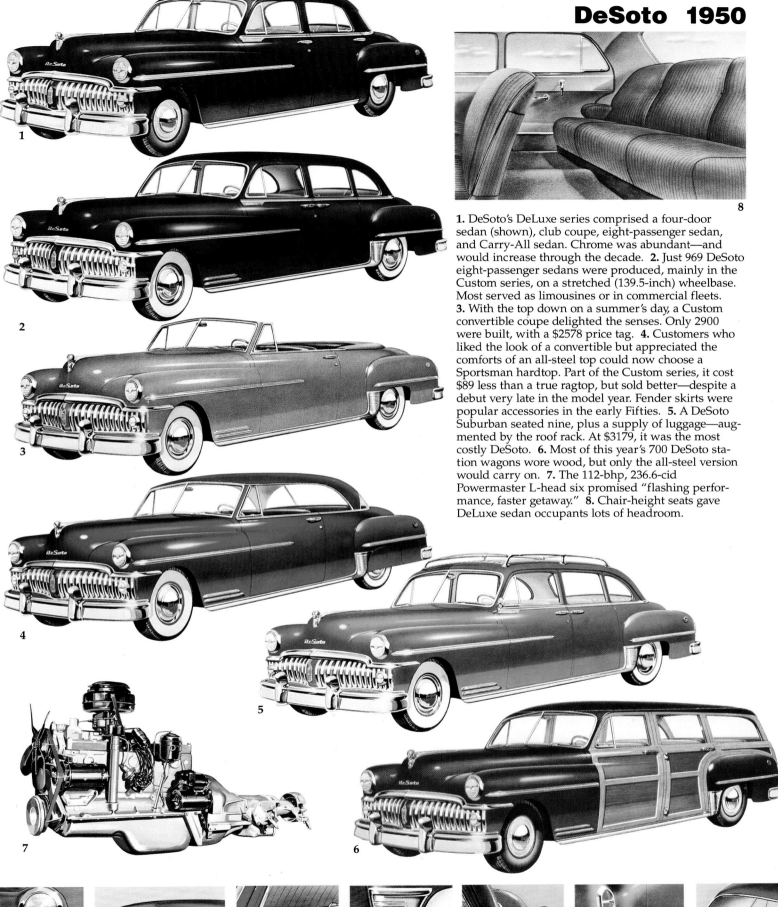

1. DeSoto's DeLuxe series comprised a four-door sedan (shown), club coupe, eight-passenger sedan, and Carry-All sedan. Chrome was abundant—and would increase through the decade. 2. Just 969 DeSoto eight-passenger sedans were produced, mainly in the Custom series, on a stretched (139.5-inch) wheelbase. Most served as limousines or in commercial fleets. 3. With the top down on a summer's day, a Custom convertible coupe delighted the senses. Only 2900 were built, with a $2578 price tag. 4. Customers who liked the look of a convertible but appreciated the comforts of an all-steel top could now choose a Sportsman hardtop. Part of the Custom series, it cost $89 less than a true ragtop, but sold better—despite a debut very late in the model year. Fender skirts were popular accessories in the early Fifties. 5. A DeSoto Suburban seated nine, plus a supply of luggage—augmented by the roof rack. At $3179, it was the most costly DeSoto. 6. Most of this year's 700 DeSoto station wagons wore wood, but only the all-steel version would carry on. 7. The 112-bhp, 236.6-cid Powermaster L-head six promised "flashing performance, faster getaway." 8. Chair-height seats gave DeLuxe sedan occupants lots of headroom.

1950 Dodge

1. Despite a shorter (115-inch) wheelbase than other models, a Wayfarer sedan also seated six. Dodge aimed the "nimble" semi-fastback—priced just above the most costly Plymouths—at "value-conscious" buyers. 2. A foursome wouldn't fit inside a Wayfarer Sportabout roadster, but it could probably carry all their clubs. Some dealers added a small rear seat to augment the three-passenger front bench. 3. Roll-up windows and vent wings could be added "at slight extra cost" to the Sportabout's $1727 base price. A mere 2903 were built. 4-5. Penny-pinchers could get a Wayfarer three-passenger coupe for just $1611, featuring a huge trunk, plus storage behind the single seat. 6. Dodge's new Coronet Diplomat hardtop cost $96 less than a convertible. 7. The rear seat in a Coronet station wagon folded forward, making a space nearly eight feet long. 8. Like Chrysler and DeSoto, Dodge had a long-wheelbase sedan with two folding seats.

1

2

3

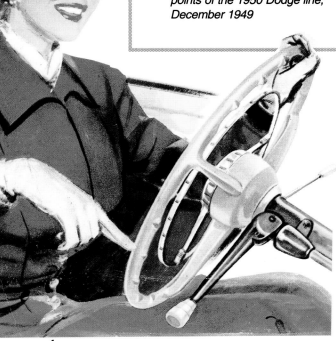

"Dodge's production and retail deliveries this year have been the highest in Dodge history. We are confident that we will do even better with our new, improved automobiles."

Dodge president
L L "Tex" Colbert, *on the plus points of the 1950 Dodge line; December 1949*

1. Like all Chrysler products, Dodge got a facelift. A Meadowbrook four-door sedan cost $79 less than a Coronet, but had the same wheelbase and 103-bhp Get-Away L-head engine. **2.** Roomy interiors allowed occupants to sit up straight "without any danger of knocking your hat off," in extra-wide seats. **3.** A restyled dashboard held three square dials and matching accessories. **4.** "Your toe does it all," Dodge claimed of its new Gyro-Matic transmission. Available only on Coronets, it had a "sprint-away" passing gear and a "power range" for steep grades. **5.** A person could enter and leave a Coronet sedan "without twisting or squirming." Because the rear footrest was fixed, leg room wasn't affected by the position of the driver's seat.

4

5

packed with value and ready to prove it!

Here's the sensational new standard for excellence in the low-priced car field — the brilliant new, value-packed Plymouth!

No other car at the price gives you anything like the new Plymouth's great engineering advantages. The speed and ease of Ignition Key starting . . . the thrilling performance of the 7.0 to 1 high compression en-gine . . . the swift, smooth stops of big Safe-Guard Hydraulic Brakes . . . the positive blowout protection of Safety-Rim Wheels.

The new Plymouth rides like a heavy, high-priced limousine yet handles with amazing ease! No wonder this fine car of great value is now — more than ever — *the car that likes to be compared!* No wonder this new American Beauty is now — more than ever — *the low-priced car most like high-priced cars!*

Plan to visit your nearby Plymouth dealer now. He'll gladly arrange for a demonstration drive. Then you can test this car and see for yourself that the new Plymouth is the most car value you can possibly buy at Plymouth's low price!

 NOW — *more than ever — the car that likes to be compared*

PLYMOUTH Division of CHRYSLER CORPORATION, Detroit 31, Michigan

1. Ads accurately pushed value and engineering, but Plymouth's 97-horsepower engine didn't quite deliver the promised "thrilling performance." Solid and reliable they were, but few folks outside Chrysler Corp. deemed Plymouths stylish. **2.** A bright Special DeLuxe convertible looked quite jaunty, despite its boxy profile. Copywriters concocted names for just about every technical feature, so Plymouths had such items as Safe-Guard brakes and Safety-Rim wheels. **3.** Only the wagon cost more than a Plymouth convertible, which featured pleated upholstery. **4.** Ice-cold root beer cost a nickel at this A&W stand in Alton, Illinois. Drive-ins and carhops already were busy, but the fast-food craze wouldn't take hold for a few more years.

2

3

4

1950 Crosley

Crosley Motors, Inc.

Just $882 buys a Crosley sedan, while Chevrolets start at $1329 . . . average full-time workers earn $2992 yearly

Super Sports roadster debuts, joining similarly low-slung Hotshot

Full line also includes sedan, station wagon, convertible

FarmORoad debuts in July—serves as car, truck, light tractor

Crosley's 44-cid engine develops 26.5 bhp

Drum brakes return at midyear, after brief flirtation with trouble-prone discs

Sales begin to sag after some success with enlarged postwar model

Only 6792 Crosleys are produced, including 742 roadsters—far below the 28,734 units issued in 1948

Price cuts in June fail to jump-start sales totals

As earnings rise and suburbs grow, Americans crave *big* automobiles, shunning this pioneering subcompact

Passenger cars are criticized for quirky handling and top-heavy shape

Crosley announces Quicksilver engine—runs on gasoline plus water-alcohol injection

Lesser-known minicars include Brogan, Imp, King Midget, Playboy

18

1

1. Crosley's Hotshot, introduced for 1949, was a genuine sports car. A mildly modified engine could push the Spartan, bug-eyed roadster to 77 mph—or even 90, if fitted with aftermarket hop-up gear. Scaled-down doors were optional. 2. Just two people fit in the down-to-basics interior of a Hotshot. Note the add-on turn-signal unit. 3. For 1950, a better-trimmed Super Sports convertible—complete with doors—joined the no-frills Hotshot. Both had a deck-mounted spare tire. Small, thrifty, inexpensive to buy and build, Crosley sedans and sportsters were two decades ahead of their time.

2

3

4. Crosley's tiny $795 FarmORoad served as a car, truck, tractor—or even a portable power source. Note the dual rear wheels. A back seat could be added.

4

Ford Motor Company

Ford, Lincoln, and Mercury get facelifts after radical '49 restyling

Ford brand slips to second place in volume, with production of 1.2 million cars—nearly 290,000 behind Chevrolet

Market share hits 24 percent—highest since 1930s

New Ford crest decorates hood and trunk lid

Pushbutton door handles replace pull units; gas filler hides beneath fender flap

Fords come with six-cylinder or V-8 engine; Mercury and Lincoln are V-8 only

Ford launches padded-roof Crestliner sports sedan . . . Lincoln Lido and Capri, and Mercury Monterey also wear padded tops

Lincolns may be ordered with Hydra-Matic, bought from GM

New York Fashion Academy names Ford "Fashion Car" for second year in a row

Lincolns again feature recessed headlights

Mercury adds short-lived Thrifty series

A Mercury wins its class in the Mobilgas Economy Run . . . another paces the Indianapolis 500 race

A Lincoln finishes ninth in the first Mexican Road Race

Ads insist V-8 engine "whispers while it works"

1

2

1. An "8" within a Ford grille "spinner" revealed the presence of the fabled flathead V-8 engine. A new hood crest, based on a 17th-century coat of arms, replaced 1949's block lettering. Taller and wider than arch-rival Chevrolet, Fords came in DeLuxe or Custom trim, with six-cylinder or V-8 power. 2. Lacking a hardtop coupe like Chevy's, Ford launched a sporty Crestliner Tudor sedan with a padded vinyl roof. Ribbed fender skirts accented its sleek look. Priced $200 above a plain Custom Tudor, Crestliners came in three vivid two-tone blends, including Sportsman Green and black. 3. Here, one of the year's 50,299 convertibles gets a fill-up with premium—and full-service attention—at a Sunoco station.

3

1950 Ford

1. Spotting twin Fords at a stoplight wasn't uncommon, as evidenced by this '50 scene in Moline, Illinois. Note the 25-cent parking-lot charge. 2. Ford wagons went to 22,929 customers, and would eventually become hot items on the used-car market. Laminated maple framing was attached to the wagon's steel body panels. 3. A DeLuxe Tudor cost $1424; the business coupe, cheaper yet. 4. Billed as "50 Ways New . . . 50 Ways Finer," Fords were much improved over '49. Bodies and frames were strengthened, handling improved, the V-8 engine quieted.

> "By taking advantage of the latest development in engine design we also have still further increased oil economy and added to the life of these engines. They are the quietest and smoothest-running engines we have ever produced."
>
> *Ford engineering vice president* **Harold T. Youngren**, *on improvements to Ford's inline sixes and V-8s for model-year 1950; November 1949*

5. Introduced in 1932, Ford's L-head V-8 engine now displaced 239.4 cid and delivered 100 horsepower. Even in stock tune the V-8 had a strong performance edge over Chevrolet and Plymouth sixes. Note separate radiator hoses for each cylinder bank. 6. Good Humor men took their jobs seriously, as evidenced by the almost military stance of these uniformed drivers. This popular fleet was made up of F-1 Ford trucks.

1. Judging by the dreary sales totals, not everyone agreed that "Nothing could be finer." Except for sunken headlights, Lincolns resembled an overweight Mercury. 2. A roomy Cosmopolitan coupe cost $3187 and rode a wheelbase four inches longer than regular Lincolns. The smaller models used Mercury body panels from the cowl back. 3. Long split rear-quarter windows on a Cosmopolitan coupe made it look more like a four-door. 4. No other car on the market had headlights like Lincoln's, but the idea failed to catch on. 5. As these lavish surroundings suggest, the fashion leader of the Lincoln line was the $3950 convertible, but only 536 went to customers. 6. Lowest-priced model, at $2529, was the basic six-passenger coupe.

1. Fender skirts helped enhance the Cosmopolitan coupe's profile, but the bulbous "bathtub" shape couldn't attract customers. Lincolns were luxurious, and rode beautifully. **2.** A Cosmopolitan sedan went for $3240. Note the three-piece rear window—a forerunner of soon-to-arrive wraparound glass. Both models contained a 336.7-cid L-head V-8, rated at 152 bhp. **3-5.** Practically every American must have seen a photo of this stretched Cosmopolitan convertible sedan with retractable running boards, built for President Truman but used by the White House until 1961. Bodywork was by Raymond H. Dietrich, Inc. A decade later, Lincoln would reintroduce the convertible sedan as a production model. Nine limos also were ordered, with bodies by Henney. All were leased to the government.

1. Mercury offered a Lincoln-like look at a lower price. The 255-cid V-8, with an Econ-O-Miser carburetor, delivered 110 horsepower—10 more than Ford's. Touch-O-Matic overdrive claimed to cut fuel costs by 20 percent. 2. A Mercury Sport Sedan cost almost $500 more than a Custom Ford Fordor. Both seated six. 3. A pillarless hardtop wasn't feasible, so Mercury issued the Monterey. This one has been lowered, and sports a load of factory extras. 4. For $177 more than a plain coupe, the Monterey got a vinyl roof—or canvas for $166. 5. Mercury's $2561 wagon seated eight. 6. An upright spare helped make efficient use of the spacious trunk. 7. New fiberglass soundproofing quieted "the soft purr of the strong, silent" engine. 8. A new Merco-Therm system delivered fresh air in any season.

1

2

3

go for a ride and you'll go for MERCURY

4

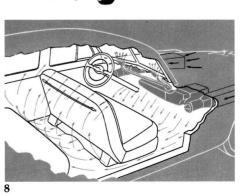
5

6

7

8

1950 Mercury

1. "Smart, sleek-looking, massive," was Mercury's description of its $2412 convertible. 2. Families liked the Sport Sedan, making it the most popular model, but teens grew to favor the brash two-door. 3. Even in stock form, a fender-skirted club coupe looked rather dashing on the street. 4. Mercury's new Safe-T-Vue dash grouped gauges behind a single plexiglass panel. 5. Lounge Rest foam-rubber seats cradled a coupe's occupants.

6. In the new-car showroom, a smooth ride and smart stance tempted shoppers. Later, the "bathtub" Merc became an auto icon after film legend James Dean drove a '49 in *Rebel Without a Cause*. 7. A Mercury convertible, painted Mirada Yellow, paced the Indianapolis 500 race on May 30. 8. Driving the pace car was Lincoln-Mercury manager Benson Ford, with former racer and Speedway president Wilbur Shaw.

1

General Motors Corporation

Corporation issues 3,653,358 U.S.-built vehicles

Pillarless hardtop coupes now available in all five GM makes

GM Motorama opens in New York; 350,000 visitors see show cars and production models

Buicks gain all-new body— so does Oldsmobile 98

Cadillac is in 48th year as "Standard of the World"

Cadillacs get new one-piece windshield, which also is phased in on Oldsmobiles

Second season for Cadillac's overhead-valve V-8 engine and Coupe de Ville body style

Chevrolets get optional Powerglide automatic

Oldsmobile issues final six-cylinder models

Rocket V-8 Oldsmobiles win 10 of 19 major stock-car races; Olds 88 sets class speed record at Daytona, reaching 100.28 mph

Pontiacs can have six- or eight-cylinder L-head engine—boast 28 styling/mechanical improvements

GM sales total a record $7.5 billion; net earnings amount to $834 million

Alfred Sloan, Jr., is GM chairman; Charles E. Wilson serves as president

"This is the car of the future only in the sense that some of its design or mechanical features may appear some day in standard motorcars.

LeSabre is purely experimental."

General Motors styling vice president **Harley J. Earl**, *on the LeSabre show car; December 1950*

2

1. Super was the mid-level Buick, selling for $2139 as a four-door sedan. Buick's Special targeted low-budget buyers, while the Roadmaster was top-of-the-line. Dynaflow, Buick's automatic transmission, was standard in Roadmasters and optional in other Buicks. Available since 1948, the torque-converter unit soon earned such derisive nicknames as "Dyna-slush," mocking its smooth but slow takeoffs. 2. Harley J. Earl, head of GM's Art and Colour Section, earned credit for many styling touches, but few were more memorable than Cadillac's tailfins. By the late '50s, virtually all American cars—and even a few imports—would be sporting fins. 3. Buick Specials came in Tourback or fastback (sedanet) form. Note this four-door DeLuxe Tourback's three-piece rear window—a popular feature this year. 4. "Buick's the fashion for 1950," said the brochure. Roadmaster interiors ranked as "ultra-regal." All models adopted a single-unit bumper/grille.

3

4

1950 Buick

1. "You're Lord of Every Highway in the Luxurious Roadmaster," Buick insisted. More so in the $2981 convertible, with leather interior. 2. Priciest by far was the $3407 Roadmaster Estate wagon. 3. Buick touted the "gracefully curved afterdeck" of its Roadmaster Tourback sedan. 4. A Super convertible's engine gave 128 horsepower (124 with stickshift). 5. Few buyers fancied a Special Jetback coupe, which seated only three. 6. The Special sedanet was billed as "spacious as a sedan, companionable as a coupe." 7. Aircraft themes were popular, so Buicks had a Pilot-Centered control panel. 8. Straight-eight engines came in three sizes—one for each series.

2

1. Edward N. Cole served as Cadillac's chief engineer from June 1946 to August 1950. Named to run a military tank plant this year, he eventually became GM president. 2. Introduced a year earlier, the luscious Coupe de Ville hardtop was the Series 62 style leader. 3. De Ville interiors were two-tone leather and cloth. Hydraulics powered the windows and front seat. 4. Cadillacs earned a reputation as top-notch road cars. Sedans came in Series 62 (shown) as well as the lower-priced 61 and larger 60 Special. 5. The overhead-valve 331-cid V-8 delivered 160 bhp. 6. Cadillac proclaimed its V-8 the "greatest automotive power plant ever built." 7. Nearly 7000 Series 62 ragtops went on sale, at $3654. 8. Leather was standard in Series 62 convertibles.

1

3

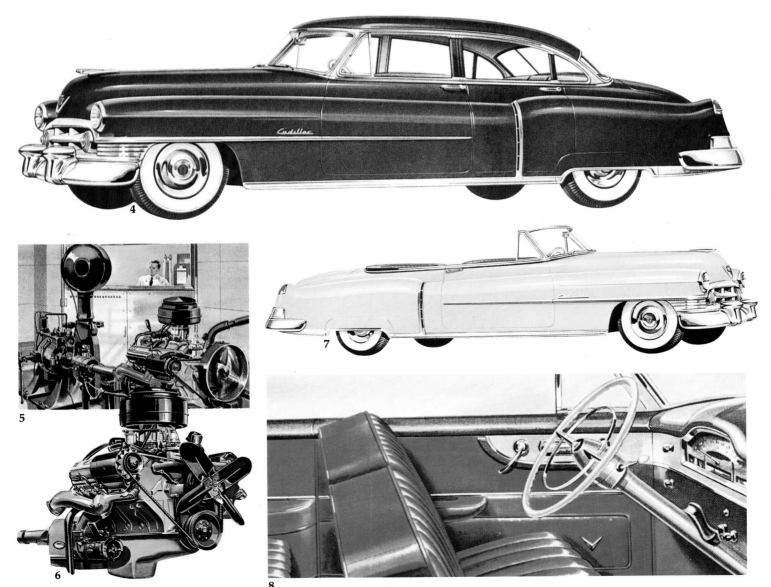

4

5

7

6

8

1950 Cadillac

1

3

4

2

5

6

1. In '49, the biggest Cadillac had kept its prewar look. This year's Series 75, styled like its smaller counterparts for the first time, came in seven-passenger sedan form, or as a divider-window limo. On a 147-inch wheelbase, it was billed as "America's most distinguished motor car." Hydra-Matic was optional on Series 61 and 75, but standard on other models. 2. This year's grille incorporated parking lights. Cadillac was consistently successful in sales, handily beating Lincoln, Packard, and Imperial in the luxury-car race. 3. Dashboards were finished in Tudor gray with a light tone pattern design insert. 4. Cadillac's sales brochure didn't call those pointed appendages fins, referring instead to the "long, low rear deck and its distinctive rear fender treatment with tail lamps in the up-sweep." Development of the V-8 engine began before World War II. 5. The 1950 Cadillacs were unveiled in January, at GM's Midcentury Motorama. Held at New York's Waldorf-Astoria Hotel, the event spotlighted past achievements and near-future ideas, as well as showcasing current vehicles. 6. When hostilities flared in Korea, GM once again enlisted in the defense effort. Here, tanks roll off production lines at Cadillac's Cleveland, Ohio, factory.

Chevrolet 1950

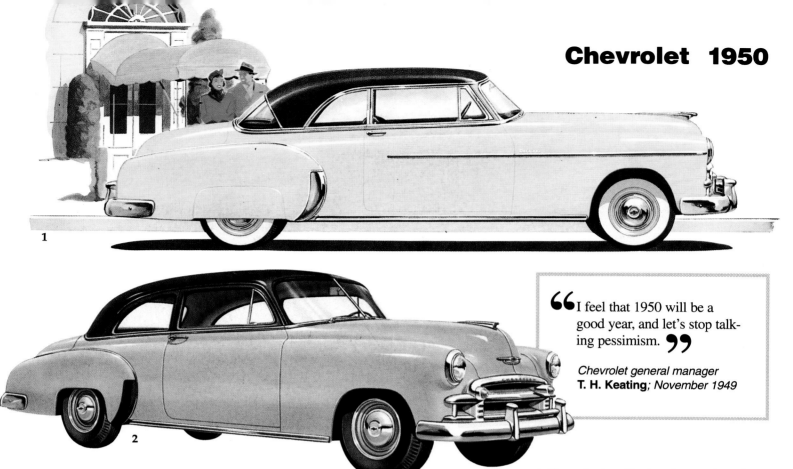

1

2

3

1. Chevrolet beat Ford to the punch with a stylish Bel Air hardtop that blended "the airiness . . . of a convertible with the coziness and permanence of an all-steel top." Leather was included for $1741. **2.** Just $1403 bought a Styleline Special two-door. Special and DeLuxe models differed in trim and interior fittings. **3.** This steel-bodied Styleline DeLuxe station wagon had removable rear seats.

4

4. Chevrolet's long-familiar "stovebolt six" engine, now rated 92 horsepower (with stickshift), featured a new Power-Jet carburetor for finer cold-weather performance. Overhead-valve engines finally were becoming a trend, offering better engine "breathing" than the L-head designs still used by Chrysler and Ford. Chevys equipped with Powerglide automatic— a new option for 1950—got a larger 235.5-cid 105-bhp engine. **5.** This Minneapolis car wash was doing a brisk business on April 8, 1950, while a pair of new Chevys waited in line at lower right.

5

29

1950 Chevrolet

1. Most popular Chevrolet was the $1529 Styleline DeLuxe four-door. DeLuxe models outsold lower-priced Specials by far.
2. Interiors featured new two-tones, while "five-foot seats" extended full-width. Heaters cost extra. 3. Dashboards were two-toned, too. Driving with Powerglide, the brochure explained, was "easy as ABC": A) start engine; B) set the "pilot control" lever; C) press gas pedal. 4. Fastbacks were fading in popularity, but not yet extinct. 5. A DeLuxe sedan nears the end of the inspection process. 6. Chevrolets sat on a box-girder frame with rear-wheel drive, front coils, rear leaf springs, and column gearshift.

1. Oldsmobile fielded three Futuramic series: redesigned 98 (*bottom*), six-cylinder 76 (*top*), and 88—which slipped the hot V-8 engine into a lightweight body. **2.** Quite a few shoppers decided to make that "date with a Rocket 8," taking Olds to sixth in sales. **3.** Most buyers chose an Olds for its luxury, not its go-power. **4.** A 98 Holiday hardtop (*foreground*) and 98 four-door sedan lead a pair of 88s through final inspection at the end of Oldsmobile's assembly line. **5.** Only the 98 had the new round taillights. This club sedan came in standard or DeLuxe trim. **6.** Copywriters were correct in branding the Olds V-8 "engine of the future," even if the revolution would take a few more years to reach full throttle. The 303.7-cid engine developed 135 horsepower.

Make a "Date with a "Rocket 8"!

OLDSMOBILE
A GENERAL MOTORS VALUE

1950 Oldsmobile

1. Only 2382 Oldsmobile 88 station wagons went to dealers. 2. Launched a year earlier, the sharp 88 Holiday hardtop got some body/trim fine-tuning. Two-tones were popular. An 88 could accelerate to 60 mph in just over 12 seconds. Olds initially down-played performance, but it signaled the beginning of the horsepower race. 3. Four-door sedans outsold all other body styles in all series; shown is a 76. 4. At $1719, a club coupe was the cheapest 76. 5. A pair of 88s stand ready to compete at Daytona Beach in 1950. 6. Despite claims of "surging acceler-ation," the 105-bhp six paled in comparison to V-8 engines. 7. Musical maestro Lawrence Welk poses with a full fleet of Olds 98s. 8. British music-hall legend Gracie Fields looks pleased with this open 98. 9. Olds promised not only swift pickup, but an "Air-Borne Ride." Coil springs soaked up the bumps at all four corners.

1

2

3

4

7

5

> "Flying Saucers Amaze You? Our New Low Payments Are Even More Amazing."
>
> *Advertising slogan,* **House of Mozes** *used-car dealership, Philadelphia; May 1950*

6

8

9

1. Factory accessories added dash to a Pontiac Chieftain DeLuxe Eight sedan. Hydra-Matic and Vent-A-Shades added well-spent dollars to the $1908 base price.
2. Backup lights cost extra, as they did on most American cars. 3. Pontiacs carried their namesake's likeness on bright red badges.
4. Ads pushed value, as well as the spirited appearance of the new Catalina hardtop.
5. "America's lowest-priced straight-eight" engine grew in size and output, reaching 268.4 cid and 108 horsepower. 6. Sixes were powered by a 239.2-cid 90-bhp engine.
7. Except for wagons, a Chieftain DeLuxe convertible was the most costly Pontiac.
8. Fastbacks came only in the lower-cost Streamliner series. 9. Options on this Streamliner DeLuxe Eight include spotlights and a rear sunshade.

1950 Pontiac

1. Pontiacs gained a bolder grille. The hood ornament could be plastic, lighting up as the headlights were switched on.
2. "Everything a Fine Car should be" was Pontiac's claim for the interior decor. Rear seats were "restfully contoured."
3. Dashboards were declared "the most beautiful in the industry," with a semicircular speedometer, round gauges, and a Handi-Grip parking brake. 4. Styling touches included a "wide horizon windshield" with slim corner posts; wide, easy-access doors, with mating floor and sill "to avoid tripping and heel-catching"; and "Carry-More" trunk. 5. A DeLuxe Catalina Eight hardtop cost $2069, but Pontiac also marketed a Super Catalina edition. Both were part of the Chieftain series. 6. An all-steel Streamliner station wagon could hold six or eight passengers. 7. Twin convertibles strutted proudly in a Chicago parade.

Hudson Motor Car Company

Modest facelift helps give "Step-down" Hudsons a lower look

"Step-down" designation refers to the dropped floorpan, surrounded by frame girders

Hudsons are applauded for toughness and handling, as well as smooth highway ride

Shorter Pacemaker joins lineup—accounts for close to half of production

Pacemaker uses 232-cid six, rated 112 horsepower

Super Six engine boosted to 123 horsepower; aluminum cylinder head is available

Super and Commodore series can have either six- or eight-cylinder engine

Commodore outsells Super Six by two to one, despite its higher prices

Hudson offers three transmission options: mechanical overdrive, Drive-Master, and new Supermatic (which included a cruising gear)

Supermatic can be locked out, using dashboard button; shifts gears when letting up on gas

All Hudsons employ a Fluid-Cushioned clutch

Hudson ranks 13th in sales—worst showing since the war—on production of 121,408 cars

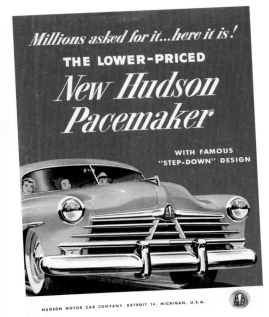

1. Owners of the "Step-down" Hudsons that arrived for 1948 cheered its low-slung design and easy-going ride. But because it was virtually impossible to restyle, Hudson had to stick with the same shape through '54. The new stripped-down, lower-priced Pacemaker line included a sedan, two coupes, two-door brougham, and convertible. **2.** A Commodore Six four-door sedan cost $2282, but an Eight brought $84 more. **3.** "Step-down" meant occupants sat within the Monobilt frame, "with box-section steel-girder protection on all sides, even outside the rear wheels." Hudson promoted the safety aspect, and riders truly felt they were "stepping down" when entering the car. **4.** Heavy metal above the windshield made Hudson convertibles easy to spot. This is a Pacemaker Brougham, but open Hudsons also came in the Super Six series, and the Commodore Six and Eight. A hydraulic top was standard, power windows optional.

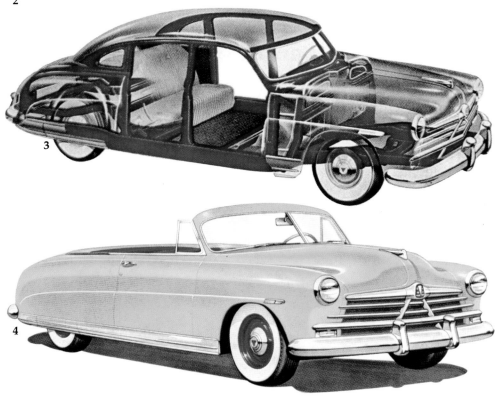

35

1950 Hudson

1. Lowest-priced Commodore Six was the $2257 club coupe, with a 123-horsepower, 262-cid engine. 2. Even in a Pacemaker, passengers had plenty of head and elbow room. Hudson seats were a whopping 64 inches wide. 3. Not only did a ragtop Commodore look glamorous, it claimed "the most room, best ride, and greatest safety of any American convertible." 4. Like most cars, Hudsons used coil springs up front. 5. Gentle-Acting rear leaf springs helped deliver a smooth highway ride. 6. Improved Center-Point steering was said to eliminate "wander" and help crosswind stability. 7. Pacemakers had a destroked version of the Super Six engine.

Kaiser-Frazer Corporation

Kaiser-Frazer markets leftover 1949 models, until restyled '51s debut in spring of 1950

"Anatomic" '51s should have been ready, but glut of '49s forces Kaiser to give leftovers new serial numbers instead

All Kaisers and Frazers carry 226-cid six-cylinder Continental L-head engine

Thunderhead engines develop 112 horsepower except in Kaiser Special, which is rated 100 bhp

Kaiser Traveler continues after 1949 debut; has dual rear doors, like station wagon's tailgate

Vagabond is DeLuxe version of Kaiser Traveler

Handful of convertible sedans and four-door hardtops built

Kaiser Virginian four-door hardtop has nylon roof

Manhattan convertible sedan, the most opulent Frazer, has unique metal-framed glass pillars

Cofounder Joseph Frazer no longer is connected with the company, having departed in spring 1949

Henry Kaiser and son Edgar are in charge

Kaiser-Frazer ranks 12th in sales, with total of 146,911 units in calendar year

1. Frazers were the upscale members of the K-F duo, offered in Standard (shown) and Manhattan trim. **2.** Joseph W. Frazer (*left*) and Henry J. Kaiser met in 1945 to develop the cars that bore both of their names. Frazer had a reputation as a super salesman; Kaiser was a shipbuilding tycoon. **3.** Because buyers of independent makes often wondered if service would stay available, K-F wisely publicized the existence of its 4,000-plus "prosperous, well-equipped distributors and dealers." **4.** Four-door convertibles disappeared before the war, but Frazer launched an open Manhattan in '49. Few were sold, partly due to high ($3295) price.

KAISER GENUINE FACTORY PARTS & SERVICE FRAZER

NORTH, SOUTH, EAST OR WEST...

KAISER-FRAZER CORPORATION, WILLOW RUN, MICHIGAN

1950 Frazer

1. A Frazer four-door sedan cost $2395 in standard form (shown), or $200 more in fancier Manhattan guise, with Bedford cloth and nylon upholstery—or full leather. Their 112-horsepower, 226-cid Supersonic L-head six-cylinder engine was designed by Continental but built by K-F. 2. Nearly 40 color combinations were available inside a Frazer. 3. Frazer claimed its 27 cubic feet of luggage space was "half again as much as in most cars." On a long (123.5-inch) wheelbase, Frazers rode pleasantly and handled adeptly. 4. Brightwork on the dashboard was common in the '50s. Frazer's speedometer and clock were identical in size, mounted ahead of a Clear-vision steering wheel.

5. Industrial designer Brooks Stevens penned a series of styling proposals for the 1950 Frazer—some of which suggest what became the '51 Kaiser. 6. Note the slight windshield dip in this three-tone "Custom Sedan," which kept much of the original Frazer's sheetmetal. 7. A full-width slot grille and wrap-around back window mark this Stevens rendering. Engineers also pondered new engine alternatives.

Kaiser 1950

1. Barely more than 15,000 Kaisers went on sale this season, as customers awaited fully redesigned models. Top seller was this DeLuxe sedan, although a Special cost $200 less. **2.** Dashboards featured a clock to match the speedometer, and a map light on the steering column shield. **3.** Kaiser seats promised "as much comfort space as your davenport at home." **4.** After styling the ill-fated 1948 Tucker, Alex Tremulis moved to Kaiser-Frazer, becoming head of advanced design. **5.** Ideas for '51 came from in-house teams, and from consultants Howard "Dutch" Darrin and Brooks Stevens. This Stevens concept has a slot grille formed into the bumper. **6.** Stevens's "Town Sedan" featured lower-body cladding. **7.** An oval grille would not be used, but the general shape of the 1951 Kaiser is evident.

1950 Kaiser

1

2

1. Practical-minded shoppers might choose a Kaiser DeLuxe Vagabond utility sedan (shown)—or the similar Special Traveler, for $200 less. Special engines made only 100 horsepower. **2.** Symmetry was a major element of dashboard design. **3.** The Vagabond's 10-foot cargo space was accessible via two hinged rear panels, with rear seat cushions folded. Note the slatted floor. **4.** Long before other automakers got the idea, Kaiser offered a four-door hardtop—the $2995 Virginian.

3

4

Nash Motors

Full-size cars change little in second year of Airflyte styling

Radical "upside-down-bathtub" design is mocked, but sells well

Nash's aerodynamic drag rating is best in the industry

Statesman with 85-bhp six replaces 600 series

Ambassador is top model, with 234.8-cid overhead-valve six

Uniscope puts all instruments—and most controls—into pod on steering column

All Airflytes have reclining front seatbacks; pneumatic mattresses can be ordered

Nash-Kelvinator president George Mason prepares a small car . . . Rambler, on 100-inch wheelbase with 82-horsepower six, is first volume-built American compact

Initial Ramblers come only in Landau Convertible form, followed by station wagon

Hydra-Matic transmission available in Ambassador; engine starts by lifting gearshift

Nash has top sales season ever, with 191,865 cars sold

Model-year output totals 171,782 cars, for 11th-place ranking

Only about 11,400 Ramblers built in first season, but sales soon will rise

1

2

4   3

1. Those who didn't scoff at the contours of a "bathtub" Nash Airflyte found a lot to like in the Wisconsin automaker's unique fleet, including a comfortable interior, cushy ride, and novel features. This Ambassador Super sedan sold for $2064. Nash claimed 25-mpg economy from the 112-horsepower six-cylinder engine. 2. No other car on the road looked anything like a Nash, especially from the rear. Note the semi-concealed wheels at front and rear. Owners often endured smirks from folks who observed that Nash seats converted into beds. 3. Despite its aero shape, an Ambassador trunk held a fair supply of luggage. 4. A Statesman two-door plays up Nash's Airflyte styling theme. 5. Ambassadors rode a 121-inch wheelbase and differed from the shorter (112-inch) Statesman only from the cowl forward.

NOW—WITH AIRFLYTE CONSTRUCTION

The Luxurious

Nash Ambassador

FOR 1950

5

1950 Nash

1

2

3

1. Other automakers had tinkered with small cars, but only Nash built one—mainly because president George Mason was intrigued by the concept of compacts. Rumored for months before its arrival in April 1950, the Rambler Landau was billed as "The Smartest, Safest Convertible in the World," promising the "safety of husky steel rails overhead." 2. Five fit snugly into a Rambler convertible. Mason knew that to survive as the seller's market eased, independents had to create cars that weren't offered by the Big Three. Note the broad cowl vent. 3. Rambler was the only open car on the market with fixed window frames and a slide-back top. 4. Nash claimed that the compact's version of unibodied Airflyte construction was "twice as rigid" as body-on-frame designs, "free of the usual squeaks and rattles." With a 100-inch wheelbase—15-inches shorter than Chevrolet's—Ramblers seemed to occupy a different world than their "bathtub" big brothers.

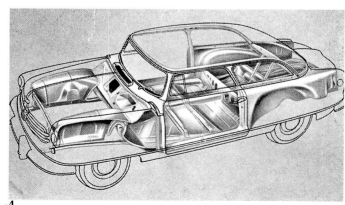

4

1

3

2

1. Two months after the convertible's debut came a Rambler Custom station wagon, for the same $1808 price. Ads claimed 30-mpg fuel economy—more with overdrive. 2. Ramblers were declared "a new beauty for the young in heart" that "steers like a dream, parks in a pocket." 3. Instruments sat in one cluster, ahead of the driver. A radio and Weather Eye Conditioned Air System were standard in the well-equipped Ramblers. 4. The 172.6-cid L-head engine was borrowed from the 1949 Nash 600. Light weight made Ramblers perky performers. 5. Big Nashes beckoned shoppers into this Oakland, California, dealership, but Ramblers were the wave of the future.

4

" Won't there come a day when people will be concerned with the cost of doing things? **"**

*Nash-Kelvinator president **George W. Mason**, on the economic virtues of small-car ownership; October 1950*

5

Packard Motor Car Company

Final season for Packard's "inverted-bathtub" shape

Late '49 and 1950 Packards show mild facelift of bulbous 1948-49 design

Twenty-Third Series of 1949-50 is known as "Golden Anniversary" Packard

Standard, Super Eight, and Custom Eight models marketed

Standard and DeLuxe Eight use 288-cid, 135-horsepower straight-eight

Super Eight engine is 327 cid and 150 bhp

Custom Eight's 356-cid straight-eight puts out 160 horsepower

Ultramatic is the only automatic transmission developed solely by an independent automaker

Ultramatic is standard on Custom series—lockup clutch gives no-slip cruising in direct drive

Rarely seen Station Sedan (wagon) uses structural wood only at tailgate

Model-year production dips to 42,627, for 15th-place ranking in industry

Company loses money, despite industry sales boom

Meager sales are attributed in part to loss of luxury image—neither midpriced nor costly Packards catch hold

1. Packards came in three series: 135-bhp Eight; 150-bhp Super Eight, yielding a "limousine ride"; and top-drawer Custom Eight, said to be "built without regard for conventional 'price class' limitations." Impressive and award-winning a few years earlier, Packards now seemed painfully portly—often derided as "pregnant elephants." 2-3. Only 707 Custom Eight sedans were built, with a $3975 price tag and 356-cid engine. Extras included a spotlight and wind wings. 4. Even the standard Eight delivered a silken ride in a plush interior. Ultramatic cost $185, but this car is equipped with overdrive—a $92 extra. 5. A Super Eight DeLuxe club sedan cost $2894, but skipping DeLuxe trim saved $286.

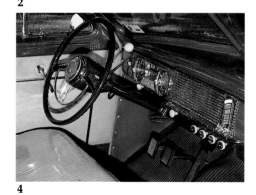

NEW PACKARD
Ultramatic Drive

The last word in automatic, no-shift control!

1. Packard issued only 77 Custom Eight convertibles, at an eye-popping $4520. An open Super Eight cost $1170 less. The mammoth Custom engine weighed half a ton.
2. Lowest-cost body was the standard Eight club sedan, shown in DeLuxe trim.
3. Standard on Custom Packards, optional on others, Ultramatic promised "no jerking, ever," and "no gasoline-wasting slippage."
4. Packard called its four-door Eights "touring sedans." 5. Even with 160 horsepower, Custom Eights set no speed records, as those ponies had to haul over 4300 pounds worth of Packard luxury.

1950 Studebaker

Studebaker Corporation

"Next Look" 1950 models debut in August 1949

Front ends display new "bullet nose," designed by Bob Bourke

Front coil springs replace outmoded single transverse-leaf configuration

Champions ride shorter wheelbase than costlier Commanders, come in three trim levels

Studebaker output soars to new record—320,884 units

Automatic Drive available after April, designed in cooperation with Detroit Gear Division of Borg-Warner

Automatic transmission includes "hill-holder" feature—an idea pioneered by Studebaker in 1930s . . . unit also promises absence of "creep" at standstill

Long-wheelbase Land Cruisers get Automatic Drive first

Champion Custom series joins during model year, to rival low-priced Big Three models

Starlight Coupe continues, featuring distinctive wraparound rear window

Body styles include convertible and three-passenger coupe, but no station wagon

Studebaker is oldest American auto manufacturer—in business since horse-and-buggy days

Sleek new Studebaker styling saves gasoline for you!

1

1. Advertisements promoted the sleek styling of the latest Studes, along with their reputation for economy. Champions came in three trim levels, larger Commanders in two. Automatic Drive cost $201 extra when it became available in spring. **2.** An 85-horsepower, 169.6-cid L-head six powered this overdrive-equipped Champion Regal DeLuxe two-door sedan. Some critics had sneered at 1947-49 models, claiming they looked the same "coming or going." This year's bullet-nose also drew snickers. **3.** No car's rear window wrapped around like that of the Starlight coupe, a body style available in all five models. Price leader was the Champion Custom three-passenger coupe, at just $1419. **4.** Dealers enjoyed a record sales year, but corporate profits failed to skyrocket.

2

3

4

1

3

1. At $2187, a long Land Cruiser cost $285 more than the cheapest Commander four-door. **2.** South Bend, Indiana, long had been Studebaker's home base, the site of most assembly. **3.** Studebakers were frugal, and this Starlight coupe enjoyed cheap gas in Los Angeles. Regional gas wars caused rival stations to slash prices fiercely. Americans collected "green stamps," issued with purchases and redeemable for special merchandise. **4.** This Commander Regal DeLuxe convertible went for $2328, but a Champion ragtop cost less.

4

1951

The New Jersey and Pennsylvania Turnpikes opened for business in '51, and the traditional nickel phone call now cost a dime in some cities. Parents began to feel guilty if their offspring didn't have music lessons and a set of encyclopedias, as the nation turned its focus toward kids—and teenagers.

Prosperity and optimism persisted. Unemployment dipped to 3.3 percent, while the gross national product grew by 15 percent. More than three-fourths of cars sold were considered "deluxe" models, as average family income continued its upward climb—

now topping $3700 a year. Americans began to indulge in an infatuation with chrome—an idiosyncrasy destined to last several decades. Growing use of two-toning also added sales appeal.

I Love Lucy appeared on TV screens for the first time, as did *The Cisco Kid* and Dinah Shore's *Chevy Show*. Color broadcasts were successful, but programs would be black-and-white a while longer.

Movie fans enjoyed Brando in *A Streetcar Named Desire* and Bogart in *The African Queen*. Rosemary Clooney sang "Come On-a My House," Johnnie Ray induced female fans to "Cry," and The Weavers had a top-ten hit with "On Top of Old Smoky."

At first glance, "More of the same" might have been the automotive slogan for 1951. With the exception of totally redesigned Kaisers and Packards, nearly all automobiles saw little more than touch-up work: a fresh grille here, revised taillights there, brightwork moved or modified.

In the wake of Nash's success with the Rambler, Kaiser launched a new compact: the Henry J, powered by Willys engines. Henry J. Kaiser insisted that the public didn't want a truly small car, but rather one "of conventional size with enough modern styling distinction to instill pride of ownership."

Chrysler joined the horsepower race by issuing a 180-horsepower Hemi V-8. Hudson unleashed the Hornet—a car destined to trounce the competition on the stock-car circuit—with the biggest six-cylinder engine on the market adding vigor to the roadholding skills of the "Step-down" design.

Hardtop coupes joined Ford and Plymouth lineups, as well as Hudson's and Packard's. As the hardtops gained in popularity, true convertibles declined.

Not every car came with turn signals or backup lights in the early Fifties. Drivers still proclaimed their intentions via hand signals.

As the Korean War intensified, production cutbacks were ordered by the National Production Authority—despite insistence by the National Automobile Dealers Association that cars were necessities. Chrome trim became thinner, curtailment of nickel limited stainless-steel brightwork, and output of steel itself was slashed by 35 percent at midyear. Whitewall-tire production was halted in order to conserve natural rubber.

The auto industry further faced government-ordered price ceilings, as well as rising labor costs. Regulation "W" limited credit terms to 15 months—increased during the year to 18 months, with a one-third down payment required. Even so, industry output wound up past 5.3 million cars, second only to record-shattering 1950.

After more than half a century of production, the 100-millionth American car was built in December. Concern about the future, on the other hand, induced some Americans to hoard consumer goods—just in case of rationing or shortages.

A Roper survey found that an "alarming" number of Americans did not trust car dealers—though most were less critical of their *own* dealers. Bootlegging was widespread—not of liquor (as in the 1919-33 Prohibition era), but of new cars. In this "gray market," a legacy of the postwar boom, used-car dealers and fly-by-night vendors managed to obtain cars and steal sales from established dealerships, typically undercutting prices.

Because many folks were unable to participate in the hot new-car market, used-car dealers also enjoyed a busy year. Still, the average used car sold for $830—hardly a giveaway sum—and prices were "frozen" during the year to prevent further hikes.

As Detroit marked its 250th anniversary, small cars were arriving from Europe. Not just exciting sports cars, but tiny sedans: Anglias, Austins, Hillmans—plus a growing number of Volkswagens, foretelling a near-future import revolution.

Chrysler Corporation

Nineteen fifty-one models don't arrive until February

Each make earns mild facelift—mainly up front—yet dowdy image persists

Chrysler launches 331-cid 180-bhp FirePower Hemi V-8 engine

Complex Hemi V-8 is most powerful engine on sale

Hemi-powered Chrysler Saratoga can accelerate to 60 mph in 10 seconds—swifter than Rocket Olds

Hemi V-8 soon commands attention of race drivers and hot rodders

Town & Country name goes only on Chrysler wagons

Hydraguide power steering debuts in top Chryslers

Fluid-Torque transmission available in Imperials

DeSotos get larger six-cylinder engine

Plymouth is sole make to lack Tip-Toe shifting

Plymouth models renamed: now called Concord, Cambridge, Cranbrook

Belvedere hardtop joins Plymouth line

Plymouth edges ahead of Buick in production race

Bill Sterling runs third in Mexican Road Race, driving a Chrysler Saratoga

Chrysler readies new Michigan proving ground

1

1. Chrysler called its new FirePower Hemi V-8 engine a "masterpiece of engineering." Standard in New Yorkers and Imperials (and later, in Saratogas), the Hemi developed a "conservative" 180 horsepower. 2. Nicknamed for its hemispherically shaped combustion chambers, the Hemi V-8, with a 7.5:1 compression ratio, ran on regular fuel. Large valves flanking center-mounted spark plugs helped produce complete, even-burning combustion. 3. A New Yorker convertible, driven by Chrysler president David A. Wallace, paced the Indianapolis 500 race on May 30, 1951. Three-time Indy winner Wilbur Shaw rode along.

2

3

THE CLUB COUPE *will easily accommodate six passengers comfortably. Extra large storage compartment in rear deck.*

CHRYSLER
The Saratoga

A 180-HORSEPOWER ENGINE; *125½ inch wheelbase; Oriflow Shock Absorbers; Hydraguide Power Steering, if desired—what a performer—what a car! Illustrated above is the beautiful Six-Passenger Sedan.*

Here is the car that is going to cause the big sensation in 1952! . . . the Chrysler Saratoga with the 180 horsepower . . . and MORE, FirePower Engine. The revolutionary Hydraguide Power Steering, and the Fluid-Torque Drive to give you even greater performance, are available as optional equipment.

THE TOWN & COUNTRY WAGON. *With rear seat folded forward, storage space is 88 inches long and 44¼ inches wide. With tailgate open, length is 116 inches.*

THE EIGHT-PASSENGER SEDAN *has a wheelbase of 139½ inches. Power Brakes are standard equipment on all Saratoga body types.*

1951 CHRYSLER MODELS

Windsor & Saratoga

New Yorker

Imperial

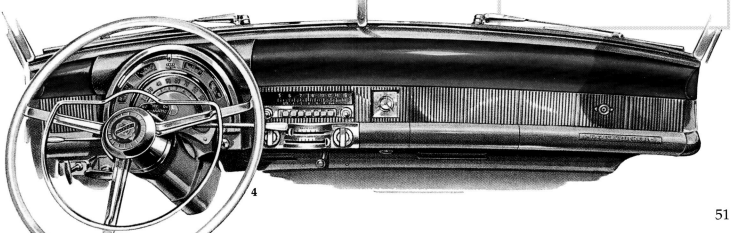

1. Offered in four body styles, Saratoga was Chrysler's least-costly V-8 series. Saratogas and Windsors rode a shorter wheelbase than New Yorkers and Imperials. Sedans gained a Clearbac wraparound rear window. **2.** A 251-cid six-cylinder engine powered Windsors, in base or DeLuxe trim. **3.** The rear seatback and cushion in a Windsor DeLuxe Traveler folded flush with the floor, to turn the sedan into a cargo carrier. A roof rack let owners haul even more. **4.** A "glance tells the story," Chrysler claimed of its new Safety-Eye instrument cluster. Gauges were grouped for easy reading. The leather-covered Safety Crash Pad was a "first."

> 66 The buying public is beginning to realize that new cars are going to be scarcer and more expensive. 99
>
> *Unidentified new-car dealer, on a sales upturn stemming from the Korean War; September 1951*

1951 Chrysler

1

2

Imperial

BY CHRYSLER

More and more the registry of its owners is a page from the Blue Book of your community... the people you know who can afford any automobile in the world.

Perhaps never before in history has any motor car expressed so well the truly discriminating point of view. In the Imperial by Chrysler is taste and beauty and quality that set new standards for America's fine cars.

The Finest Car America Has Yet Produced!

4

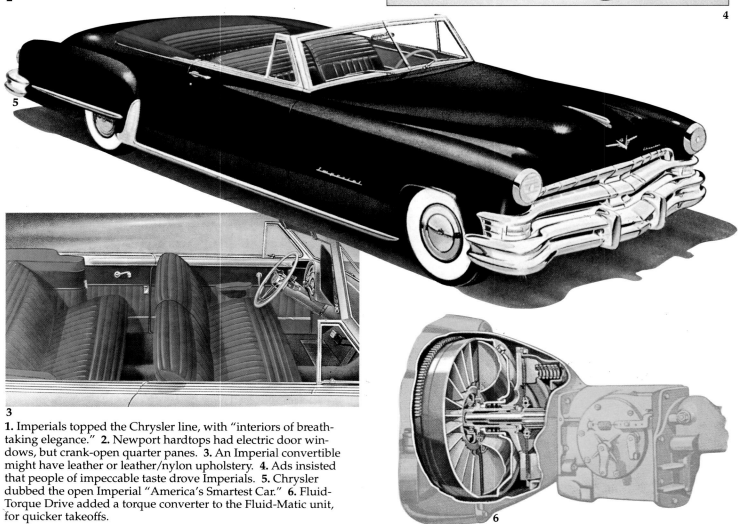

5

3

6

1. Imperials topped the Chrysler line, with "interiors of breath-taking elegance." **2.** Newport hardtops had electric door windows, but crank-open quarter panes. **3.** An Imperial convertible might have leather or leather/nylon upholstery. **4.** Ads insisted that people of impeccable taste drove Imperials. **5.** Chrysler dubbed the open Imperial "America's Smartest Car." **6.** Fluid-Torque Drive added a torque converter to the Fluid-Matic unit, for quicker takeoffs.

52

1. All DeSotos, including this Custom sedan, wore a new grille and larger windshield. 2. A lower, but wider, rear window gave the DeSoto driver a wide-angle view. 3. Three circular gauge units graced the instrument panel. 4. DeLuxe and Custom DeSotos were said to be designed "expressly for you." The line included a club coupe, convertible, Sportsman hardtop, Suburban, and station wagon. 5. DeSoto's Carry-All utility sedan featured a fold-down rear seat. 6. The Carry-All's rear seatback and cushion folded to create a 6½ x 3½-foot cargo space. 7. Displacement of DeSoto's Powermaster six-cylinder engine grew to 251 cubic inches.

1951 Dodge

1. Engineering had always been Number One at Chrysler Corporation. So, Dodge ads promised such practical virtues as a smooth ride from the new Coronet Diplomat hard-top. **2.** Safety-Rim wheels held a blown or deflated tire in position until the car came to a stop "under complete driver control." **3.** Like other Chrysler products, Dodge promised dials that were easy to read, and controls that were easy to reach. A new cane-type lever operated the parking brake. Dodge's Gyro-Matic transmission was billed as "America's lowest-priced automatic." Actually, the unit operated *semi*-automatically, with a "sprint-away" gear for passing, plus a low-ratio "power range." **4.** Seat covers were popular Dodge add-ons, in a choice of colors, fabrics, and patterns. Buyers could also order back-up lights and a marbleized plastic steering wheel.

Smoothie

When The Going Is Rough !

When a new owner gets his hands on a Dodge, here's something he learns in a hurry . . . and enjoys for a long time.

It's just this: Dodge is the smoothest-riding, easiest-going car a man could want *on any kind of road*. It's no "boulevard prima donna" that has to be babied over bumps!

Comfortably, you take a gravel or "washboard" road at a clip that would have you fighting the wheel in cars that lack the great "roadability" of this staunch and sturdy Dodge.

"Shockmeter" tests give Dodge a rating of "excellent" on road performance—the *highest rating* a car can achieve.

You know the answer. Better suspension-engineering. Road-taming Oriflow shock absorbers. And the same honest ruggedness that gives this "smoothie" such a great record for *long road life*.

This is the time to *step up* to a big, beautiful Dodge . . . and *step out* in the smoothest riding car on the road.

Specifications and equipment subject to change without notice.

Dodge

DEPENDABILITY

54

1. Barely more than a thousand Dodge Wayfarer Sportabouts went on sale in '51, the model's final year. 2. Dodge billed the three-seat Sportabout as "America's lowest-priced full-size completely convertible open car." At just $1924, it cost $644 less than a Coronet ragtop. 3. Economy-minded shoppers could select a semi-fastback Wayfarer two-door sedan. 4. Wayfarers rode a 115-inch wheelbase, versus 123.5 inches for Coronets. 5. Interstates weren't even envisioned yet, but a Dodge was the first car to enter the brand-new Pennsylvania Turnpike, at Pittsburgh, on August 7, 1951.

1951 Plymouth

1

1. Plymouth got a hardtop coupe, named Belvedere—part of the new Cranbrook series.
2. Plymouths wore a fresh face with a wider grille. The lineup included a mid-level Cambridge and short-wheelbase Concord series. 3. Four-door sedans might have Cambridge or Cranbrook dress. 4. Lowest-priced Plymouth was the Concord business coupe. 5. Plymouth's Concord series included Savoy and Suburban wagons.

3

4

5

2

Gas Stations Get a New Look

A Standard Oil station in Detroit shows the trend toward Fifties modernization. Even though the basic structure did not change shape during remodeling, new architectural porcelain surfacing gave the brick building a friendly nature.

Crosley Motors, Inc.

Base convertible dropped; now only offered in Super trim

Hotshot wins Index of Performance at Sebring

Powel Crosley, Jr., spends $3 million to keep company alive

Powel Crosley, Jr., insisted that his '51s were "the most-improved cars we have ever built," but even the new "spinner" grille failed to jump-start sales. Model-year output skidded to 6614 units (including 646 roadsters). Crosley spent $3 million to try and shore up the company, but its days were numbered. **1.** Fred Koster (behind wheel) and Ralph Deshon drove this Hotshot to victory in the Collier Race, earning the Sam C. Collier Memorial Trophy. Crosleys chalked up an impressive total of race wins, including the Index of Performance at Sebring. **2.** Sedans may have been tame, but Crosley's sport roadsters were adept in road races or on banked ovals. Riding an 85-inch wheelbase, the Hotshot could hit 90 mph. **3.** In addition to pumping gas, this Gulf station on Long Island, New York, served as a Crosley dealership.

1

2

3

Ford Motor Company

New Ford Victoria is the only low-priced hardtop coupe with standard V-8 engine

Three-speed Ford-O-Matic and Merc-O-Matic transmissions become available—blend torque converter with planetary gearset

New automatics, built in cooperation with Warner Gear, garner favorable comments from road testers

Ford Crestliner Tudor reappears, but is eclipsed in sales by new Victoria hardtop

Victorias account for 11 percent of Ford production total

Ford's model-year output tops a million—but that doesn't beat Chevrolet's

Lincoln output rises to 32,574—but ranking drops to 18th

Specially-geared Lincoln wins its class at Mobilgas Economy Run, delivering 25.44 mpg—despite 4100-pound weight

Special-edition Lincolns—Lido and Capri—on sale again

Monterey special-edition remains—but neither Mercury nor Lincoln has a hardtop coupe

Lincolns, like many makes, get larger back window

Ray Crawford runs eighth in Mexican Road Race, driving a Lincoln

Mercury edges up to sixth in production, with 310,387 built—a new high

1. Crestliner Tudors got a revised two-tone pattern, with five color choices—including all-black. Only 8703 were built. 2. Not enough new-car customers were tempted by that Ford crest for the company to overtake Chevrolet in sales. 3-4. "Continental kits" were popular extras on many cars, including this Custom DeLuxe convertible. This "loaded" Ford sports oversize bumper guards, a massive hood ornament, extra lights, and a bundle of brightwork.

1

2

3

1. Woody station wagons wore Country Squire badging. A total of 29,017 were built. 2. Ford's new asymmetric dashboard featured a Safety-Glow control panel, Chanalited instruments, recessed controls—and new ignition-key starter switch. Ford-O-Matic added $159. 3. Suburbanites shunned them, but no-frills business coupes drew respectable sales: 20,343 produced this season, at just $1324. 4. Ford V-8s had long been popular with both cops and criminals. A collectible today, this DeLuxe Fordor sedan started life as an Illinois State Police car. 5. Here, a State Police Ford stops at a service facility in Springfield, Illinois.

4

5

1951 Ford

1

2

3

4

5

6

1. Ford's facelift included a new "dual-spinner" grille and chromed windsplits ahead of twin-point taillights. Victorias came in 10 color combinations. **2.** Despite a late debut, the new Custom Victoria outsold Chevrolet's hardtop. **3.** Priced at $1925, a Victoria cost just $24 less than the convertible on which it was based. Gordon Buehrig earned credit for the body. **4.** Steep-roofed gas stations, like this Phillips 66 outlet, were common in rural areas. Note the rack of oil cans. **5.** This Fordor participated in the 1951 Mobilgas Economy Run, from Los Angeles to the Grand Canyon. **6.** Light-duty trucks gained a bold restyle, including a wider cargo box with wood floor for this F-1 half-ton V-8 pickup.

1

2

3

1. This year's modest facelift gave the Mercury-based Lincoln coupe a revised grille, cleaner bumpers, and upright taillights in squared-up rear fenders, replacing the round lenses. 2. Lincolns, the brochure insisted, were "produced with a jeweler's painstaking precision," intended to deliver satisfaction as steadfastly and long-lasting as that of a historical memorial. Not everyone agreed, evidently, as sales failed to reach great heights. 3. A special-edition Lido coupe went on sale again, at $2702, with a "vinyl-leather-covered safety-steel roof." Seats in the "master-crafted" Lido featured leather shoulder bolsters.

1951 Lincoln

1. Only 857 Cosmopolitan convertibles went on sale, priced at $3891 and tipping the scales at a burly 4615 pounds. Painted chartreuse, a well-loaded Cosmo was quite a sight. **2.** As before, Sport Sedans came in both standard Lincoln (shown) and top-of-the-line Cosmopolitan guise. *Motor Trend* named Lincoln "one of the best cars on the market." **3.** Lincoln's "sturdy, comfort-secure chassis" with "skyscraper braced cross members" promised "relaxing comfort . . . from the road up," allegedly filtering out fatigue-building vibration. The brawny InVincible 8 L-head engine produced 154 horsepower this year.

1. Cosmopolitans rode a wheelbase four inches longer than standard Lincolns, and cost considerably more—$629 more, in the case of the four-door Sport Sedan. Production of Cosmopolitan Sport Sedans shot up 47 percent, to 12,229. Unlike those on the smaller Lincoln, rear fenders did not protrude. 2. A padded roof gave the $3350 Cosmopolitan Capri some extra flair, but coupes failed to attract much attention in the marketplace. Only 2727 were built, in basic or Capri trim. Capris came in a choice of three colors, with harmonizing "vinyl-leather" roofs. Cosmopolitans added a full-length sidespear, replacing the controversial airfoil trim. 3. Capri interiors featured custom-tailored cord and leather upholstery. Formerly woodgrained, Lincoln dashboards now were painted to match the body color.

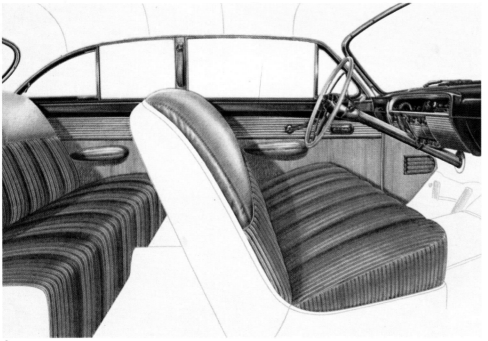

66 Statistics recently told us that Ford Motor Co. could produce about 6,300 cars a day. That was our total capacity—on paper. But that didn't stop us from boosting our production to nearly 9,000 units a day. . . . Now there's the difference between statistics and what actually can be done. 99

*Lincoln-Mercury general manager **Benson Ford**, on the tendency of statistical projections to underestimate American productivity; February 1951*

1951 Mercury

1

2

1-2. Like Lincoln, Mercury faced its final season in this "bathtub" form, adding a bolder grille and extended rear fenders with upright taillights. The longer, lower silhouette looked particularly pleasing in the club coupe body, which sold for $1947. Outside sun visors and fender skirts still were among the most popular extra-cost accessories. Mercury's V-8 engine added two horsepower (now 112). **3.** Browsers had plenty to choose from in Mercury showrooms, "styled just for you." The selection of models again included a Monterey coupe, with "vinyl-leather" or canvas top and leather or leather/cord interior. Newly optional Merc-O-Matic Drive featured a "natural" selector dial. Swiftest acceleration was attained by starting off in Low range, then shifting manually into Drive.

3

1

2

3

1. Least-popular Mercury model was the eight-passenger station wagon. Only 3812 were produced. Note the jumbo fender skirts and such extras as a grille guard, sun visor, and spotlight. 2. A Mercury Sport Sedan tows a float in the Santa Claus Parade down Chicago's State Street, on November 17, 1951. Partly because TV had not yet taken hold of kids' attention, parades often drew enormous crowds. 3. Mercury's four-door Sport Sedan was the most popular, with an even $2000 price and 157,648 produced. Many considered this year's brightwork and extra size excessive, detracting from the clean look of the 1949-50 models—especially the coupes. 4. Rear-fender script reveals that this convertible has the new Merc-O-Matic.

4

1951 Buick

General Motors Corporation

Buicks get restyled front end

Hardtop joins Buick Special line

Buick drops to fourth in production, behind Plymouth

Final Cadillac Series 61 models built

Four Cadillac series on sale; all have Hydra-Matic

Chevrolets get slightly protruding rear fenders and cleaner-looking grille

All Oldsmobiles have V-8 engines, and switch from rear coils to rear leaf springs

Restyled Oldsmobiles win 20 of 41 stock-car starts

Super 88 joins Oldsmobile line, on new 120-inch wheelbase

Slow-selling Oldsmobile station wagons discontinued

Standard Olds 88, with Chevrolet bodyshell, includes only sedans

Self-winding watch available in Oldsmobile steering-wheel hub

Pontiacs come in 28 models—production is second-best ever, clinching fifth-place ranking

Four-door Pontiac fastbacks extinct . . . two-doors soon dropped

Pontiac marks 25th anniversary

1. A toned-down grille marked this year's "Smart Buy" Buicks. **2.** Buick initially used the Riviera nameplate for four-door sedans as well as two-doors. This Roadmaster Riv went for $3044, with a 152-horsepower straight-eight. Roadmasters wore an ample quantity of chrome—but far more would be coming later in the decade. Two-tone paint sparked sales. **3.** Not a strong seller, the Buick Roadmaster Estate wagon cost $3780. As usual, the ad copywriters stayed busy formulating lavish praise. Roadmasters, for instance, were described as the "brilliant master of the road in performance, prestige, and the sheer luxury of its travel."

1. Buick engineers helped design wild show cars, including the XP-300. Inside are Mr. and Mrs. C. E. Wilson, accompanied by chief engineer Charles Chayne. 2. Both the XP-300 and Le Sabre held an aluminum 215-cid V-8. Note the fine-toothed grille and teardrop headlight nacelles—styling touches coming in 1954. 3. GM used the XP-300 to promote other products. The supercharged engine used an AC oil filter. 4. Harley Earl, head of GM styling, sits behind the wheel of the LeSabre show car. 5. Buick Specials now carried the same size engine as Supers. 6. Convertibles came in all three Buick series.

1951 Cadillac

1. Cadillacs added small grilles under the headlights, but otherwise changed little. 2. Except for interior trim, the basic Series 62 hardtop was similar to a Coupe de Ville. 3. Top seller by far: the Series 62 sedan. 4. The Series 62 convertible cost nearly $4000. 5. Series 62 Coupe de Ville. 6. Series 61 coupe. 7. Though "every inch a Cadillac," the Series 61 failed to attract buyers. 8. Hollywood starlet Jan Sterling looks dwarfed behind the wheel of this Series 62 ragtop. 9. Biggest model: the Fleetwood 75.

1

3

2

1. This ambulance was used by the police department of Cicero, Illinois. 2. Don E. Ahrens served as Cadillac's general sales manager from 1950 to 1956. 3. GM's XP-300 and Le Sabre "cars of the future" served as test beds for engineering ideas. Le Sabre's top closed when rain began, while the XP-300 had an adjustable-height steering column—plus built-in jacks. Le Sabre's wrap-around windshield and protruding bumpers soon would appear on production models.

"Madman" Muntz turns from TVs to cars

One of the most publicized low-production sport models was the Muntz Jet, built in Evanston, Illinois. After creating an envelope-bodied car in 1949, Frank Kurtis sold his firm to Earl W. Muntz, a former car dealer and maker of TV sets, known as "Madman" for his promotional antics. Four-seat Jets first carried Cadillac engines, then switched to Lincoln V-8s. Original aluminum bodies were replaced by steel, with a removable hardtop. A Jet could top 120 mph. Muntz had ambitious hopes for 1000-a-day production and factory-run showrooms, but only 394 were built from 1950–54.

1951 Chevrolet

1.

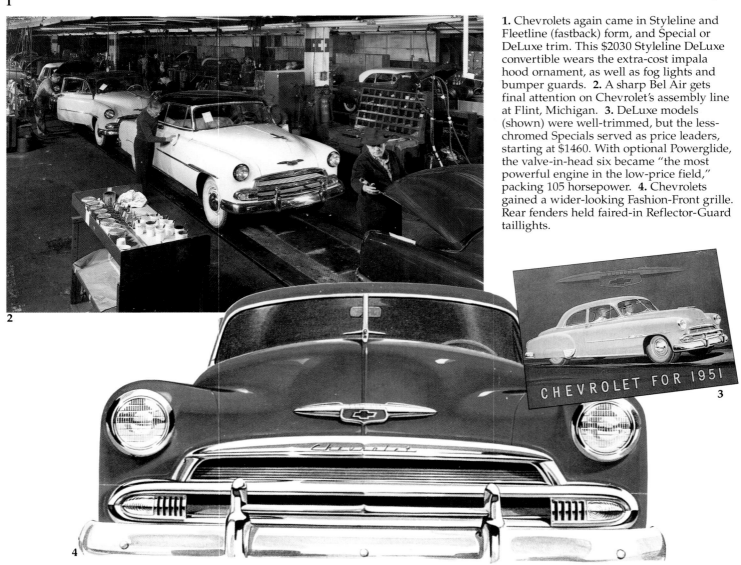

1. Chevrolets again came in Styleline and Fleetline (fastback) form, and Special or DeLuxe trim. This $2030 Styleline DeLuxe convertible wears the extra-cost impala hood ornament, as well as fog lights and bumper guards. 2. A sharp Bel Air gets final attention on Chevrolet's assembly line at Flint, Michigan. 3. DeLuxe models (shown) were well-trimmed, but the less-chromed Specials served as price leaders, starting at $1460. With optional Powerglide, the valve-in-head six became "the most powerful engine in the low-price field," packing 105 horsepower. 4. Chevrolets gained a wider-looking Fashion-Front grille. Rear fenders held faired-in Reflector-Guard taillights.

2.

CHEVROLET FOR 1951

3.

4.

1

2

3

4

1. Though handily outsold by sedans, the Styleline DeLuxe Bel Air hardtop proved to be a hot number. 2. Nearly any street scene included Chevrolets. This one is in Skokie, Illinois. 3. Fleetline fastbacks would last only one more season, but a DeLuxe two-door looked dashing when loaded with GM accessories. Inside was a new Safety-sight dash. 4. Even with six-cylinder power, Chevrolets were called on for Police duty. Stickshift models used a 216.5-cid engine; Powerglide, 235.5-cid. 5. Polishing the car on a Saturday was a regular ritual on suburban driveways.

71

1951 Oldsmobile

1. First seen at the Chicago Auto Show in February with a chubby B-body akin to Buick's Special, the Oldsmobile Super 88 series appeared in five body styles. Design touches differed from both the regular 88 and posh 98 series. New rear leaf springs produced a stable ride with little body lean. **2.** A Super 88 DeLuxe Holiday hardtop coupe promised to be "your midsummer day's dream," for a mere $2558. **3.** Basic A-bodied 88s looked similar to their 1949-50 predecessors—and to Chevrolets—and were dropped early in the year. **4.** The standard 88 line included only two- and four-door sedans. **5.** All 88s now warranted a Rocket-engine emblem, since six-cylinder engines were gone. **6-7.** This Super 88 two-door sedan started at $2265, but the slower-selling club coupe was cheaper yet.

Oldsmobile 1951

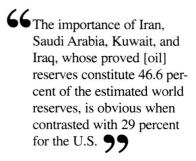

5

1. Oldsmobile's 98 Series served the near-luxury market. This DeLuxe Holiday hard-top shows new spear-like stainless steel trim on rear fenders. 2. Only the 98 convertible topped the $3000 mark. 3. In the 98 Series, four-door sedans were top sellers. 4. Though modern in appearance, this dealership's showroom had not yet acquired cars or customers. 5. The V-8 got a new distributor and carburetor, but output remained the same: 135 horsepower. 6. Olds buyers could opt for a steering-wheel-mounted Maar self-winding watch.

6

1951 Pontiac

1. Except for a new V-motif grille and fresh bodyside trim, Silver Anniversary Pontiacs showed only mild change. This visored Chieftain DeLuxe sedan holds a six-cylinder engine, but eights were gaining favor. Both engines gained horsepower—and could get an optional high-compression head. Pontiac was GM's most conservative division, using value as its major theme. Even so, copywriters managed to call it "the most beautiful thing on wheels,"as well as "America's lowest-priced straight-eight."
2. The four-millionth Pontiac was an eight-cylinder hardtop, rolling off the line in August. 3. Dealers again had a variety of Pontiacs: Chieftain or Streamliner, Six or Eight, plain or DeLuxe. Four-door fastbacks were gone, but two-doors hung on.
4. Workmen apply Blue Coral protective finish to a Pontiac hardtop.

1

2

3

4

5

7

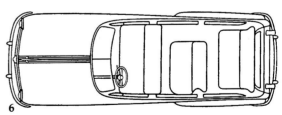

6

1. Virtues or demerits of its two-tone glamour aside, the Chieftain Eight Super DeLuxe Catalina hardtop deserves a prize for most breathless nomenclature. 2. Pontiacs also saw commercial service in the form of the sedan delivery. 3. A Chieftain DeLuxe convertible cost $2314 with the six, $74 more with an eight. 4. The Chieftain DeLuxe sedan coupe disappeared during the year. 5. All-steel Streamliner station wagons came in two levels. 6. Pontiac's DeLuxe station wagon seated six; the standard model (shown) held eight. 7. In contrast to today's self-service pumps, gas station attendants performed quite a variety of duties. Here, a Mobil mechanic helps with an outboard motor, delivered via '49 Pontiac.

1951 Hudson

Hudson Motor Car Company

Hot Hudson Hornet debuts with 145-bhp, 308-cid six

New engine is the largest, most powerful L-head six ever

Hornets come in four body styles, priced identically to Commodore Eights

Hudsons may now be ordered with Hydra-Matic—costs $158 extra

Supermatic semi-automatic transmission disappears

Instrument panel restyled; gauges now ahead of driver

Standard Pacemaker and Super Eight dropped

Hollywood hardtop joins body-style list late in season

Hornet becomes the most popular series

Factory soon offers "severe usage" parts for Hudson Hornet to boost its already-swift performance . . . they're really thinly disguised racing modifications

Stock-car racer Marshall Teague claims to get 112-mph speed from Hornet certified as stock

Hornets begin to earn long list of stock-car race victories—would prove nearly invincible from 1951–54

Total output climbs to near 132,000 . . . Hudson stays in 13th place

1

2

1-2. Like all Hudsons, the hot new Hornet displayed a more prominent grille. This $2568 French Gray four-door has Hydra-Matic, wheel trim rings, and an outside mirror—not a standard item on all cars. Veteran road-tester Tom McCahill called Hudsons "America's finest road cars [for] roadability, cornering, and steering." 3. Hudsons enter the final assembly process before going off to eager customers.

3

1

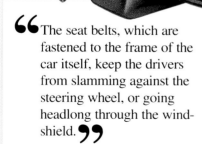

2

3

4

5

1. A Hollywood hardtop became available in all but the Pacemaker Custom series. This Hornet has been fitted with a 7X high-performance engine, which wasn't offered until late in 1953. 2. Rear-seat occupants had plenty of elbow room. 3. Instruments now sat ahead of a Hudson driver, with a Dura-fab top to cut reflections. 4. Initial Hornet engines had a single carburetor, but Twin H-Power later lured high-performance fans. 5. A Hornet's H-145 engine promised "Miracle H-Power." 6. A "Badge of Power" suggested Hornet capabilities. 7. After winning his first race in February, Marshall Teague posed with his wife.

6

66 The seat belts, which are fastened to the frame of the car itself, keep the drivers from slamming against the steering wheel, or going headlong through the windshield. **99**

NASCAR spokesman, on a new safety innovation designed to protect stock-car drivers; August 1951

7

Kaiser-Frazer Corporation

Final year for Frazers

Frazers earn rather radical restyling—actually, they're modified 1949-50 Kaisers

Hydra-Matic now available in Frazers

Compact, Kaiser-built Henry J economy car debuts

Henry J sedans lack glovebox and trunk lid

Henry J named "Fashion Car of the Year"

"Anatomic" restyled Kaiser, penned by Howard "Dutch" Darrin, debuts early in 1950 as '51 model . . . sales are strong

Kaisers have the lowest beltline of any car . . . economy of design whispers "elegance"

Kaiser output rises sharply—near 140,000, for 12th place

Kaiser promotes safety with padded dashboard, narrow-post pop-out windshield, recessed instruments

All Kaisers have 115-horsepower six—no V-8 available

Kaisers appear in International Home Furnishings Market, called "living room on wheels"—first time a car is recognized as an integral unit of home living

Supersonic Kaiser engines come with choice of three drives

1

2

1. Despite ad claims of "new handcrafted body styles," this year's cars were unused Kaisers—impressively remodeled for one final outing of the Frazer badge. The line included a four-door sedan and Vagabond, and Manhattan convertible and hardtop sedans—the latter with or without a nylon-covered roof. 2. By now America's only four-door convertible, the Frazer Manhattan was even more noticeable with this unusual color scheme. Only 131 were built, plus 152 hardtops. 3. Final Frazers had a new spear-motif design in front. Dealers were eager, but "The Pride of Willow Run" was about to expire, now that Kaisers were redesigned.

3

1. Neither the window frames nor the glass pillar retracted in the Manhattan hardtop sedan—evolved from the Kaiser Virginian—or the convertible. Either model cost $3075. **2.** Some called the final Frazer grille cumbersome, but the facelift actually was ingenious, producing a new look on the same bodyshell used since 1947. **3.** Biggest seller in Frazer's final season was the standard $2359 four-door sedan, but the make was dead regardless. **4.** Billed as 2-cars-in-1, Frazer Vagabonds were claimed to convert from a luxury sedan to spacious carrier in 10 seconds. Frazer called it a "successor to the station wagon."

The NEW handcrafted 1951

FRAZER VAGABOND

For you...sportsman, estate owner or commuter...here is the 1951 successor to the station wagon...truly a car built to better the best on the road! The Frazer Vagabond fills the needs of all who require a handsome sedan on one trip and a large-capacity carrier on the next. For merchant, farmer, technician or professional man the Vagabond serves double use in transporting products or equipment. With its new Supersonic Engine (Hydra-Matic Drive optional at extra cost) and handcrafted quality the Vagabond has the performance and value to make it the year's smartest buy for smart people. KAISER-FRAZER SALES CORPORATION, Willow Run, Michigan.

Converts in 10 seconds from 6-passenger sedan to spacious carrier.

The Pride of Willow Run

1951 Kaiser

1

2

3

5

6

4

1-4. Switching to an all-new body didn't mean the twin-hatch Kaiser Traveler utility sedan had to disappear. In fact, Travelers could have either two or four doors. Note "sweetheart dip" in the upper portion of back window—repeated in the split windshield. **5.** Clean lines looked uniquely appealing in a Special business coupe, or similar club coupe, with short quarter windows and long deck. **6.** All Kaisers, including this Special, now had a 115-horsepower L-head six-cylinder engine. **7.** Top seller: the Deluxe four-door sedan. **8.** These Kaiser bodies still needed work before leaving the assembly line. Note the brick floor.
9. Opera singer—and noted antique-car buff—James Melton (*left*) visited the Kaiser plant.

7

8

9

1-2. Most exotic Kaiser was the Golden Dragon, a $125 option for the Deluxe sedan. Fabric/color expert Carlton Spencer helped develop "dragon" vinyl—a heavy-duty plastic that looked like alligator hide. Note the wire wheels and Continental spare tire. **3.** No other car sported an interior like the Golden Dragon. A padded top in "dinosaur" pattern vinyl also became available. **4.** Ads promoted a variety of virtues, led by the fact that 600,000 Kaiser cars existed. **5.** Armed animal trainer Clyde Beatty received this "Safari" Kaiser from the company, upholstered in untreated lion and zebra pelts. It was one of four exotically trimmed sedans exhibited at the Chicago Auto Show.

1951 Henry J

1

2

3

4

5

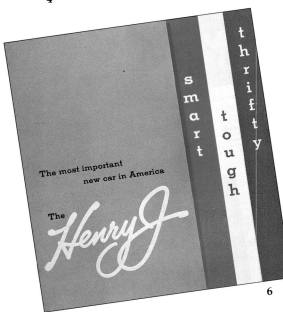

6

7

1. Henry J. Kaiser poses with his compact. Thousands entered a contest to name the new model, but the company planned all along to call it Henry J. 2. K-F displayed the Henry J at fairs across the country under the banner "The Most Important New car in America." Four- and six-cylinder versions were offered. 3. Henry J was to be the "affordable" car. 4. This Deluxe six has vent windows and turn signals. 5. Early models lacked a glovebox. Seat covers were common. 6. The Henry J brochure touted the compact's benefits. 7. Fins were prominent on the two-door sedan—the sole body style.

Nash Motors

Country Club hardtop coupe joins Rambler lineup in June, but wagons sell best

Final "bathtub" Nashes on sale, with prominent "jet" rear fenders instead of rounded bustleback

Each big Nash model comes in Super and Custom trim

Restyled Pilot Panel dashboards on big Nashes abandon Uniscope gauge cluster

Nash dubs Airflyte line "the world's most modern car," publicizing records for speed, stamina, and economy

Statesman promises over 25 mpg at average highway speed

New two-seat Nash-Healey sports car wears bodywork by Donald Healey, atop a Nash chassis with tuned Ambassador engine

Nash-Healeys are built in England, in cooperative effort between Healey and Nash Motors

All 104 Nash-Healeys built this year go to U.S. market, priced at $4063

Nash-Healeys stand just 38 inches high—can hit 125 mph

Big-Nash production drops a bit, but slack is more than taken up by increased Rambler output

Italian stylist Pinin Farina meets with Nash officials in Detroit, in June, and agrees to consult on styling for future Nash models

1

2

1. Some of the final "bathtub" Nashes near completion, with new vertical-bar grilles and protruding rear fenders. **2.** Statesman and Ambassador models wore the big-Nash crest again. Both could have Hydra-Matic, but overdrive was actually more popular. **3.** Is this Ambassador Custom really a police car? Sorry, the "Metropolis" on the door is a dead giveaway that it's not. The sedan was converted in 1990, inspired by the old *Superman* TV series. **4.** The $2501 Ambassador Custom sedan tempted fewer buyers than its cheaper Super stablemate.

3

4

1951 Nash

1. An open Rambler looked different from any convertible on the market, attracting a modest—but avid—following. 2. All three models were promoted as Airflytes: Ambassador, Statesman, and Rambler. Nash claimed them as the "first cars to apply the modern developments of aviation to the building of an automobile." 3. A sliding-top Rambler convertible cost $1993, the same as a Custom station wagon. A cheaper Super wagon also became available.
4. Nash added the Rambler Country Club hardtop in June, starting at $1968—including $300 worth of Custom equipment.
5. An aluminum-bodied Nash-Healey debuted at the Chicago Auto Show, with a 125-horsepower Ambassador engine. A true sports car, it handled capably on both track and highway

Nash Presents the World's Most Modern Cars, the 1951 Airflytes

Packard Motor Car Company

Packards gain modern squared-off profile, styled by John Reinhart on 122- and 127-inch wheelbases

Packards get new model designations

Lower-priced 200 series joins Packard lineup . . . Patrician 400 tops the line . . . 250 and 300 hold down the middle

Packard named "most beautiful car of the year" by Society of Motion Picture Art Directors

Top Packard engine is 327-cid straight-eight . . . 356-cid unit fades away

Ultramatic standard only on the Patrician 400 sedan, optional on other models

Packard persists in focusing on moderately priced cars: some Packards cost up to $500 less than the cheapest Cadillac

Mayfair hardtop coupe joins line in midseason

Some claim the 200 isn't a true, traditional Packard

"Real" Packards—250, 300, 400—are well-built, comfortable, high-speed road cars

Series 250/300 use same engine as 400, but at five fewer horsepower with manual shift

Larger 300/400 series cars ride 127-inch wheelbase, five inches longer than 200/250 models

1. Packard tried to convince customers that they would get more than mundane transport in the dramatically redesigned models, but Cadillac kept its lock on the luxury-car market. Perhaps alluding to the broad price range, the line was promoted as "America's most democratic fine-car family." 2. A Series 250 convertible cost $3391, with a 327-cid straight-eight. 3. The new Tele-Glance instrument panel included a pull-out drawer. Like most car models, Packard gave the driver "idiot lights" to show oil pressure and charge rate. Dealer response to the lower, roomier new Packards was called "electrifying."

1951 Packard

1

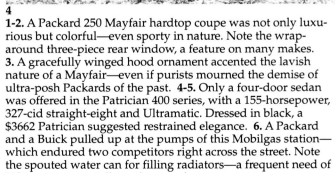

2

3

4

5

1-2. A Packard 250 Mayfair hardtop coupe was not only luxurious but colorful—even sporty in nature. Note the wraparound three-piece rear window, a feature on many makes. **3.** A gracefully winged hood ornament accented the lavish nature of a Mayfair—even if purists mourned the demise of ultra-posh Packards of the past. **4-5.** Only a four-door sedan was offered in the Patrician 400 series, with a 155-horsepower, 327-cid straight-eight and Ultramatic. Dressed in black, a $3662 Patrician suggested restrained elegance. **6.** A Packard and a Buick pulled up at the pumps of this Mobilgas station—which endured two competitors right across the street. Note the spouted water can for filling radiators—a frequent need of Fifties cars, especially as they aged.

6

Studebacker Corporation

Studebaker Commanders and Land Cruisers get V-8 engine

V-8 displaces 232.6 cid and delivers 120 horsepower

Studebaker's is first overhead-valve V-8 from an independent, and first in low-price field—expected to spark sales

V-8 contributes to small-block engine technology—and helps topple price barrier between popular-priced and luxury cars

Engineers had considered overhead cams—even a hemi—but chose overhead-valve design

Commanders now ride Champion's shorter (115-inch) wheelbase—lose 200 pounds

Land Cruiser sedan drops from 124-inch to 119-inch span

Though criticized, "bullet-nose" look is popular, and draws considerable attention; second chrome circle is added

Automatic Drive available, after introduction during 1950

Overdrive-equipped Studebaker accelerates to 60 mph in less than 13 seconds

Studebaker is first auto manufacturer to install Orlon convertible tops

U.S. production drops to 246,195 in abbreviated model year; Stude ranks ninth

1

2

3

1. A procession of '51s looks nearly finished on the Studebaker assembly line.
2. Economy-oriented Champions stuck with their 169.6-cid L-head engine. This two-door sports bumper guards, wheel covers, and chrome window trim. 3. The new 120-horsepower Commander V-8 promised "a thrill for your throttle foot," as well as frugal running. Two V-8s with overdrive got better mileage than all eights and most standard sixes at the 1951 Mobilgas Run. 4. A Studebaker rear end peeks past the carport of a tract home—typical of 1950s suburban style.

4

1952

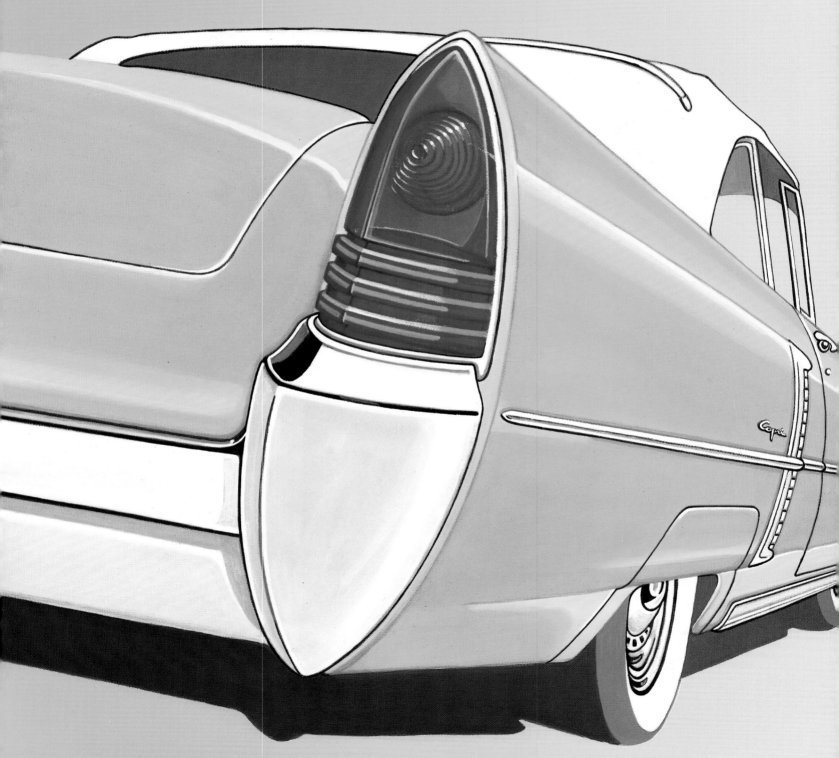

Despite the Korean War, Americans considered themselves to be prospering. They were, too, as judged by continually rising incomes and modest unemployment—down as low as three percent. Median family income approached $3900 a year, and the average full-time worker earned just over $3400—just about the price of a Packard convertible (or a pair of Fords). College teachers could expect about $5100 yearly, lawyers around $9000.

Three out of five families had a car, and two-thirds of homes had telephones. Already, one in three American households watched television—perhaps with one of the new TV trays propped in front of each family member. The traditional evening ritual of eating—and conversing—around the dinner table was in jeopardy.

The family automobile was turning into an *extension* of the home. More and more cars were loaded with comforts and conveniences, from power steering and sofa-plush seats to outside mirrors and even the new automatic-dimming headlights. Radios, on the other hand, were AM-only, just as they were in most homes, and nobody thought—yet—about playing music recordings in an automobile.

Some 56 million viewers saw vice-presidential candidate Richard Nixon's "Checkers" speech, in which he told of his 1950 car, mortgage, and "Republican cloth coat" for wife Pat. Dwight Eisenhower trounced Adlai Stevenson in the presidential election. TV premieres included *The Jackie Gleason Show*, Jack Webb's *Dragnet*, and the first *Today Show*, starring Dave Garroway.

Kay Starr sang "Wheel of Fortune," the Four Aces crooned "Tell Me Why," and Teresa Brewer waited "Till I Waltz Again With You." The "penny postcard" now cost a whopping two cents, but urban residents got two mail deliveries a day. The average American woman married at age 20, looking forward to a family—but seldom continuing in a career.

Fast-food restaurants had been scattered around the country for years, but Americans were taking a fresh interest in no-wait service. Some of the new drive-ins even had carhops to take orders right at car-side, and deliver the food on trays that hooked onto the open car window.

Gary Cooper won an Oscar for *High Noon*, Gene Kelly was *Singin' in the Rain*, and the comedy duo of Dean Martin and Jerry Lewis captured laughs from young moviegoers. Three-D glasses appeared, but neither that fad nor big-screen Cinerama would last more than a few years.

Anxious Americans began to scan the skies for (alleged) flying saucers, entertain themselves with new Paint-by-Numbers kits, or peruse *Mad* magazine. Travelers might stay at one of the new Holiday Inns. On a less pleasant note, the scourge of polio hit more than 50,000, subversives were barred from teaching in public schools, and unions—including auto workers—were accused of harboring "Reds."

The Korean conflict placed a limit on auto production. As a rule, most automakers were restricted to 80 percent of their output in 1950. The National Production Authority set a specific limit of 4,342,000 cars, and actual calendar-year output turned out to be just a few thousand under that figure. Price ceilings were in effect, too.

Cadillac upped the output of its V-8 to 190 horsepower, complete with dual exhausts. Ford launched an overhead-valve six, Lincoln got a new ohv V-8, and Hudson adopted Twin H-Power (a fancy designation for twin carburetors).

Ford came out with a totally redesigned line of cars, while each rival made do with facelifts. Shoppers could even buy a car at Sears: the new Allstate, a thinly-disguised clone of the Henry J.

More than two million automatic transmissions were installed, despite a temporary limit, early in the model year, on the number of cars that could have automatic. One-third of cars had a V-8 engine. Sixes would hang on for many more years, but straight-eights were nearing the end of their era. Automotive gadgets proliferated, as aftermarket manufacturers had their inventors ponder more and more comforts and conveniences.

At a typical gas station, regular fuel cost about a quarter a gallon—considerably more than today, when allowance is made for inflation. In May, government limits on credit were dropped, with 24-month finance terms seen likely. Dealers anticipated a serious upswing in sales if customers could spread their payments over a longer period.

No new models debuted until November '51, and many waited until early 1952. Some experts recommended a return to autumn launches, which had been the rule before World War II.

State license plates came in 34 lengths and 15 heights, and Charles Chayne of GM called for a standard size. Fort Worth, Texas, proposed banning cars to create a pedestrian shopping mall. That change didn't happen, but it served as a portent for the future.

Crosley production ceased in July, as the company merged into General Tire and Rubber. Americans bought the occasional imported minicar, but home-grown minis weren't yet in demand. As usual, several more independents—Autoette, Skorpion, Woodill—tried their hand, but few survived.

Prosperous or not, Americans weren't able—or willing—to snap up everything the automakers produced. In contrast to the recent past, when they were able to sell every last vehicle the factories turned out—with a hefty profit—dealers were seeing cars languish on the lots. Kaiser, in fact, touched up thousands of leftover '51s and remarketed them as '52 models, until a mildly redesigned replacement was ready.

In some dealers' minds—and in the plans of certain Detroit executives—the answer to a buyer's market was obvious: Sell 'em hard, and move the merchandise at any cost. The industry was preparing for a sales blitz, a full-scale assault on the consumer led by Ford and Chevrolet, whose repercussions are still felt today.

Chrysler Corporation

Mild facelifts given to '52 models, which differ little in styling or technical details

Chrysler, DeSoto, and Dodge continue to offer only *semi*-automatic shifting

Imperial series retrenches a bit by dropping its convertible coupe

Traveler utility wagons depart from Chrysler lineup . . . final Saratogas on sale

Windsor sixes can get Hydraguide power steering . . . all Chryslers may have electric windows and tinted glass

Six-cylinder Chrysler engine gains three horsepower; Hemi stands pat at 180 bhp

FireDome Hemi V-8 power now available in DeSotos—only the tiny Crosley engine produces more horsepower per cubic inch

DeSoto V-8 with 160 horsepower is produced in new plant

Dodge Wayfarer line trimmed to two models . . . roadster gone

Plymouth clings to Number Three production position, followed by Buick and Pontiac . . . Dodge remains in seventh spot

Motor Trend magazine awards V-8 Chrysler the title of "Best Engineered" car

Chrysler exhibits experimental Ghia-built C-200 convertible, evolved from K-310 coupe . . . other show cars follow, most powered by Hemi V-8 engines

1

1. One of a series of Chrysler "idea cars" in the early '50s, the D'Elegance coupe followed an earlier K-310. On a cut-down New Yorker platform, its "2+1" body held a sideways rear seat. **2.** Like most Chrysler "dream cars" of the period, the Special was designed by a team under Virgil Exner and built by the Ghia company in Italy. Note the snug spare-tire compartment. **3-4.** An open companion to the K-310 coupe, the C-200 show car also rode a stock Saratoga chassis. Distinctive "gunsight" taillights would be seen again on 1955-56 Imperials. Full wheel cutouts were a typical Exner styling touch. Both the K-310 and C-200 were considered for production, but rejected. Note the dual exhaust pipes.

2

3

4

1

2

3

1-2. Chrysler's Ghia-built, one-of-a-kind show cars didn't always disappear after their debuts. This fastback Special coupe was updated by the factory during its three-year active life by replacing its original semi-automatic transmission with PowerFlite. After 1955, it was released from active service. The body is aluminum from the cowl back, with steel front fenders and an aluminum hood. Chrysler's 331-cid Hemi V-8 powered most show cars of the period. 3. Chrysler advertisements focused on the fashionable show cars: (*top to bottom*) K-310, C-200, Special, and D'Elegance. 4. Occupants of this Ghia-built coupe could swivel into position. Note the large round gauge units, and the seatbelt buckle—safety belts were rare except on race cars.

4

1952 Chrysler

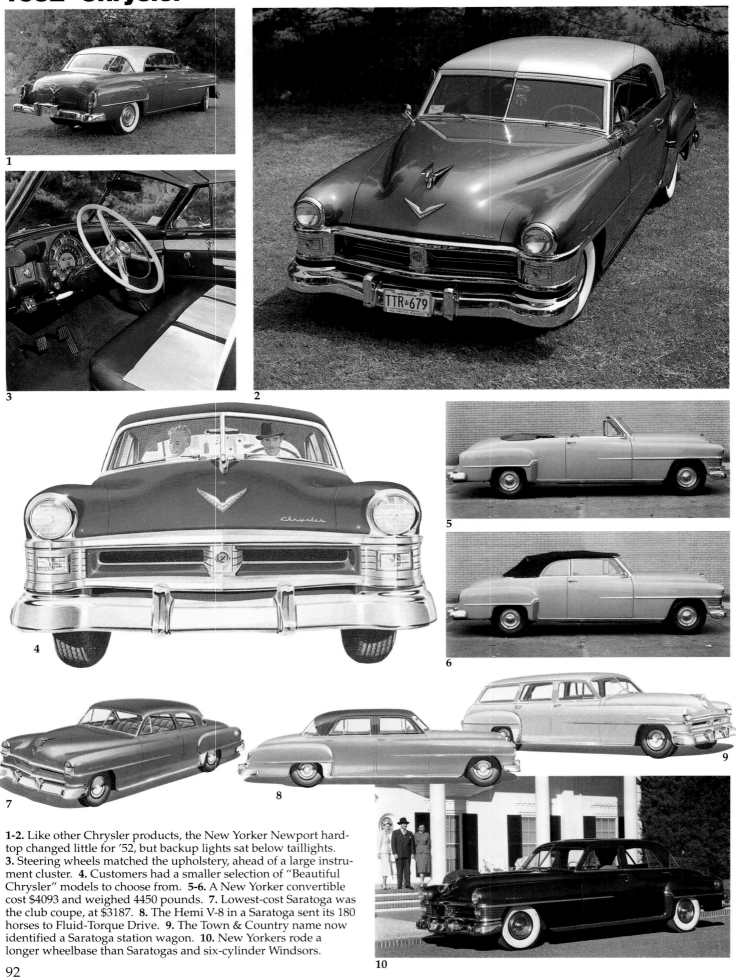

1-2. Like other Chrysler products, the New Yorker Newport hardtop changed little for '52, but backup lights sat below taillights. 3. Steering wheels matched the upholstery, ahead of a large instrument cluster. 4. Customers had a smaller selection of "Beautiful Chrysler" models to choose from. 5-6. A New Yorker convertible cost $4093 and weighed 4450 pounds. 7. Lowest-cost Saratoga was the club coupe, at $3187. 8. The Hemi V-8 in a Saratoga sent its 180 horses to Fluid-Torque Drive. 9. The Town & Country name now identified a Saratoga station wagon. 10. New Yorkers rode a longer wheelbase than Saratogas and six-cylinder Windsors.

Cunningham Shifts from Racing to Limited Production

Famed sportsman Briggs Cunningham sent a series of fast roadsters to the Le Mans race. Note the four carbs on the Chrysler Hemi V-8. Only a handful of Italian-built race-and-ride C-3 fastback coupes went on sale, at $9000 each. Three C-4R Cunninghams ran at Le Mans, as Briggs himself drove to a fourth-place finish.

1. DeSoto got its own version of the Hemi engine. Named FireDome, this scaled-down 276.1-cid V-8 yielded 160 horsepower—20 fewer than Chrysler's, but equal to the output of the new Lincoln. 2. DeSoto sponsored Groucho Marx's popular quiz show, *You Bet Your Life*. On radio or TV, major entertainers typically had a single sponsor, cleverly weaving the brand name into scripts. 3. Only a fingertip might be needed for parking, but power steering gave the driver little road "feel."

1952 DeSoto

1. Bumper-to-bumper traffic stretching into the horizon is nothing new, as seen in this view of Boston's Boylston Street. Note the parked DeSoto. 2. Like most body styles, the Sportsman hardtop came as either a FireDome Eight or Custom Six. 3. A convertible cost $2996 with a 116-bhp six, or $3183 with the new V-8. 4. With either engine, an all-steel wagon cost $637 more than a four-door sedan. 5. Nearly every gas station offered full mechanical service—including this Gulf outlet in Bronxville, New York. Note the coin changer hooked to the man's belt. 6. A $3183 FireDome Eight convertible promised 160-bhp performance, full power steering, and power braking.

5

6

1

2

3

1. Dodge continued to promote practical features and dependability. Only minor detail changes were evident. A Diplomat hardtop commanded $2602. 2. In the conformity of quickly expanding suburbia, neighbors' opinions mattered. Few were likely to find fault with a $2908 Coronet Sierra station wagon. 3. Lightweight Wayfarers went on sale for the last time, in two-door sedan and business coupe form. All Dodges stuck with the 103-horsepower L-head six. 4. In a Dodge, the brochure insisted, "you sit normally erect and comfortably relaxed on knee-level seats." This Coronet sedan cost $90 more than the same-size Meadowbrook.

4

1952 Plymouth

1

3

2

1. Plymouth touted 46 improvements, most of them hidden. They included modified springs/shocks, revised starting and braking hardware, plus easier shifting. A new rear nameplate, integrated with the trunk handle, replaced the former script. Style leader was the Cranbrook Belvedere hardtop, at $2216. 2. Fabrics blended with the instrument panel and door panels in Tone-Tailored interiors. Solex safety glass was optional. Note the flat two-piece windshield and the plaid seat covers—a popular add-on. 3. Do-it-yourselfers in thousands of driveways could install new Champion plugs—and handle tuneups of the easy-to-service L-head engine.

1

2

3

1. No other manufacturer offered a two-tone paint scheme similar to that of the Plymouth Belvedere. 2. Most Plymouth improvements were beneath the surface. President D. S. Eddins promised "the most gentle ride, the smoothest engine performance and the greatest safety ever built into a car for the lowest price field."
3. Overdrive engaged as the driver's foot lifted off the gas pedal at 25 mph or more.

Crosley Motors, Inc.

Lineup continues with little change; even some prices remain the same

Cooperative development with Union Pacific Railroad produces shipping boxcar that can hold 16 Crosleys

Power again comes from 44-cid four-cylinder engine with cast iron block

Only 2075 Crosleys are built in 1952 model year as automobile production halts in July

Final tally includes 358 Hotshot and Super Sports roadsters—still able to make strong showings on race courses

Crosley Motors is acquired by General Tire and Rubber Company, which gets controlling interest for about $60,000

Corporate assets amount to $5,728,208 at time of sale

Powel Crosley, Jr., has spent $3 million in a valiant attempt to stay afloat

Reasons for failure include trend away from no-frills transport in the "Bigger is Better" Fifties

America has shown it isn't yet ready for a domestic minicar

Crosley engine remains in production, used in power boats and for portable refrigeration

Ralph Roberts and Jack Wills develop kit to transform a Crosley sedan or station wagon into shapely Skorpion sports car

1

1. Jingle contests were popular pastimes. Thousands of Americans took pen in hand to compose rhapsodic prose about a product—typically, 25 words or less—hoping to win a valuable prize. In this challenge sponsored by Mission Orange soda pop, young folks simply had to write the last line. Top prizes: an orange grove and Crosley Super Sports roadster. 2. Crosley was represented at the Chicago Auto Show by this Super convertible, priced at $1059.

2

Ford Motor Company

Ford Motor Company is only automaker to fully restyle all its cars this year

Fords get overhead-valve Mileage Maker six-cylinder engine . . . flathead Strato-Star V-8 adds 10 horsepower

Fords come in three series: Mainline, Customline, Crestline

All-steel Ford station wagons debut, including woody-look Country Squire

Country Sedan and Crestlines come only with V-8 engines

Veteran road-tester Tom McCahill calls totally restyled '52 "the best looking Ford ever built"

Hardtop coupe now available in Lincoln and Mercury lines

Lincoln adds ball-joint front suspension and 317.5-cid overhead-valve V-8 engine for restyled Cosmopolitan and Capri

Power steering and four-way power seat available on Lincolns

Mercury V-8 boosted to 125 bhp, via higher compression and improved carburetion

Overdrive-equipped Mercury wins class in Mobilgas Economy Run

Lincolns take top four spots in 2000-mile *Carrera Panamericana* road race, beating Ferraris, Chryslers—and Hudson Hornets

Continental 195X "Car of Tomorrow" holds phone, dictaphone, automatic jacks

1

2

3

1. Helmsmen of Ford Motor Company included Lincoln-Mercury chief Benson Ford (*third from left*), executive vice president Ernest R. Breech (*fifth from left*), and president Henry Ford II (*sixth from left*). **2.** Led by George Snyder and Tom Hibberd, these artists at work on a full-scale rendering of the 1952 Ford were close to the final design. The basic shape—boxy lower body with fenders near hood-height—was decided fairly early in the process, which began in 1949. **3.** A few redesigned '52s get final inspection.

1952 Ford

1

2

3

4

5

6

7

1. Three Crestline models topped the Ford line, including this $2027 Sunliner convertible. 2. In the mid-range Customline series, a Tudor sedan cost $1570. Customlines sold best, by far. 3. Country Sedan station wagons had plain bodysides, while the higher-priced Country Squire wore simulated wood. 4. Ford originally was to get an overhead-valve V-8, like Lincoln's, but that would have to wait. 5. Ford issued 77,320 hardtops in the new shape. This Crestline Victoria sports such extras as full-disc hubcaps, skirts, Continental kit, and dual exhausts. 6. Without add-ons, a Victoria cost $1925. Ford-O-Matic added $170.
7. Owners loved dealer-installed and aftermarket goodies. This Sunliner has oversize V-8 emblems, rocker moldings, grille guard, and more. 8. Not many young fellows enjoyed service of this sort at the local Sohio station.

8

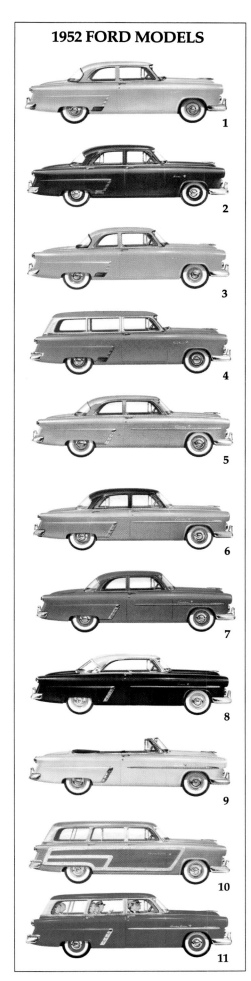

1952 FORD MODELS

1
2
3
4
5
6
7
8
9
10
11

12

13

14

15

1. Mainline Tudor sedan. 2. Mainline Fordor sedan. 3. Mainline business coupe. 4. Mainline Ranch Wagon. 5. Customline Tudor sedan. 6. Customline Fordor sedan. 7. Customline club coupe. 8. Crestline Victoria hardtop coupe. 9. Crestline Sunliner convertible. 10. Crestline Country Squire. 11. Customline Country Sedan. 12. This Customline Tudor served the Houston Police Department. 13. Ford's new six developed 101 horsepower. 14. A series of contests sponsored by soap companies gave away 20 Fords. 15. Note the hooded gauge cluster in this Victoria.

1952 Lincoln

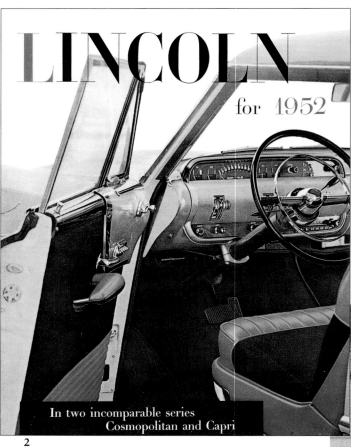

1. Lincolns looked sharp and performed deftly, with the new Y-block V-8 and ball-joint suspension. A Capri hardtop cost $3518 with Dual-Range Hydra-Matic.
2. Interiors offered "a rich, yet smartly informal atmosphere" with aircraft-style dash. Cosmopolitans wore two-tone broadcloth, while Capris used leather, nylon, and whipcord. 3-4. Cosmos cost less but rode the same 123-inch wheelbase as Capris.

1-2. Only 1191 Lincoln Capri convertibles were built, versus 5681 hardtops. William Schmidt led the styling team, while Earle S. MacPherson (later to develop MacPherson struts) helped with engineering. Lincoln's integrated bumper/grille became a styling trend, as did the gas filler hidden behind the license plate. In the sales race, Lincoln aimed less at Cadillac than at buyers of big Ninety-Eight Oldsmobiles.

1952 Lincoln

1. Whether buying a car or a home, every American was presumed to crave the "modern living" that Lincoln offered. 2. Capris came in three body styles, Cosmos only as a hardtop coupe and four-door sedan. 3. A Capri Special Custom sedan cost $3331, or $133 more than its Cosmo equivalent. 4. Hardtops, in particular, showed a resemblance to the restyled Mercury. "No other production car," insisted *Speed Age*, "can equal Lincoln's roadability, ease of handling and excellent overall driving characteristics." 5. Saturday cleanup duties included the car's tires.

1. Mercury promoted both the styling and frugality of its redesigned models. Sharing bodyshells with Ford, Mercs rode a longer wheelbase—identical to 1949-51. **2.** For the first time, Mercury had a hardtop coupe, in both the Custom and upscale Monterey series. **3.** Mercury showed clean lines in an assertively angled profile. **4.** All-steel wagons replaced the woody, with either six- or eight-passenger capacity. **5.** Eight-passenger wagon seats could be set up three ways for various cargo/passenger requirements.

1952 Mercury

1

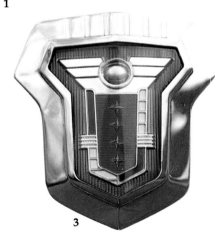

3

2

1. Sleek is the word for a top-down Mercury Monterey convertible—far different from its rounded 1949-51 predecessor. Note the wide nonfunctional hood Jet-scoop. Most Mercs wore extra-cost grille guards, which enhanced the front-end look. 2. Power windows and seats cost extra on the $2370 Special Custom convertible, while curb buffers and rear fender shields were standard on all Montereys. The familiar flathead V-8 gained 13 horsepower. 3. Mercury's crest reappeared on '52 hoods after a one-year absence. 4. Early in the year, the New Jersey Turnpike opened for business. Note the variety of cars at this rest stop.

4

1. Mercury's new ladder-type box-section frame, with five cross members, provided "an extra-strong foundation" as well as mounting for "sea-leg" rear shock absorbers. Merc might have gotten an overhead-valve V-8 this year, but lack of manpower and tooling restricted that engine to Lincoln. **2.** Especially with blackwall tires, a Mercury Custom four-door sedan looked rather plain. **3.** The Custom series also included a $2100 two-door hardtop. Factory accessories included Solex Sea-Tint windows, backup lights, and road lamps. **4.** Two-tone paint added glamour to a Monterey four-door sedan. Mercury promoted the virtues of its new Mono-pane curved windshield and wraparound back window. Customers liked the Interceptor aircraft-style instrument pods with their toggle switches.

1952 Buick

General Motors Corporation

GM mainly fields facelifted '51 models

Dual-Range Hydra-Matic installed in GM cars—operates through either three or four gear ratios

Power steering available on upper-level Buicks . . . also new on Cadillacs and Oldsmobiles

Cadillac marks Golden (50th) Anniversary

Cadillac installs dual exhaust outlet tips in rear bumpers as standard equipment

Cadillac engines have highest horsepower (190) in the industry, with new four-barrel carburetion

Sales manager J.M. Roche calls Cadillac "the pinnacle of styling perfection"

Chevrolet output drops to 818,142 cars—but Ford builds only 671,733 in slack year for the industry

Super 88 Oldsmobile engine puts out 160 horsepower

"Ninety-Eight" nomenclature replaces "98" on top-line Oldsmobiles

Autronic Eye automatic headlight dimmer available late in season . . . device may be installed in Cadillacs and Oldsmobiles for $53

Oldsmobile revives Valiant Car program, to provide specially equipped cars for amputee and paraplegic veterans

1

1. Wearing new trim atop rear fenders, each Buick series included a Riviera hardtop coupe, often sold with two-tone paint. (Riviera badging no longer went on sedans.) Automakers announced specific dates when cars would appear in showrooms, and dealers frequently turned the occasion into a high-profile event. "When better automobiles are built, Buick will build them" was the company's slogan for years. 2-3. Just $2115 bought a Special sport coupe with a 263.3-cid straight-eight.

2

3

1. A Buick Roadmaster Riviera hardtop coupe started at $3306, with Dynaflow and a 170-horsepower engine—18 more than in 1951, courtesy of a new four-barrel carb. 2. Only the seldom-seen station wagon cost more than a $3453 Roadmaster convertible—$524 more, to be precise. 3. Special was the lowest-cost Riviera hardtop, at $2295. Super hardtops sold far more copies. 4. A little-known Marilyn Monroe appeared in the film *Niagara*, waiting near a Buick Special. 5. Power steering cost a "moderate" $199 extra on a Roadmaster, billed as similar to a "hydraulic slave."

1952 Cadillac

1-2. Lots of buyers ordered their colorful Cadillacs "loaded." Motorists of all ages began to yearn for a Coupe de Ville, but even without extras, the top Series 62 hardtop commanded $4013. 3. Output from Cadillac's 331-cid V-8 leaped by 30 horsepower to a lively 190. Dual-Range Hydra-Matic was standard on all models, except the big Series 75. Its "performance" range skipped one gear. 4. No longer a transitory styling touch, Cadillac fins were beginning to symbolize everything right (or wrong) with American automobiles. 5. Tipping up a taillight revealed the Caddy's gas-filler opening.

Announcing the Golden Anniversary — Cadillac

...WITH THE FINEST PERFORMANCE OF ALL TIME!

1902 1952 — STANDARD OF THE WORLD

HIGHLIGHTS OF THE GOLDEN ANNIVERSARY ADVANCEMENTS

NEW 190-HORSEPOWER ENGINE ★ NEW HYDRA-MATIC DRIVE ★ NEW CADILLAC POWER STEERING
BEAUTIFUL NEW INTERIORS IN ALL MODELS ★ NEW FRONT AND REAR END APPEARANCE ★ NEW DUAL EXHAUST SYSTEM

YOUR CADILLAC DEALER

1

IT'S A "WHO'S WHO" OF THE HIGHWAY!

THE GOLDEN ANNIVERSARY

Cadillac

STANDARD OF THE WORLD

YOUR CADILLAC DEALER

2

Cadillac

More Eloquent Than Words!

YOUR CADIL[LAC]

3

8

1. Series 60 Specials rode a 130-inch wheelbase. **2.** In Cadillac ads—and in the public mind—most owners were "distinguished persons." **3.** Cars were symbols of success, and nothing represented it better than the Cadillac crest. **4.** Convertibles came only in Series 62. **5.** Series 62 hardtop coupes had light/dark broadcloth or cord upholstery. **6.** Convertibles wore two-tone or solid leather. **7.** Sedan back seats had tufted cushions. **8.** Whitewalls were scarce for a time, due to Korean War cutbacks.

4

5

6

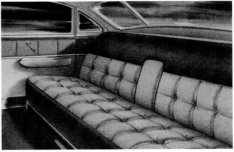

7

1952 Chevrolet

1. Not every Bel Air hardtop has as many goodies as this one, featuring a gold impala hood emblem, skirts, bumper tips, beauty rings—and seat covers inside. Stickshift models kept the 92-horsepower engine, while Powerglide again brought the bigger truck-based six, with 105 horses and a new automatic choke. 2. Facelifted one more time, "America's most beautiful low-priced car" gained a set of grille teeth and rear-fender brightwork. 3-4. A Styleline DeLuxe convertible cost $2128.

1. Some automakers ignored them, but Chevrolet's "OK Used Car" tag helped dealers move trade-ins. Each car was reconditioned. 2. Ads pushed plain sedans as well as flashier models. 3. Like its rivals, Chevy promoted value. This is a Styleline DeLuxe sport coupe. 4. Fastback Fleetlines went on sale for the last time. 5. An all-metal wagon offered function as well as beauty for $2297. 6. Long-term owners eventually had to think about an overhaul—or a remanufactured engine.

1952 Oldsmobile

1

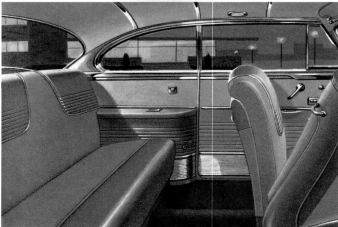

2

3

1. Breathing through a Quadri-Jet carburetor, output of Oldsmobile's fabled Rocket V-8 engine rose to 160 horsepower. Hydra-Matic added a second range for hill climbing and peak performance. DeLuxe 88s had the Super's body, but a 145-bhp V-8 engine. 2. Olds promised a Custom-Lounge "Rocket Ride" with "deep-decked comfort." 3. Roomy back seats featured "rich, durable fabrics in a choice of harmonizing colors." A new rear stabilizer helped handling. 4. Wheelbases of Ninety-Eight models grew by two inches, perhaps accounting for the promised "ultra-long look." The big convertible cost $3229. 5. A $3022 Ninety-Eight hardtop sold better than the convertible. Power steering allowed "1 finger" parking.

114

EVERY INCH A
classic!
(and 213 inches over-all!)

5

Tomorrow's Classic

4

1952 OLDSMOBILE SUPER 88 and DELUXE 88 MODELS

1

2

3

4

5

6

7

8

9

1. Most popular Olds was the four-door Super 88. 2. Super 88 convertible. 3. Super 88 Holiday hardtop. 4. Super 88 two-door sedan. 5. Club coupe was the lowest-priced Super 88. 6. Cheapest Olds was the DeLuxe 88 two-door. 7. DeLuxe 88 four-door sedan. 8. Super 88 four-door. 9. Motorists saw few roads other than two-lanes in mid-America. Here, an Olds and Pontiac approach an intersection outside of East Peoria, Illinois. Note the Skelly gas sign and roadside fruit market.

White Castle—Fast Food Pioneer, Still Going Strong

In 1921, Walter Anderson opened the first White Castle restaurant in Wichita, Kansas. Its specialty: small-scale burgers and trimmings—in a hurry. Patrons were encouraged to "Buy 'em by the sack." This White Castle outlet stood on South Western Avenue, in Chicago. White Castle still grills "sliders" today, their little burgers being loved by millions. Other early fast-food emporiums—Twinburger, Henry's, Chicken in the Rough—faded after a time. Already, in many parts of the U.S., drive-ins were becoming the favored meeting spot for teenagers.

1952 Pontiac

1. Except for a fresh grille, new full-disc hubcaps, and altered rear trim, the only big change at Pontiac was Dual-Range Hydra-Matic. Auxiliary "Drive" range gave quicker acceleration in traffic and on hills, while "Low" now delivered a second-gear start—handy on slippery pavement. 2. A Chieftain DeLuxe Eight convertible cost $2518 (up $130). Price-leader business coupes were gone, and the passenger-car line included just nine models—each with a six- or eight-cylinder engine. Both L-head engines went unchanged from '51. 3. More than 80 percent of Pontiacs had automatic shift, and 93 percent had straight-eight engines. Note the large box-style Hydra-Matic selector unit, and the clock built into the central radio speaker. A power antenna could now be ordered, as could "E-Z Eye" glass. 4. Pontiac's easy-to-spot hood ornament changed shape this season.

1

2

3

1. A Pontiac Chieftain Standard Six two-door sedan could be had for $1956, but this one has extras—including underseat heater and Hydra-Matic. 2. Standard Chieftains got a simpler steering wheel (shown) than DeLuxe models (opposite page). Climate controls are at the base of the steering column—hardly convenient. 3. Pontiac's trademark was still the Indian chief. Body trim changed, but Pontiac used the same sheetmetal from 1949 to '52. 4-5. A sedan delivery looked impressive with side trim borrowed from DeLuxe passenger cars. This stickshift Eight served as a flower car for a Wisconsin funeral home. Only 984 sedan deliveries were built, starting at $1920.

4

5

1952 Hudson

Hudson Motor Car Company

Hudson launches Wasp series, replacing Super Six

Full line also includes Pacemaker, Hornet, and Commodore Six and Eight

Hornets come in four body styles, with minor revisions in grille and body trim

All models get revised trim details, and all can have Hydra-Matic transmission—including budget-priced Pacemaker

Twin H-Power, featuring dual carburetors, arrives as option during '52 model year

Dual carbs available on all sixes, but mainly installed on Hornets, boosting their already-strong performance

Hudson promises "jet-like acceleration" from Twin H-Power engine

Marshall Teague wins 12 of 13 stock-car events at wheel of Hudson Hornet . . . Hudsons also claim 27 NASCAR victories

Tim Flock wins 250-mile Detroit race in Twin H-Power Hornet . . . Hudsons also take second and third

Ads push Hudson's stock-car race record

Model-year output drops to lowest level since 1942—just over half are Hornets

Aging "Step-down" design still revered for superior handling characteristics and roadability on the highway

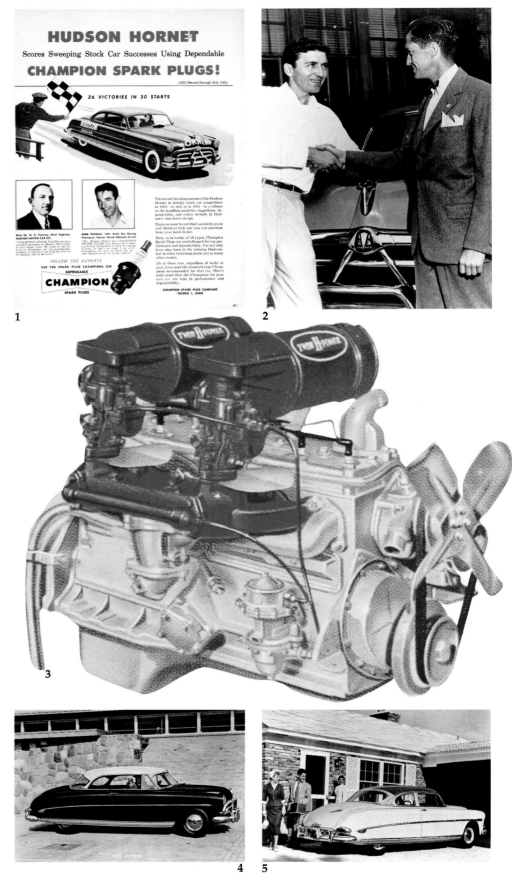

1. Even parts manufacturers took advantage of the hot Hornet's racing prowess for their advertising messages. 2. Tim Flock (*left*), youngest of the "Flying Flock" brothers, picked up a new Hudson Hornet at the Detroit factory, greeted by assistant sales manager Roy Chapin, Jr. 3. Every Twin H-Power engine sported bright red air cleaners. 4. The new Wasp mixed a Pacemaker platform with the old Super Six's 262-cid engine. 5. At $2742, the club coupe was the cheapest—and lightest weight—Hornet. Note the long trunk lid and wraparound back window.

1

1. "Road handling," insists this two-tone Hornet sedan's owner, was "second to none in its day." With a 145-bhp, 308-cid six-cylinder engine, the four-door sold for $2769. Hydra-Matic cost extra. **2.** Chicago's Courtesy Motors ranked as the country's largest Hudson dealer. Owner Jim Moran appeared regularly in the dealership's TV commercials and generated a long series of innovative promotions that pushed sales to the limit. Even the roof held Hudsons, as customers arrived in throngs to scan the newest Hornets. Car-shopping was becoming a major family event. **3.** Hornets got the most publicity, but Hudson had a full range of cars, from the thrifty Pacemaker and fresh Wasp to the last Commodore Eights. **4.** This dealership operated by M.L. "Red" Townsend used plenty of neon for its signage and decoration.

2

3

4

Kaiser-Frazer Corporation

Sears, Roebuck markets new compact Allstate sedan (a Henry J with different badging)

Allstates marketed mainly in southern states—and only through Sears stores carrying auto products

Regional Sears catalogs list the Allstate along with mail-order merchandise

Sears offers its traditional guarantee of satisfaction "or your money back"

Allstate brand fails to catch on; only 1566 cars issued this season, then half that number as '53 models

Interim Henry J Vagabond wears "Continental" (outside) spare tire in rear

Redesigned Henry J appears later in season, bearing Corsair badge

Leftover Kaisers are marketed as Virginians, sporting Continental kits and two-tone paint

Facelifted Kaiser sedans arrive late in season, with modified grilles and enlarged taillights

Frazers are gone, so top Kaiser gets Manhattan nameplate

Dual-Range Hydra-Matic available in Kaisers

Final Kaiser coupes built

No Kaiser Dragons issued this year, but a few Manhattans have Dragon-type padded tops

1

2

1. Kaiser-Frazer dealers weren't happy when Sears, Roebuck announced that its new Allstate two-door sedan started at just $1395. The Henry J cost more and had less standard equipment. 2. Allstates contained many Sears components (spark plugs, battery, tires). 3. Despite the U.S. map on its badge, Allstate sales were limited to Sears stores in the south and southeast. 4. Late in the '52 model year, taillights were moved into the protruding tailfins.

3

4

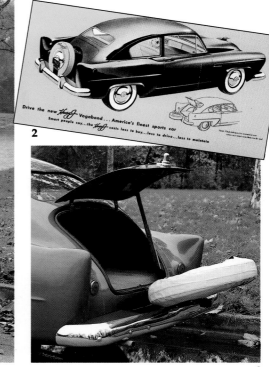

1

4

5

6

3

1. Kaiser-Frazer disposed of its leftover Henry J sedans by tacking on a Continental kit and Vagabond badges, selling them as '52 models. 2. Copywriters indulged in gross excess when they called Vagabond "America's finest sports car." 3. Vagabond's outside spare tilted outward to reveal a trunk lid, for more cargo space. 4. In this ad, the comedy team of George Burns and Gracie Allen spent a "typical" day with their Henry J. 5. Gauges sat in a Spartan dashboard. That bulging horn button would probably send shivers through today's safety experts. 6. Prices rose sharply when the Corsair arrived in March wearing fin-mounted taillights.

Excalibur Goes to the Races—Helped by Henry J

Who would guess that a Henry J chassis lurked beneath this racy body? Industrial designer Brooks Stevens devised a race-and-ride sports car based on the compact Henry J. Three Excalibur "J" roadsters were planned, with a Willys F-head or Alfa Romeo engine, to evaluate racing potential. They fared rather well, actually. A lightweight tubular structure held an aluminum skin. Note the cycle-style fenders. Years later, Stevens launched a neoclassic Excalibur roadster.

1952 Kaiser

1

5

2

1-2. Most costly Kaiser, at $2654, was the Manhattan four-door sedan. Deluxe was now the junior version. **3.** Manhattan interior fabrics hailed from the studio of Carlton Spencer. Note the hooded instrument cluster and row of controls, plus the short Hydra-Matic selector. **4.** Kaisers adopted large teardrop taillights and a heavier bumper/grille. Chrome plating during the Korean War was thinner than usual. **5.** Edgar F. Kaiser (son of the co-founder) served as company president.

66 We are in the auto business to stay. We have completed work on our '53 jobs and have frozen designs on '54s. 99

Kaiser-Frazer president **Edgar F. Kaiser**, *responding to rumors that K-F was in a transition out of the auto business; March 1952*

3

4

Nash Motors

Italian stylist Pinin Farina helps redesign senior Nash line, replacing bathtub look with squared-off shape

Pinin Farina earns credit for new design, though most of the changes stem from Nash stylists

Dual-Range Hydra-Matic and Solex tinted glass available on big Nashes

New Country Club hardtop, in Statesman and Ambassador lines, resembles tiny Rambler version

"Golden Airflyte" Nashes mark the company's 50th anniversary—started with "Little Red Rambler," issued in 1902

Nash sticks with unibodied construction; hawks strength, "life-saving safety," and absence of squeaks and rattles

Nash-Healey restyled by Pinin Farina . . . roadsters are assembled in Italy, built upon a chassis from Wisconsin— after tuning by Healey in England

Reworked Nash-Healey appears first at Chicago Auto Show in February 1952

Dual Jetfire Ambassador engine in Nash-Healey uses two carbs

Nash-Healey wins first in class, third overall at Le Mans race

Nash continues to study NXI experimental two-seater, renamed NKI—will become Metropolitan of 1954

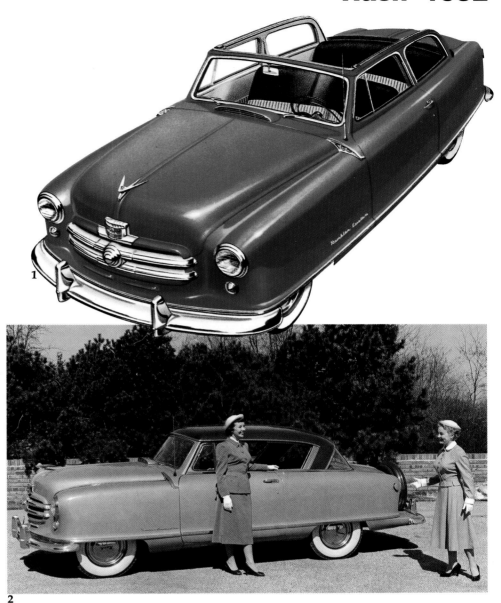

1. Nash dubbed its open Rambler a "convertible sedan," promising not only safety and rattle-proof construction but "dazzling performance, featherlight handling, down-to-earth economy." Its price rose to $2119. 2. Women with hats could sit comfortably in a $2094 Rambler Country Club hardtop. The outside spare tire added to the compact's panache. 3. Station wagons helped Rambler gain a following in suburbia. Two were issued: Super Suburban and this costlier Custom.

1952 Nash

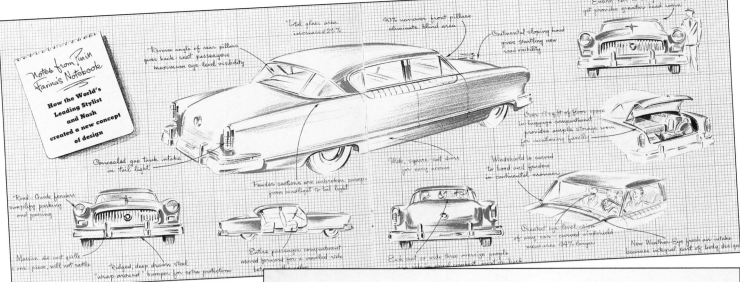

1. Immodestly billed as "the world's leading stylist," Pinin Farina was charged with re-creating the big Nash. Gone was the distinctive but outmoded "bathtub" look, replaced by a bulbously rounded box shape, as suggested in these drawings. Farina's two proposals played a role, notably the inclusion of a simple square grille and three-section rear window, but the end result was the work mainly of Nash stylist Edmund Anderson. Nevertheless, the cars carried "Pinin Farina" badges, and Nash promoted the contribution of the well-known Italian designer. 2. "Golden Airflyte" Nashes kept the prior model's integral-skirted front wheels, which limited the turning circle and impaired tire-changing. 3. Ambassadors rode a wheelbase seven inches longer than the Statesman, and carried a 120-horsepower, 252.6-cid engine.

3

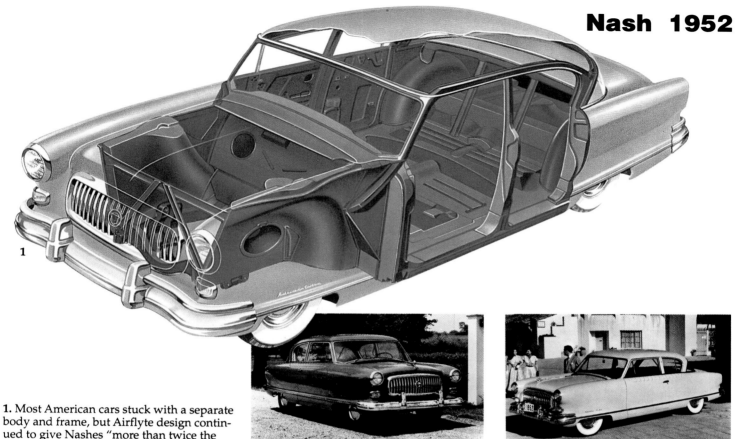

1. Most American cars stuck with a separate body and frame, but Airflyte design continued to give Nashes "more than twice the torsional rigidity of ordinary construction." Nash claimed it "made possible the elimination forever of body-bolt squeaks and rattles." 2. The $2144 Statesman Super two-door sedan rode a 114.3-inch wheelbase; its 195.6-cid six rated 88 horsepower. Both the Statesman and Ambassador came as Super and Custom sedans, along with a Custom Country Club hardtop. 3. This Ambassador Custom two-door sedan cost $174 more than an equivalent Super. 4. Pinin Farina gave the Nash-Healey a handsome new steel body, with a one-piece windshield and inboard headlights that would appear later on senior Nashes. 5. A Nash-Healey paced the Bridgehampton Race. During the year, a larger engine replaced the original Le Mans Dual Jetfire Ambassador Six.

To push its Car Plate wax, S.C. Johnson & Son bought a Nash-Healey and asked William Flajole to design and build a one-of-a-kind roadster body. Winners of the "name-it" contest earned a World Series trip. Baseball great Ted Williams got the car after a promotional tour, but never drove it.

1952 Packard

Packard Motor Car Company

Twenty-Fifth Series Packards tout more than 70 mechanical revisions and improvements

Main changes affect side trim, hood badge and ornament

DeLuxe 200 gets same grille as upper Packards—differences between junior and senior lines fade even further

Business coupe dropped

Packards get Bendix Easamatic power brakes—a $39 option

Former Hotpoint exec James Nance takes Packard helm, promising new focus on luxury automobiles

Fashion consultant Dorothy Draper creates colorful new interiors—notably two-tones

Instead of 20-percent output cut, mandated by Korean War, Packard is granted 5-percent hike in production

Three special Packards appear at Chicago Auto Show, including convertible with Continental kit and a Patrician 400 trimmed in mouton lamb

Experimental Packard Pan-American, created by Henney with modified Thunderbolt engine, appears at New York Motor Sports Show—will evolve into Caribbean

Brochure claims that more than 53 percent of all Packards built since 1899 are still in use

Packards are sold at 1457 dealerships

1. The Packard 200 (*right*) just got filled with regular—at 25.4 cents a gallon. 2. Top-line Patrician 400 got its own brochure. Inside, Packard refers to it as "the most advanced, most luxurious motor car in the world." 3. Aftermarket firms encouraged consumers to buy accessories.

Most luxurious motor car in the world.....
New Packard Patrician '400' for 1952

1952 PACKARD INTERIORS

Patrician 400

300

1

2

1-3. Only Packard's 250 series included a Mayfair hardtop—a stunner when two-toned. Ultramatic added $189 to its $3318 price. Power came from Packard's 327-cubic-inch straight-eight, offered since 1948. Mated to Ultramatic, it produced 155 horsepower; with stickshift, 150.

3

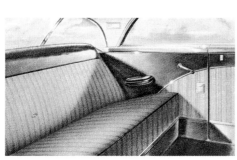

250 Mayfair hardtop

250 convertible

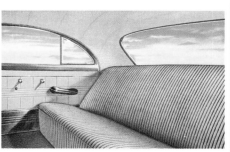

200 DeLuxe

1952 Studebaker

Studebaker Corporation

Studebaker celebrates 100th anniversary—still turning out vehicles mainly in South Bend, Indiana

Unibodied "N-Series" with evolutionary bullet nose is developed, then abandoned, due to government restraints and growing military production

Studebaker joins pillarless hardtop ranks with new Starliner body style

Final facelift hits 1947-51 bodyshells, prior to all-new 1953 model

Bullet-nose front ends gone, replaced by wraparound split grille ahead of longer, lower hood

Studebakers take two class wins at Mobilgas Economy Run: 27.8 mpg for Champion, 25.6 mpg for Commander V-8

Car/truck volume slips to 231,837 units in slowdown year for the industry

Studebaker maintains ninth-place ranking in American passenger-car production

Corporate earnings set records at $586 million, but profits amount to only $1.4 million

Commander convertible paces Indianapolis 500 race

Indy event is preceded by parade of 25 historic vehicles, led by float with Conestoga wagon, in "Caravan of the Century"

Race victor Troy Ruttman takes home the pace car—plus prize money

1

2

1-2. Finally, Studebaker issued the increasingly popular hardtop coupe body style. The Commander State Starliner with V-8 engine started at $2488, but a six-cylinder Champion ran $268 less. This overdrive-equipped Commander Starliner sports a gas-door guard, full wheel discs, and two-tone paint (for the first time). **3.** Starliner hardtops sold well, in both "sprightly" Champion and potent Commander guise, accounting for 15 percent of Studebaker's total. "Sparkling with verve and vigor in every line," the brochure insisted, "it's a remarkable gas saver . . . free from power wasting excess weight." Upholstery was fabricated in button-tufted nylon or optional leather. Each Champion body style came in three trim levels: Custom, DeLuxe, or Regal.

3

1. Studebaker began as a wagon maker, as shown in this centennial ad. 2. Stude was hardly alone in tying design themes to "jets," even though most planes were propeller-driven. 3. Soon-to-be President Eisenhower paraded in a Commander. 4. From left, designers Robert Bourke, Raymond Loewy, and Holden Koto pose with a prototype of the Champion Starlight coupe. 5. Frugal operation was always a top selling point. 6. First Studebaker of the second century leaves the plant on February 18, 1952.

1952 Studebaker

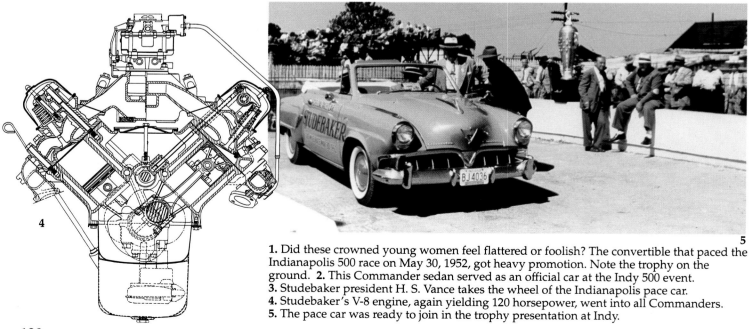

1. Did these crowned young women feel flattered or foolish? The convertible that paced the Indianapolis 500 race on May 30, 1952, got heavy promotion. Note the trophy on the ground. **2.** This Commander sedan served as an official car at the Indy 500 event.
3. Studebaker president H. S. Vance takes the wheel of the Indianapolis pace car.
4. Studebaker's V-8 engine, again yielding 120 horsepower, went into all Commanders.
5. The pace car was ready to join in the trophy presentation at Indy.

1. Studebaker's Commander four-door sedan came in Regal or State trim—or as a longer-wheelbase Land Cruiser. Stickshift and overdrive models continued to offer the Hill-Holder, to keep the car from rolling backward. 2. A Champion Regal Starliner hardtop cost $2220 with the 85-horsepower L-head six. 3. Four-door sedans stuck with "suicide" (rear-hinged) back doors. 4. Starlight coupes, with distinctive wraparound rear/side windows, appeared for the last time. 5. Studebaker wasn't far off the mark in claiming itself as "the originator of the modern look in cars." 6. On this day, Hodak Motor Sales featured a Starliner hardtop and four-door sedan.

131

1952 Willys

Willys-Overland Motors

Unibodied Willys Aero sedans arrive, with L-head or F-head six-cylinder engines

Both engines measure 161 cubic-inch displacement

Aero series issued in three levels: Lark, Wing, and Ace . . . Eagle hardtop comes later

Sole postwar products had been civilian versions of Jeep, steel station wagons, and unique Jeepster phaeton of 1948–51

New design borrows elements from aircraft—thus the Aero name

President Ward M. Canaday insists that Aero's "gasoline economy is unsurpassed"

Canaday predicts trend toward smaller cars in 1952— cites high taxes, costs, and possible shortage of high-octane gasoline

Cars reach dealers in January, promising 90 features

Two-door Wing and Ace sedans arrive first, joined by economy Lark and Eagle hardtop—then four-door sedans

Willys finishes the year in 17th place, just ahead of Henry J, with 31,363 cars produced

Willys-Overland also continues production of Jeep-based station wagons

Since the start of World War II, Willys-Overland has built a total of 700,000 Jeeps—400,000 of them for military use

1. Smaller than Big Three offerings, all 1952 Willys were two-doors; yet this contemporary photo shows a four-door (which didn't "officially" debut until '53) wearing 1952 hubcaps. Perhaps it's a prototype. **2.** This Aero-Wing shows off its fashionable profile. Its F-head Hurricane six developed 90 horsepower, while the L-head version (used in Larks) made 75 bhp. **3.** The color-coordinated dashboard held basic controls. Prices ranged from $1731 for a Lark to $2155 for an Eagle hardtop, but the $1989 Wing was the most popular.

> ❝ The Willys Aero Ace is an aeronautically designed luxury car with all-around visibility comparable to that of an airport control tower. ❞
>
> *Willys vice president*
> **Howard P. Grove**; *April 1952*

1

2

3

4

1-2. With gray paint and blackwalls, a Willys Aero-Lark tended to blend into the background. As on many low-priced cars, an oil filter was optional. So was the hood ornament. **3.** Two-toning gave this $2074 Aero-Ace extra character. With 90-bhp six and overdrive, an Aero was a frugal—and impressive—performer. **4.** Dashboards were simple but functional. Note the horn ring—an element of most steering wheels. **5.** Willys continued to offer the Jeep station wagon, with two- or four-wheel drive and a four-cylinder engine. Wheel covers are not original.

5

Woodill Wildfire—Fluid Lines Meet Willys Parts

Dodge/Willys dealer B. Robert "Woody" Woodill liked sports cars. So, he built his own—mainly with Willys parts. The one-piece body was supplied by the Glasspar Company, a pioneer in fiberglass. The Woodill Wildfire first appeared at a Los Angeles Motorama, then went into production—in both kit and assembled form. Here, while the two-seater was on display in Detroit, reporters interview company president William Tritt (center), as representatives of U.S. Rubber look on. The body, just ³⁄₁₆-inch thick, weighed 180 pounds. With a Willys engine, the whole car weighed 1620 pounds. Note the cut-down door.

1953

Voracious as Americans were becoming in their quest for consumer goods, they couldn't—and wouldn't—buy everything on the market. Dismayed at slackening car sales, the Big Three automakers pondered ways to rekindle interest in their wares. The folks at Ford thought they had the answer: send scads of new cars to dealers, and let them discover ways to dispose of the glut. Chevrolet followed suit with its own retailers.

Thus began the sales blitz of 1953–54, a period of flamboyant promotions, high-pressure tactics, and frenzied dealers—an age of excess that set the stage for government action later in the decade. Production controls had been lifted in February, as Dwight Eisenhower took the presidency from Harry Truman, so showrooms ballooned with unordered vehicles. As a nasty side effect, the "blitz" helped to kill off several independent automakers in the next few years— led by Kaiser and Willys, whose ultimate destiny was not enriched by a merger in the spring of 1953.

Not that the '53 models weren't tempting on their own merits. Buicks, Chevrolets, and Pontiacs got new squared-up silhouettes. So did all four Chrysler products. Ford stood pat, for the most part, with the restyled bodies that had arrived a year earlier. Stunner of the season, though, was the new Studebaker coupe—a milestone design that nevertheless failed to reverse the company's failing fortunes.

Having fallen in love with styling, Americans were easy prey to hard-sell techniques—especially since those luscious hardtops and roomy wagons could be bought on "easy" time payments.

Delayed gratification—postponing purchases until cash was at hand—was a vestige of the past, not a theme for the prosperous present, much less the future. That was how their *parents* had lived, surviving the Great Depression. Now, it was time to fill the split-level's larder—and the carport—with bigger and better merchandise, and worry about the payments later on.

Fashionable hardtops, in fact, accounted for 14.5 percent of total output. Half of new cars had automatic transmissions, and many makes offered power steering and other goodies.

Sure, engineering was important; but in the increasingly status-conscious suburbs, people began to define their personalities by their possessions. Owning a big, fully loaded car, suggested some psychologists, allowed a person to feel more significant.

Conformity was becoming the norm, and workers sought careers rather than mere jobs. Union influence stood near its peak, as membership approached 18 million. Fringe benefits were gaining importance in the wage package, and employees learned to expect regular hikes to keep pace with inflation—which was below one percent, but steadily rising.

It took an average of 30 weeks' work to buy a new car, as opposed to 37 weeks back in 1925—before the 1930s Depression. Bread cost 16 cents a pound in 1953, round steak 92 cents. Eggs were 70 cents a dozen, coffee 89 cents a pound. Traveling coast-to-coast (one-way) cost almost $57 on a Greyhound bus, or $99 via TWA. An off-brand air conditioner went for $289 at Macy's, while a new Buick Special ran $2197 and Chevrolets started at $1524.

Seats for Rodgers & Hammerstein's *Me & Juliet* on Broadway ranged from $1.80 to $7.20. Motels already outnumbered hotels, two-to-one.

With wage and price controls halted, and unemployment dipping to just 2.9 percent, median family income edged past $4200. Workers earned an average of $3581 annually. The average employee grossed $64 a week at his $1.61 hourly rate. Auto workers made $88 per week. Teachers collected an average $4254 per year. Workers looked forward to ever-increasing prosperity and an expanding number of consumer goods.

TV viewers got to see Steve Allen on *The Tonight Show*, and Danny Thomas in *Make Room for Daddy*. Bob Hope hosted the first Academy Awards show on TV. Mary Martin and Ethel Merman celebrated Ford's 50th anniversary on CBS and NBC. Frank Sinatra revived his flagging career in the role of Maggio in *From Here to Eternity*, which was named best picture. Alan Ladd and Jack Palance dueled in the saloon in *Shane*. Three-D movies appeared, but the use of special glasses limited their popularity.

Tony Bennett sang "Rags to Riches," and Patti Page warbled about a "Doggie in the Window." Hugh Hefner launched *Playboy* magazine in Chicago, and *TV Guide* appeared on newsstands. The first successful open-heart surgery was performed—and a young Elvis Presley paid four bucks to cut a record to celebrate his mother's birthday.

Americans spoke derisively of intellectuals as "eggheads," a term applied to Adlai Stevenson in his losing battle for the presidency in '52. Former GM chief "Engine Charlie" Wilson, named secretary of defense in the new Administration, uttered one of the most noted phrases of the decade: "What was good for our country was good for General Motors and vice versa." Mildly misquoted in the present tense, the seemingly arrogant assertion drew flak for years afterward.

As the Korean War ended on July 26, 1953, those who earned the 75-cents-an-hour minimum wage might have been worried. But most Americans gazed avidly forward, foreseeing even greater prosperity for themselves and the nation. The average motorist drove 10,000 miles yearly—a figure that's remained surprisingly steady. Who wanted to pile up those miles in an old clunker—or a stripped-down Ford Mainline or Chevrolet One-Fifty—when a host of more inviting choices beckoned? Best of all, one of these new beauties could be driven home for "just a few dollars down."

Chrysler Corporation

Restyled Chrysler products wear one-piece windshields and squared-off rear ends

PowerFlite two-speed fully automatic transmission installed in Chryslers late in model year

More than half of Chryslers are six-cylinder Windsors

New Yorker adds DeLuxe range; standard New Yorker replaces Saratoga

Air conditioning now available in Chryslers and DeSotos

DeSoto rises to 11th place in production . . . Dodge remains in seventh, Plymouth third again

Wire wheels offered on each make

Red Ram 241.3-cid V-8 engine available in new-look Dodge, delivering 140 horsepower

Gyro-Torque transmission available in Dodges

Dodge is one of first production cars styled by Virgil Exner

Danny Eames drives Red Ram Dodge V-8 to 102.62 mph

Overdrive-equipped Dodge V-8 averages 23.4 mpg in Mobilgas Economy Run; also breaks 196 AAA stock-car records at Bonneville

Plymouth marks 25th anniversary

Plymouths get Hy-Drive option, mixing manual shift with torque converter

1

2

1-2. An extensive reskin made this year's Chryslers more shapely, less bulky—but big enough to attract customers who expected plenty of metal in an expensive automobile. Most costly New Yorker DeLuxe model was this $3945 convertible, with only 950 built. 3. Once again, the New Yorker's FirePower Hemi V-8 engine developed 180 horsepower. New Yorkers now rode a 125.5-inch wheelbase, like the six-cylinder Windsors. 4. Legendary Hollywood singing cowboy Roy Rogers, and wife Dale Evans, posed with a Chrysler station wagon. Note the Kelsey-Hayes wire wheels—a $300 factory accessory.

3

4

1

2

1. Two-tone paint and wide whitewalls were popular on stylish hardtops, including the New Yorker DeLuxe Newport.
2. Dressed in black, a Chrysler Imperial limousine looked stately. Both Custom and Crown Imperials were sold. 3. This Imperial limo, produced by Carrozzeria Ghia in Turin, Italy, saw service at the Vatican. Note the glass roof panels.
4. Chrysler's D'Elegance show car was a close-coupled hardtop coupe with "gunsight" taillights, sculpted metal, and wire wheels within full cutouts.

3

5

4

5. A cut-down windshield reveals the race intentions of a C-5R Cunningham. Briggs Cunningham himself finished third at Le Mans. 6. The entire front end tilted to reveal the hopped-up (310-horsepower) Hemi V-8, breathing through four carbs. 7. Cunningham's production C-3 coupe wore a striking oval grille and carried a 220-bhp Chrysler V-8. It was built by Carrozzeria Vignale in Italy.

6

7

1953 DeSoto

1. DeSoto grilles added a couple of teeth, and bodies gained some glitter—a typical move in the '50s. This FireDome V-8 sedan cost $2643. 2. FireDome DeSotos sold far better than their six-cylinder counterparts, and cost a lot less than a comparable Chrysler. 3. The club coupe was the lowest-priced V-8 DeSoto, and the second-best seller. 4. Long-wheelbase models kept the prior year's rear-end profile. Note the rear-hinged back doors on this six-window FireDome V-8 eight-passenger sedan. 5. Like most 1953 station wagons, the $3351 FireDome V-8 was all steel. 6. Only 1700 FireDome V-8 convertibles were built, with a $3114 price tag. Note the abundance of brightwork. 7. DeSoto called its 160-horsepower V-8 the "most advanced engine design in America." Domed combustion chambers and central spark plugs promised "greater power per drop of regular gasoline," plus "enviable" fuel mileage.

1. With a 116-horsepower L-head six under its hood, a DeSoto Powermaster Six Sportsman hardtop coupe cost $2604—or $289 less than a V-8 equivalent. Oddly, DeSoto still promoted Floating Power engine mounts, an idea from the early '30s.
2. About a third of this year's four-door sedans were six-cylinder. DeSoto offered a total of 11 models. 3. "Richly-grained" dashboards, blending with body colors, featured a new vinyl top to cut glare. 4. Full hydraulic power steering pledged to make "parking child's play," adding that "your feel of the road is always steady, reassuring." 5. Just $2334 bought a DeSoto Powermaster Six club coupe. 6. DeSoto's Adventurer I show car featured full wheel cutouts over wire wheels, plus an outside exhaust system. Production of the four-seat coupe was weighed briefly, but overly cautious Chrysler executives nixed the idea.

1953 Dodge

1. Dodge heralded the "power-packed beauty" of its Coronets—an accurate description, with the new Red Ram V-8. 2. Interiors promised more space than ever, despite trimmer outside dimensions. Instead of Gyro-Matic, shoppers could pay $233 for a Gyro-Torque transmission with torque converter and selector dial. 3. Modest weight made the V-8 Coronet club coupe a car to be reckoned with, especially if equipped with new $98 overdrive. 4. When not performing useful work, a Coronet Sierra wagon was said to be suitable "at country club or mountain lodge." 5. Only 4100 convertibles were built, all V-8 Coronets. 6. Hoods were decorated with a ram's-head ornament, a symbol that would be revived during the 1980s on the company's trucks. 7. Like other Coronets, the Diplomat hardtop was upholstered in two-tone Fashion-Fiber fabric, along with vinyl.

140

1

2

3

1. Dodge encouraged shoppers to observe "the clean flow of the smart fender lines" on a Meadowbrook Six four-door sedan. **2.** All Meadowbrooks, including this club coupe, had the familiar 230.2-cid L-head engine, again rated at 103 horsepower. **3.** Whether moving freely or anchored in traffic, Dodge drivers faced a Pilot-Control instrument panel and Pilot-View one-piece windshield. **4.** Dodge was close to correct in claiming its '53 as the "most completely new car." Shorter than the competition, it looked almost compact—even on the longer (119-inch) wheelbase used by club coupes and four-door sedans. **5.** A new suspension joined the double-channel frame to make a Dodge "master of all kinds of roads," according to the brochure. Even mundane features had names: Safeguard brakes, Oriflow shocks, Stabilizer springs. **6.** Dodge's Get-Away Six was long known for dependability and low upkeep costs. Price-leader Meadowbrook Specials didn't last long, but six-cylinder Coronets became available later.

4

5

6

1953 Plymouth

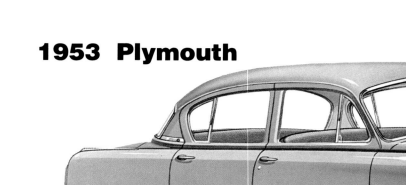

1

2

1. Aircraft themes influenced low-priced cars, too, as Plymouth's new one-piece windshield delivered Control Tower Visibility. Shown is a Cranbrook sedan. 2. "Exciting to look at," Plymouth insisted, a Belvedere hardtop also was "thrilling to drive." Maybe so, but teenagers generally favored V-8 Fords. 3. TV host Art Linkletter showed off a Belvedere with extra-cost wire wheels. Despite a wheelbase similar to rivals, Plymouths looked stubby—which might have hurt sales. In Fifties America, bigger equaled better. 4. Plymouth ads continued to stress reliability, even when showcasing the Belvedere—now with conventional two-toning. 5. Most drivers rolled the side glass down when a Cranbrook convertible was on the road. The power top contained a full-width window.

3

4

5

Plxmouth 1953

1. With Borg-Warner overdrive, the brochure insisted, the 100-bhp L-head engine "loafs its way to longer life." 2. All two-doors, including this club coupe, held a new E-Z exit front seat, the outer third of which folded forward. 3. Plymouth touted the all-purpose nature of its Savoy wagon. 4. Cranbrook interiors mixed fashion and utility. 5. Belvederes looked spiffy inside, using fabrics that complemented the body colors. 6. Glove compartments sat in the dash center. Even steering wheels came in harmonizing colors. 7. Unlike club coupes, the Cambridge club sedan had a rear wing window. 8. Though popular, the Cambridge four-door was handily outsold by its costlier Cranbrook mate. 9. Unlike outmoded vacuum units, electric wipers ran at a constant speed.

Ford Motor Company

Ford celebrates 50th anniversary on June 16 . . . festivities include special *Ed Sullivan Show* and dedication of Engineering and Research Center

Ford distributes two million Norman Rockwell calendars and publishes book *Ford at Fifty*

Ford production comes within 100,000 of Chevrolet's 1.35 million cars . . . Mercury output soars, but fails to overtake Oldsmobile and Dodge

Flathead V-8 engine in final season

Sales blitz underway as Ford chases Chevrolet: cars go to dealers whether ordered or not . . . discounting is rampant, hard-sell promotions common

Ford Sunliner convertible paces Indianapolis 500 race, driven by William Clay Ford; limited run of replicas built

Power brakes and steering available on Fords, starting in mid-season; also available on Lincoln-Mercury models

Ford six with overdrive gets 27.03 mpg at Mobilgas Run

Lincoln V-8 boosted to 205 horsepower, with four-barrel carburetion

Lincoln offers four-way power seat—an industry "first" . . . power windows offered, too

Lincolns take first four spots in Mexican Road Race—again

1. A mid-range Ford Customline sedan, said the sales brochure, was "big in size and long on beauty." 2. A Customline club coupe was "smart for two—with room for six." 3. Mainline Fords lacked the brightwork of Customline and Crestline, but offered the same styling and technical features. 4. Each year, automakers came up with lists of new features—some worthy, others not. Ford promoted an array of "Worth More" qualities, valuable not only while the car was new, but when it came time to resell.

Lightweight Sports Car Packs V-8 Punch

Well-known for its work with fiberglass, the Glasspar Company of Santa Ana, California, began building two-seat sports car bodies in 1950. Though most of the approximately 200 G-2s sold through 1955 were in kit form, a tubular steel frame was eventually made available, and Glasspar sold some completed versions powered by Ford and Mercury V-8s. Note the roll bar and separate monocle-like windscreens.

'53's leader is the '53 Ford !

1. Like most hardtop coupes, Ford's $1941 Crestline Victoria looked best when two-toned. The sales brochure called it "sedan snug—convertible smart." **2.** The $2043 Crestline Sunliner convertible featured a Breezeway top with large zip-out window. **3.** Switching from an eight-passenger car to a cargo carrier took a claimed three minutes with a Ford Crestline Country Squire station wagon. Center seats folded into the floor. Body panels were trimmed with genuine maple or birch wood. Ford also offered a plain-bodyside Customline Country Sedan. **4.** Ford's K-bar frame, with deep channel struts, delivered added twist resistance. A variable-rate rear suspension used extra-long springs, and Hydra-Coil front springs were tailored to model weight. **5.** A view through the windshield demonstrated the value of Full-Circle visibility. Steering wheel hubs held a 50th-anniversary medallion. **6.** Ford's Mileage Maker six gave 101 horsepower. **7.** In its final season, the Strato-Star flathead V-8 delivered 110 bhp.

> **"** Wait until the figures are in for this fourth quarter. We have some pretty nasty things in store for Chevrolet. **"**
>
> *Unidentified* **Ford spokesman**, *on the anticipated Ford sales victory over Chevy during the month of October 1953; November 1953*

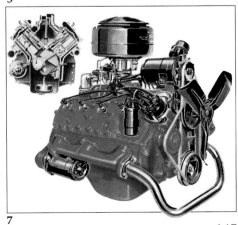

1953 Lincoln

1. A Lincoln Capri hardtop not only felt luxurious, it looked rakish—especially viewed from down low. Even so, Lincoln continued to lag far behind Cadillac in popularity. 2. A 205-horsepower V-8 drove the $3226 Cosmopolitan sedan and every other model—45 more horses than in '52, and just five short of Cadillac's output. 3. Lincoln unflinchingly promoted the virtues of its vehicles for women, noting that the "smallest lady can fit easily" and "power brakes respond to the touch of a ballet slipper." No automaker today would promise to give "feminine hands control they've never known before." 4. The top-selling Capri hardtop cost $3549, with standard Hydra-Matic. Newly optional power steering also came from General Motors.

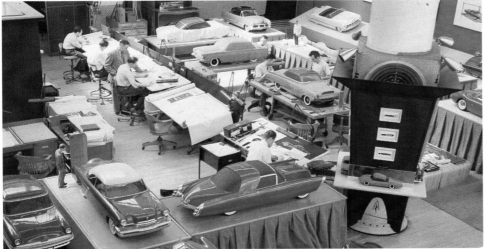

1. A fleet of pre-production '53s drove in the Mexican Road Race. Lincoln eagerly promoted its cars' impressive showings, as well as a first-in-class finish at the Mobilgas Economy Run. 2. Bob Estes was chief driver in the *Carrera Panamericana*. 3. Engines of Lincolns in the Mexican race were fitted with Champion spark plugs. Naturally, Champion suggested that owners of other cars might expect similar performance. 4. Stylists stayed busy not only with production Lincolns, but created Ford's show cars. 5. Three Ford brothers pose with a pair of dream cars: Henry Ford II in foreground, alongside the Continental Fifty-X; and in the rear, Benson Ford and William Clay Ford with the XL-500. 6. The front portion of the Fifty-X top retracted automatically into the rear. Gadgetry included automatic jacks. 7. By 1953, the family automobile—plain or plush—was a major part of "modern living," and everyone was presumed to want to "leave the past far behind."

1953 Mercury

1. New full-length bodyside spears helped give Mercury a longer, more integrated look. This Custom sedan cost $2057, while a Monterey four-door went for $2133.
2. Small fender skirts enhanced the sleek profile of a $2390 Monterey convertible.
3-4. Outside visors were fading out of popularity, but the Monterey sedan—with standard skirts and two-toning—attracted a healthy share of customers. **5.** Mercury pushed "Unified Design," enhanced by bullet-shaped front bumper guards.

1. No air entered a Mercury flathead V-8 engine via the decorative hood scoop. This Monterey Sport Coupe featured Stedi-Line steering and variable-rate rear springs. Seven models went on sale. 2. A Monterey station wagon seated eight and cost $2591. 3. The Custom series included two- and four-door sedans. 4. A Custom two-door was not only attractive but also frugal—especially with overdrive. 5. Ford's 40-millionth vehicle, an open Mercury, appeared with three brothers: (*from left*) Henry Ford II; Benson Ford, then head of Lincoln-Mercury; and William Clay Ford. 6. Polishing up the Merc with Bodygard Liquid Car Wax was meant to yield a "showroom shine." A 12-ounce can of Simoniz—probably the best-known product of its kind—cost 98 cents.

1903 40,000,000th 1953
FORD MOTOR COMPANY VEHICLE BUILT IN U.S.A.

General Motors Corporation

GM Motorama tours for six months—1.7 million visitors see show cars

Buick celebrates 50th anniversary

All Buicks except Special adopt V-8 engines; most carry improved Twin-Turbine Dynaflow

Buick offers limited-production Skylark convertible with lowered beltline and top, rounded wheel openings, and wire wheels

Eldorado and Fiesta are limited-edition ragtops from Cadillac and Oldsmobile; $7750 Eldorado is most costly car of the year

Because of fire at Hydra-Matic plant, many Cadillacs and Oldsmobiles come with Dynaflow, while some Pontiacs carry Chevrolet's Powerglide

Full-size Chevrolets are restyled—squarer in shape . . . Pontiacs get comparable treatment

Chevrolet fields three series: Bel Air, mid-range Two-Ten DeLuxe, and low-budget One-Fifty

Fiberglass-bodied Corvette sports car debuts at GM Motorama, then enters production with 150-bhp six-cylinder engine

Just 300 Corvettes are built in first short season

1

2

3

4

1. To spot a Roadmaster, just count the fender portholes: four, versus three for a Buick Super. 2. A Roadmaster Riviera hardtop cost $3358, but Riv sedans sold better. 3. Last of the woody wagons, the Roadmaster Estate was made of "seasoned wood and sturdy metal." 4. A six-seat sports car? That was the Buick Skylark, on a Roadmaster chassis, wearing cut-down doors and a hunkered-tight top. Owning this "corsair of the highway," the brochure said, delivered "scintillating life on wheels." Kelsey-Hayes wire wheels had 40 spokes. 5. Only the budget-priced Special stuck with straight-eight power.

BROTHER, GIVE IT ROOM!

BUICK

5

1. Buick Supers carried a 170-horsepower version of the new 322-cid V-8 engine (164 bhp with manual shift). Roadmasters now rode the same wheelbase, but had a 188-bhp engine, with Twin-Turbine Dynaflow and power steering standard. 2. A Super convertible cost $3002, but ragtops also came in cheaper Special form, as well as in the high-dollar Roadmaster series. 3. Even those who accepted the Special as a "thoroughbred Buick through and through" might view its straight-eight performance as tepid rather than "pure thrill," despite company assurances. 4. Four body styles made up the Special line, including this $2197 Tourback sedan. The Special's engine offered its highest horsepower (125/130) and compression ratio ever. 5. GM planned its five-make lineup so a Chevrolet owner might look forward to driving a Pontiac or Olds—or slipping behind a Buick Roadmaster's wheel one day. 6. For half a century, Buicks had been tempting moderately affluent families.

1953 Cadillac

1. Despite a modest claim that it was merely "a special sports convertible built in the finest Cadillac tradition," the new Eldorado served as the foundation for a heritage all its own. Inspired by a '52 show car, only 532 were built this season—but the splendid name would last for decades. 2. Eldorados featured a freshly cut-down Panoramic wraparound windshield, notched beltline, chromed wire wheels, and flush-fit metal boot for the convertible top. All that style and lavishness commanded an eye-popping $7750, yet its powertrain was identical to other models. 3-4. The Series 62 convertible sat three inches higher than an Eldorado and lacked its special touches—but cost a mere $4144. 5. Though less luxurious than an Eldo's, the Series 62 interior looked inviting—especially done in red. 6. Countless Americans looked forward to the day when they, too, might experience the "delight" of stepping into a Cadillac. Ads often showed the Cadillac crest alongside fine jewelry—a none-too-subtle appeal.

152

1

2

3

1. Runaway best-seller was the Series 62 sedan at $3666. All Cadillacs weighed well over two tons. **2.** Protruding bumpers, dubbed "Dagmars" in reference to a buxom TV personality of that name, were trendy this year. None outdid Cadillac's in size or boldness. **3.** The Fleetwood 75 series included an eight-passenger sedan and Imperial sedan, each on a 146.8-inch wheelbase. **4.** A fire destroyed GM's huge Hydra-Matic plant in Livonia, Michigan, on August 12, 1953. As a result, some late '53 Cadillacs and Oldsmobiles were fitted with Buick's Twin-Turbine Dynaflow automatic, while a few Pontiacs got Chevrolet's Powerglide. **5.** Americans saw the Eldorado on TV, carrying newly elected President Dwight D. Eisenhower to his inauguration. No modern President could ever stand so nonchalantly—and unprotected. **6.** Suave film actor Gilbert Roland slouches on a Cadillac—still the choice of many celebrities.

4

5

6

1953 Chevrolet

1. All-new front-end styling, Chevrolet asserted, "accentuates the appearance of power and fleetness." The squared-off profile served as a bridge between the 1949–52 era and the phenomenal '55 models. Like many publicity photos, this one came with a warning that it not be published before afternoon newspapers came out on a specific date. Many cities had a selection of morning and afternoon papers—engaged in heavy rivalry. 2. Bel Air was the top-ranked series, sporting unique two-toning on rear fenders. A Cadillac or Buick might be considered ostentatious by neighbors, but any Chevrolet looked proper in the carport of a split-level suburban ranch house. 3. A little more luxurious than its lower-priced mates, the Bel Air lineup included a convertible, plus a sport coupe and two- and four-door sedans. 4. This Atlas tire ad showed the license plates of all 48 states and the District of Columbia, as well as Canadian provinces. The need for uniform size is evident. Motorists, Atlas insisted, needed a "dependable car, equipped with dependable products, backed by dependable service."

154

1

1. A Chevrolet Two-Ten convertible lacked the Bel Air's bodyside decorations, but whitewalls and full discs were common. Just 5617 were built, priced only $82 below a Bel Air ragtop. 2. Two-tone paint turned an ordinary Two-Ten sedan into a modest charmer, especially with skirted rear wheels. The One-Fifty series wore rubber moldings. 3. Chevrolet's sedan delivery was basically a station wagon without windows, priced at $1648. 4. GM affiliates offered a staggering range of parts and accessories, including Delco batteries, Rochester carburetors, and Hyatt roller bearings. 5. A mechanic was on duty at this Texaco station in El Paso, Texas. Today's facilities aren't as likely to promote availability of a rest room. Note the Chevrolet taxi.

2

4

3

5

1953 Chevrolet

1

1. Long known for family cars, Chevrolet sought a youthful image to match Ford's reputation as a hot-rodder's dream. Thus came the Corvette, first appearing in January 1953 as a show car at the GM Motorama. By the end of June, production was underway on an initial batch of fiberglass-bodied two-seaters—each painted Polo White. 2. Corvettes looked equally sharp inside, trimmed in red and white. Gauges stretched across the twin-pod dashboard, making readings difficult. 3. Three carburetors fed air and fuel to a modified 235.5-cid Blue Flame six-cylinder engine. All early Corvettes came with two-speed Powerglide.

> 66 It is a feeling of being part and parcel of the vehicle; of intimacy with the machine and its functioning; of close, accurate control; of feeling the road, the engine; the feeling of being the master of a tight, concise, safe bundle. 99
>
> *MG Club of America president* **Norman E. Carlson,** *on the allure of sports cars; February 1953*

2

3

1-2. Corvette development took 30 months, a joint effort between Harley Earl's Art & Colour Studio and Chevrolet engineers. Enthusiastic public response convinced Chevrolet to turn the two-seater into more than a display model. Styling touches included screened headlights, extended pod-style taillights, and a wraparound windshield. **3.** Americans were eager to ogle sports cars, even if they had no intention of purchasing one. Corvette Number One drew eager crowds at the New York Motorama, as did the selection of other GM "dream cars." **4.** Just 33 inches tall to the cowl, the Motorama Corvette looks minuscule next to a Bel Air sedan. Corvettes rode a 102-inch wheelbase and had quicker-than-usual steering. Nearly all '53s went to VIPs.

1

2

3

5

> **66** We are exploring a new field. **99**
>
> *Chevrolet general manager* **T. H. Keating**, *on the fiberglass-bodied Corvette; March 1953*

5. Corvettes go down in history as the first fiberglass-bodied series-production cars. Bodies consisted of 46 pieces, supplied by the Molded Fiber Glass Company. **6.** The six-cylinder engine sat aft of the front axle, in a cut-down passenger-car frame with a low center of gravity.

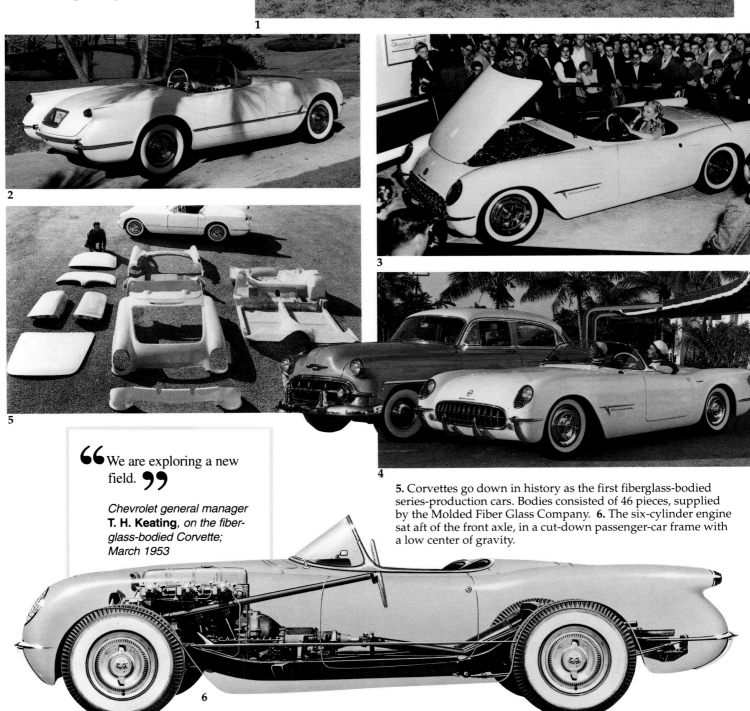

4

6

1953 Oldsmobile

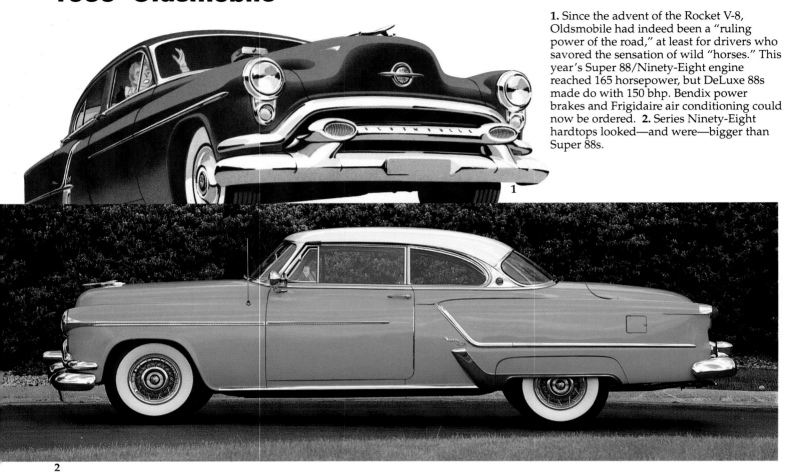

1. Since the advent of the Rocket V-8, Oldsmobile had indeed been a "ruling power of the road," at least for drivers who savored the sensation of wild "horses." This year's Super 88/Ninety-Eight engine reached 165 horsepower, but DeLuxe 88s made do with 150 bhp. Bendix power brakes and Frigidaire air conditioning could now be ordered. **2.** Series Ninety-Eight hardtops looked—and were—bigger than Super 88s.

3. Vying for attention against Cadillac's Eldorado and Buick's Skylark, Oldsmobile launched a limited-edition Ninety-Eight Fiesta convertible with panoramic windshield and 170-horsepower engine. Only 458 customers got one, for $5717. Its distinctive spinner wheel covers soon appeared as aftermarket add-ons. **4.** Ads still asked readers to "Make a date" with a Rocket Olds. **5.** A Ninety-Eight could get Safety-Padding atop its symmetrical dashboard. A new Quick-View Hydra-Matic quadrant sat below the speedometer.

MOST *Glamorous* CAR TO DATE !

MAKE A DATE WITH A "ROCKET 8"

OLDSMOBILE

158

1

2

3

1. Oldsmobile pushed both the glamour and comfort of the Ninety-Eight, which featured new squared-off seatbacks and Custom-Lounge cushions. 2. Two-tone upholstery was common in 1953 models, including the Super 88. 3. Oldsmobile called its new front end the "power look." Shown is a Super 88 sedan. 4. Super 88s blended the more potent V-8 with a smaller body—resulting in greater performance. 5. Oldsmobile officials celebrated the production of the company's four-millionth car in May of 1953. 6. This AC ad spotlighted the experimental Olds Starfire, with a 200-horsepower V-8 and 9:1 compression. AC spark plugs had been used on all Oldsmobiles since 1911.

6

5

1953 Pontiac

1-2. Pontiac was attempting to shed its stodgy image. New styling on a longer wheelbase helped, but continued use of the familiar inline L-head engines did not. Continental spare tires, shown on a top-of-the-line Custom Catalina hardtop, were gaining a modest following as extra-cost accessories. Subtle rear-fender kick-ups gave a suggestion of tailfins. **3.** Buyers could pay extra to get illumination for the Indian-head hood ornament. **4.** All Pontiacs, including the Chieftain DeLuxe convertible, came with either a 239.2-cid six or 268.4-cid eight. The six produced 115/118 horsepower (manual/automatic), the eight, 118/122. Twin spotlights weren't standard fare. **5.** Only $66 separated the DeLuxe Catalina hardtop (shown) from a costlier Custom model. **6.** Even a practical-minded Pontiac sedan delivery looked good in two colors with DeLuxe bodyside trim.

1

2

3

4

5

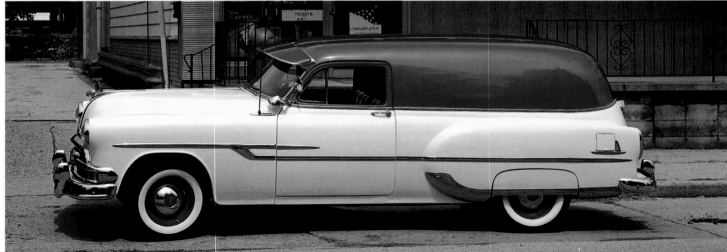

6

1

2

3

4

1. In addition to a new wraparound windshield, Pontiacs had panoramic back windows. 2. Pontiac continued to extol the economic virtues and dependable operation of its 26-model Chieftain lineup. Six- and eight-cylinder engines now differed only slightly in horsepower (the six gaining about 15 bhp this year), but eights delivered considerably more torque. 3-4. Station-wagon fanciers could choose from a full dozen Pontiacs, including this woodgrained DeLuxe Eight. 5. Pontiac's offering at the GM Motorama was this Parisienne town car. 6. Outside, the Parisienne looked more stock than some show cars, but bucket-style seats and super-plush carpeting weren't like those fitted to any production Pontiacs.

6

5

1953 Hudson

Hudson Motor Car Company

Economy-priced Hudson Jet debuts, following $12 million development program

Jets ride 105-inch wheelbase and carry 202-cid engine; marketed in standard and Super Jet form

Jets employ same Monobilt construction as large Hudsons

Jet sales fail to take off as hoped—demand for compact cars remains marginal, despite Rambler's success

Ultimate failure of Jet also is attributed to slab-sided styling and too high price

Twin H-Power (dual carburetion) available for all Hudson engines—even the Jet

7-X race engine for "severe usage" yields as much as 210 horsepower . . . regular Hornet sixes are rated 145 or 160 horsepower

Big Hudson lineup is cut to three series: Wasp, Super Wasp, and Hornet

Full-size Hudsons get fresh interiors and detail changes

Hudson claims its 64-inch seats are roomier than any other car's

Pacemaker and Commodore models are gone; so is the Commodore's straight-eight engine

Production sags slightly, sending Hudson down a notch—to 15th position in the industry

1

2

3

1-2. Nearly all American cars had a one-piece windshield by 1953, but not Hudsons. This Hornet not only has Twin H-Power, but backup lights and an accessory spotlight. 3. Copywriters used good sense in writing this ad. Over a six-year period, Americans had gotten to know that Hudson's "Step-down" design, with its low center of gravity, made for a fine-handling road car. A powerful one, too, with the Twin H-Power version of the big Hornet six-cylinder engine. Hudson promised "smooth, lightning-quick acceleration" coupled with "mighty reserve power," but also mentioned the Wasp and new, low-priced Jet. 4. At first glance this photo looks old, but these two Hudsons are in far better shape than the Texaco station behind them.

4

1. Super Wasp was Hudson's new mid-range model, offered in five body styles. Note the center-mounted radio antenna—a Hudson "trademark." **2.** Champion spark plugs were installed in a number of top stock cars, including Oldsmobiles and the course-tromping Hornets. Hudson pilots pictured are Dick Rathman (*second from top*) and Fonty Flock (*third from top*). **3.** A modified 1953 Hudson and a 1947 Hudson pickup hauled parts for Bill Hermann, Detroit's oldest Hudson dealer. **4.** Like many models before and since, the Hudson Jet drew plenty of attention at dealerships when it was introduced. Nearly one-third of the Hudsons built were Jets. **5.** Hudson Jets and police work don't seem to intertwine, but officers in Peru, Indiana, obviously disagreed. Here, they're taking delivery of two Super Jet sedans. **6.** With the compact Jet, Hudson gained an entrant into the low-price field. Spacious enough for six, despite its modest outside dimensions, the Jet held a 202-cid six-cylinder engine, producing 104 to 114 horsepower. Hydra-Matic Drive and Twin H-Power were optional. Prices started at $1858. **7.** The Super Jet four-door sedan cost $1954; a two-door version went for $1933. Note the extra window trim.

1953 Kaiser

Kaiser-Frazer Corporation

Posh Kaiser Dragon wears gold-plated trim and embossed-vinyl padded roof

Though publicized as a "hardtop," Dragon is actually a four-door sedan

Dragons are loaded with standard equipment, including Hydra-Matic and tinted glass, for $3924—just 1277 are produced

New chromed body moldings accent front-to-rear lines of Kaiser Deluxe and Manhattan sedans

Stripped-down, value-leader Carolina series Kaisers debut, but few are sold

Redesigned Kaiser interiors again stress safety, including pop-out windshield . . . outside trunk hinges are gone

Henry J gets engineering tweaks, but few other changes

Production of DKF-161 sports car announced in February; fiberglass two-seater will go on sale as '54 model, called Kaiser-Darrin

Kaiser-Frazer buys Willys-Overland company in March—merger is taken as a sign that Kaiser is not about to give up auto production

Assets of new combined company total $200 million; GM has assets of $3.6 billion, Ford $1.5 billion, and Chrysler $913 million

Kaiser sells its Willow Run plant to General Motors for $26 million

1

2

3

1-2. Wearing gold-plated badges and ornaments, the Kaiser Dragon had a wild interior of Bambu vinyl and Laguna patterned cloth.
3. Despite Kaiser's elation at manufacturing its 730,000th car, and a $62 million expansion program, the company's days were numbered.
4. Though priced higher, Manhattans easily outsold Deluxe Kaiser models.

4

1

3

2

1. Tailfin-mounted taillights gave the Henry J Corsair an attractive rear appearance. Except for a fresh hood ornament, little was new. The four-cylinder sedan cost $1399; a six-cylinder DeLuxe version with padded dashboard, $1561. 2. All gauges went into a single panel, with the radio tacked below the lip of the few-frills dashboard. 3. Of the list of 39 ways a Henry J was "easiest," most shoppers doubtless considered price a top drawing card. A total of 16,672 were built this year, and a handful of leftovers went to customers as '54 models. 4. Claimed to be the first fiberglass-reinforced car in volume production (ahead of Corvette), the Kaiser-Darrin sports car was designed by Howard A. Darrin. It stood only 36 inches tall, to the cowl. Note the tiny grille.

4

❝ We've been knocked from the ring but we've got to come back in. ❞

Kaiser Motors president **Edgar F. Kaiser**, *on Kaiser's faltering sales; July 1953*

Nash Motors

Le Mans option for Ambassadors includes dual carburetors and high-compression head, for 140 horsepower . . . it's based on Nash-Healey's latest engine

Statesman's L-head engine gains a dozen horsepower . . . Rambler's smaller six adds three

Pinin Farina earns credit for Rambler modifications

Dual-Range Hydra-Matic available on all Nash models, including Ramblers

Outside spare tire is standard gear on Rambler hardtop and convertible, also available on full-size Nashes

Air intake of Weather Eye heating system is redesigned—extends full width of hood, on all three models

Full-size Nashes called "America's travel car," featuring drawer-style glovebox and full-width parcel shelf

Le Mans coupe body joins Nash-Healey convertible . . . wheelbase is six inches longer on closed version

Both Nash-Healeys hold bored-out 253-cid engine, phased in during 1952

Nash-Healey wins Italian International Concours d'Elegance

Nash production sinks to 121,793 cars, sending the company down to 12th place in industry ranking

1

2

3

4

1-2. This was largely a stand-pat year for Nash. Note the fender-mounted mirrors and upper window trim on this Ambassador sedan, plus unique two-tone paint. **3.** In addition to the standard 120-bhp six (shown), Nash offered a 140-horsepower Le Mans option for Ambassadors. **4.** Once again, the Nash badge graced three series: Rambler, Statesman, and Ambassador. **5.** In 1953, a family really could choose to sleep inside their Nash. Front seatbacks folded all the way down, to form a bed-like flat surface.

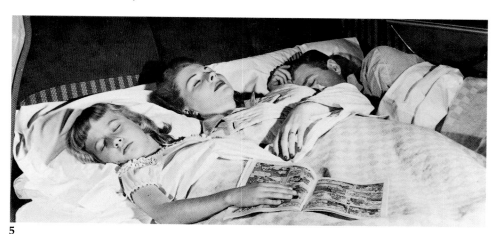

5

1

2

3

4

5

6

1. Ambassador sedans came in Custom (shown) or lower-cost Super trim, as well as a Country Club hardtop coupe. 2. All instruments in an Ambassador ran along the panel top, with a glovebox at the center. Note the Hydra-Matic selector atop the steering column. 3. The interior of an Ambassador Custom sedan looked inviting; the center seatback folded down as a large armrest. Meanwhile, the mid-range Statesman's 195.6-cid engine got a boost to 100 horsepower. 4. Nash-Healey roadsters now were known as convertibles, selling for $5908. No more than 162 were built this year. 5. A Le Mans sport coupe version of the Nash-Healey debuted in mid-season, on a longer (108-inch) wheelbase with a $6399 price. 6. A Continental spare tire became standard on the Rambler Custom convertible and Country Club hardtop.

1953 Packard

Packard Motor Car Company

Packards earn new grille and bodyside trim, and modernized "pelican" ornament—but change little otherwise

Former 300 and 400 now named Cavalier and Patrician

New four-barrel carburetion helps boost output of Packard 327-cid engines to 180 horsepower

Mid-priced Clipper series joins upper-level Packards, allows sale of "junior" and "senior" models . . . Clipper name had been used in 1940s

Mayfairs are now full-fledged Packards, with plusher trim

Packard shows signs of refocusing on luxury market, after concentrating on mid-range cars since World War II . . . limousines and Executive sedans offered

New Packard-designed power steering available; air conditioning is offered later in the year

Packard prices range from $2544 all the way to $6900

Ultramatic transmission promises 21 advancements this year—cruises in direct drive

Glamorous Caribbean convertible outsells Cadillac's Eldorado

Production rises to 90,287 cars, boosting Packard by a notch—to 14th place—in industry standing

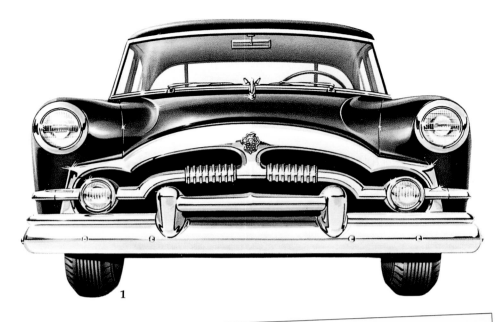

1. Packard touted the "advanced contour styling" of "America's most individual cars." Grilles and side trim were freshened. 2. Two separate lines went on sale: "distinguished" Packard, plus a moderately priced Clipper series. The posh Packard, said this ad, was "built expressly for those who demand the finest in motoring comfort and pleasure." 3. "Tomorrow's advanced engineering," said Packard of the Patrician sedan, "meets yesterday's finest traditions of careful craftsmanship." The 180-horsepower Thunderbolt engine ran in nine main bearings, billed as America's highest-compression straight-eight. Packard declared its Patrician the "Most beautiful car on the road." 4. Packard crests graced the upper grille bars of the '53 models.

3

> "We haven't been inspiring enough people to 'ask the man who owns one.' "
>
> *Packard president* **James J. Nance**, *on Packard's plans to revitalize its product and expand its dealer network; January 1953*

4

5

6

1. An "easy-handling Cavalier" with 180-bhp engine, the brochure insisted, "all but drives itself." 2. "Lithe, low and rakish—as modern as tomorrow," the convertible promised "advanced contour styling in the Continental manner." 3. All a reader had to do to win a Caribbean convertible was to come up with a new name for this Hollywood starlet. The winner also got a trip to the film capital—or $7500 in cash. (A Caribbean sold for $5210.) Note the clean bodyside and rounded wheel openings. 4. An outside spare was said to give a Mayfair hardtop "a new note of continental swank." 5. Less-affluent folks could ponder a Packard, now that the Clipper club sedan sold for just $2544. 6. Packard's Pan American drew much attention at the International Motor Sports Show; it evolved into the Caribbean.

169

Studebaker Corporation

Studebakers enjoy Euro-style redesign by Robert Bourke of Raymond Loewy studio

Company managers fail to anticipate extent of positive public response—especially for dramatically low-slung coupes

Demand for stunning Starlight and Starliner coupes tops sedans four-to-one, to the surprise of Studebaker executives

Coupes stand just 56.3 inches tall—an astoundingly low profile to 1953 eyes, accentuated by long (120.5-inch) wheelbase

Studebaker coupe earns flurry of styling awards, serves as landmark of modern design

Too-tall sedans fail to take full advantage of Loewy team's lovely lines

Six-cylinder Champions and V-8 Commanders on sale

Chassis is designed to flex and absorb road shocks—but leads to creaks and groans in body . . . rust woes also develop later in cars' lives

Strike at Borg-Warner plant curtails availability of automatic transmissions

Only 151,576 Studebakers are produced in U.S.—fewer than in 1952 model year—dropping the company to 10th in the industry

Studillac, built by outside company, mixes light Studebaker coupe body with Cadillac V-8 power

1

2

3

1-3. A Studebaker Commander Starliner hardtop looked particularly attractive in red and white. Few automobiles, before or since, captured the imagination as forcefully as the new Stude. What should have been a magnificent sales year for Studebaker became a ho-hum season, due largely to an initial focus on sedans rather than coupes. Production ills also developed, as front sheetmetal wouldn't quite fit the coupe body at first. **4.** Even the dashboard of the new Studebaker seemed to have a European tone.

4

1

2

3

4

1. Studebaker gave a Starlight badge to the pillared version of the Commander V-8 Regal coupe. The low-slung two-doors held five passengers. Sadly, convertible versions were never produced. **2.** The magnificent European-aimed profile penned by the Loewy team failed to come across as well in sedan body styles. Shown is a Commander V-8 DeLuxe two-door with six-passenger seating. **3.** Wide doors and low floors made sedan entry/exit easy. Four-door sedan and Land Cruiser models had rear doors hinged at the center post. Coupes had extra-wide right front seatbacks that swung out of the way to permit easy entrance into the rear seat. **4.** Mechanical power steering, available on all Studebaker models, promised its operator "a thrill." **5.** Studebaker claimed to have introduced nylon into auto upholstery—gold striped in this Regal Commander sedan. **6.** Claims that a Starliner hardtop delivered "the sleek-lined smartness of a costly foreign car" weren't considered much of a stretch of the truth.

5

THE NEW STUDEBAKER WITH
THE EUROPEAN LOOK

**Styling
straight out of the
dream book!**

'53 Studebaker

6

1953 Studebaker

1. No '53 car deserved the Fashion Academy Award more than Studebaker. As *Motor World* reported, Studebaker "made every other American car look ten years older." **2.** Raymond Loewy (seated) studies a freehand design with fellow stylists Robert Bourke and Holden "Bob" Koto (*right*). **3.** Ungainly is the word for a Champion Deluxe sedan—at least when compared to the sweeping coupe silhouette. Sedan wheelbases were four inches shorter. **4.** Champions, represented by this Custom two-door, kept their 85-bhp L-head six-cylinder engine. The Commander V-8 line included a Land Cruiser sedan. Coupes and sedans shared few common parts. **5.** President Harold S. Vance inspects a Champion Starliner, claimed to be "setting a new trend in American automobile design." Note the fender-mounted vent door—later to be a focal point for rust. **6.** Studebakers near the end of the assembly line. **7.** Dealers were pleased to see those new Studebakers coming—but they'd rather have had more coupes once the public had taken a close look.

1

Willys-Overland Motors

Four-door sedans available this year, along with two-doors—Willys taxis also on sale

Lineup consists of Aero-Lark, Aero-Ace, and Aero-Falcon sedans, plus the pretty Aero-Eagle hardtop coupe

Prices start at just $1646 this season for Aero-Lark two-door

Old four-cylinder engine available only in Aero-Lark series, aimed at export

Aero-Lark and Aero-Falcon get 75-horsepower six-cylinder engine; Aero-Ace and Aero-Eagle Hurricane six is rated 90 bhp

Only minor appearance change is evident . . . gold-plated "W" in grille denotes company's 50th anniversary

Hydra-Matic joins option list late in model year

Willys ads promise "immense visibility," solid unibody construction, and "unbelievable gas mileage". . . customers also are encouraged to "drive with pride"

Production totals 42,057 cars for model year—up by one-third from 1952 figure

Willys ranks 16th in production race, just ahead of Lincoln

In March, Kaiser-Frazer takes over Willys-Overland company

2

1. Not everyone considered the Willys Aero-Eagle hardtop to have "distinctive charm in every line," as one ad proclaimed, but the compact sold reasonably well. "Nimble in traffic," the text continued, a Willys "cruises at 65 [with] ample reserve power for safety." 2. The seven reasons to buy a Willys just happened to consist of the seven Aero models. The base Aero-Lark could now be fitted with Willy's old 134.2-cid F-head four, but these were primarily for export. 3. Style leader was the $2157 Aero-Eagle hardtop. 4. Aero-Falcon sedans, with either two or four doors, replaced the Aero-Wing. 5. Aero-Ace gained a four-door sedan bodystyle in '53 to add to this two-door model, which used center pillars in combination with the Eagle hardtop's wrap-around rear window.

3

4

5

173

1954

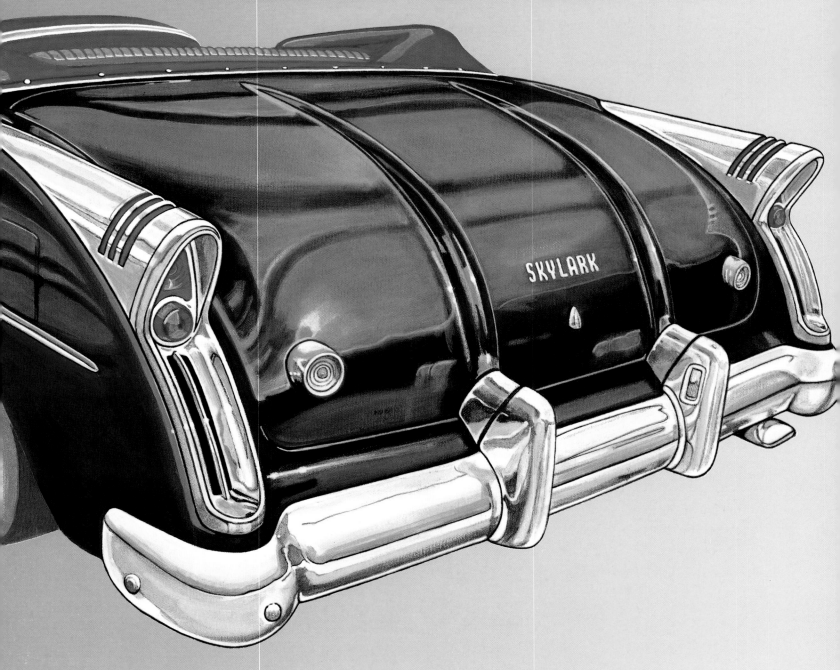

As car dealers struggled to recover from the impact of the sales blitz that began in 1953, Ford and Chevrolet accountants tallied their sales totals—each eager to claim victory. Some critics decried the high-pressure tactics and carnival-like atmosphere that had prevailed. A modest outcry emerged against misleading ads and shady practices.

Meanwhile, consumers began to hold back on purchases. Every make except Oldsmobile showed a production slump in the '54 model year.

Biggest losers were the independent makes, facing the opening salvo of a shakeout that was destined to thin their ranks sharply. Nash took over an ailing Hudson company in the spring. Then, in autumn, Studebaker and Packard merged into one—neither firm having been on solid financial footing. Both Kaiser and Willys were about to disappear. A U.S. congressman even charged that Ford and GM were trying to monopolize the industry and called for a full-scale investigation.

Except for a cute little British-built Metropolitan from Nash, a short-lived Kaiser-Darrin roadster, and a reappearance of the Century in Buick's lineup, there was little in the way of model shuffling or new introductions in '54. Under the hoods, however, existing engines grew stronger and the overhead-valve V-8 increased its foothold in the market. In all, 15 out of the 18 car makes announced higher engine outputs.

Ford launched a pair of new Y-block V-8 engines, elbowing aside the long-lived flathead design. Chrysler's hottest Hemi leaped to 235 horsepower. Oldsmobile's V-8 grew bigger. Packard had no V-8, but enlarged its long-familiar straight-eight to mammoth dimensions. Pontiac made do with its L-head inline eight for another season—but everyone knew a modern V-8 was waiting in the wings.

Big General Motors cars adopted Panoramic windshields, setting a trend for the decade. Packard took the lead with tubeless tires—soon to become standard across the industry. Chrysler tucked a gas turbine engine into a Plymouth Belvedere—the first serious test of that breed of powerplant.

Mid-priced cars showed signs of growing appeal, as Buick nipped closely at Plymouth's heels in the production race for Number Three. GM and Ford warned dealers about "bootleg" sales of new cars by unauthorized retailers—a practice some attributed to overproduction, or to indifference on the part of automakers. An Atlanta dealer drew attention in the trade press simply for hiring female salespeople, whom he felt improved showroom morale.

A recession that stretched from 1953 into '54 subsided quickly—and completely. Unemployment reached 5.5 percent—well above the 1953 figure—though inflation remained modest, and the economy in general continued to grow.

Millions of Americans looked forward to a ranch home in the suburbs, with one (or more) cars in the garage—plus shorter work hours to allow more leisure time. As more wives entered the labor force, families also grew to expect more in terms of education, nutrition, and medical services. Few seemed to care that GM president Harlow Curtice received a mind-boggling $637,233 in 1953.

Workers were encouraged—by advertising and by fellow employees—to buy the American dream for "no money down." Even youngsters were rapidly absorbed into the blossoming consumer society, led down that path by both peers and parents.

"The average American male," declared *Reader's Digest*, "thinks the ability to run a home smoothly and efficiently is the most important quality in a wife." In that vein, *Father Knows Best* premiered on TV, starring Robert Young as the "perfect" Dad. Color sets went on the market, but programs still aired in black-and-white. Smiling pianist Liberace attracted a wide female audience on TV. Senator Joe McCarthy initiated the Army-McCarthy hearings—also attracting a sizable share of television viewers.

Marlon Brando starred in the film version of *On the Waterfront*. He also portrayed the rebellious Johnny in *The Wild One*, inspiring millions of young fellows—many sporting "ducktail" haircuts—to exhibit sullen expressions and mumbled responses.

Even more suggestive of the times that would be a-changing, the theme music for *Blackboard Jungle*, a hard-hitting movie filmed in 1954 dealing with juvenile delinquents, featured Bill Haley and the Comets performing "Rock Around the Clock." New York disc jockey Alan Freed was one of the first to play rock 'n' roll—to the eagerly expressed displeasure of millions of parents. Down Memphis way, Elvis Presley cut his first commercial record.

Elsewhere on the cultural front, such "beat" poets and writers as Jack Kerouac and Allen Ginsberg gathered at the City Lights Bookshop in San Francisco. Teens and adults alike danced the cha-cha and mambo, ate the new frozen TV dinners—and began to fret about radioactive fallout from nuclear testing.

Willie Mays led the National League in hitting with a .345 average, Bill Vukovich won the Indy 500 for the second year in a row, and Englishman Roger Bannister was the first man to run a mile in under four minutes. Children began to receive Salk polio vaccine, Boeing tested the first 707 jet, and the first atomic-powered submarine was commissioned.

A trend toward do-it-yourself projects began to develop—including maintenance tasks on the family automobile. Gasoline cost about 29 cents a gallon—equivalent to $1.30 or so in today's currency.

William Littlewood, president of the Society of Automotive Engineers, decried the lack of focus on safety, insisting that the horsepower race "isn't engineering—it's a fight between sales forces." Of the million vehicles participating in a Check Your Car program, one-fourth flunked the safety test.

Like it or not, the die was cast. Nearly every automaker planned to play engine-performance leapfrog by '55, as the remaining members of the Big Three—and newly merged independents—readied new bodies and small-block V-8 engines.

1954 Hudson

American Motors Corporation

Nash-Kelvinator and Hudson Motor Car Co. combine to form American Motors Corporation on May 1

Merger is viewed as a Nash takeover of Hudson

Hudson production continues briefly in Detroit, then moves to Kenosha, Wisconsin

Because Nash is senior partner, George Mason becomes president

Following Mason's death six months later, George Romney is named chief of new company

Full-size Hudsons get restyle in final "Step-down" year

Power steering available in Hudsons

Hornet engine gains horsepower

Hornet Special and Jet-Liner models debut, plus price-leader Jet Family Club sedan

Nash-Healey production ceases during 1954

Four-door Rambler sedans and wagon join lineup

All-season air conditioning available in Ramblers

Nash markets colorful little Metropolitan hardtop and convertible, built in Britain . . . 13,905 arrive in North America by end of 1954

Dramatic aluminum-bodied Hudson Italia, built in Italy, sees minimal production

1

2

3

4

1. Top executives of the newly formed American Motors Corporation posed for a photo on April 22, 1954, near the time of the Hudson-Nash merger. Pictured are (*left to right*) Abraham E. Barit of Hudson, president/chairman George W. Mason from Nash-Kelvinator, and fellow Nash executive George Romney, who took the helm after Mason's death. 2. Hudsons earned a long-overdue restyle, as shown by this Hornet Brougham convertible. Each "Step-down" model had a one-piece windshield and fender-tip taillights. New sheetmetal below the beltline gave a squarer, more contemporary profile. These were the last "true" Hudsons. After '54, they would be little more than rebadged Nashes. 3. As usual, dashboards were loaded with bright metal. Power steering joined the options list. Note the large Hydra-Matic selector. 4. No one could mistake the presence of Twin H-Power under a Hornet hood. The 308-cid L-head six got a compression increase to 7.5:1, boosting horsepower to no less than 170.

1. In March, a value-leader Hornet Special joined the Hudson lineup; shown is a club coupe. 2. "Step-downs" continued to pile up victories on the stock-car circuit.

3. Bright body colors showed off the reshaped lines of a Hornet Hollywood hardtop. Note the hood scoop. 4. A new top-of-the-line Jet-Liner came as a four-door (shown) or club sedan. Both featured unique body trim and upmarket interiors. Basic Jets might now have either two or four doors. 5. Three Wasp body styles went on sale again, plus five Super Wasp models—including a hardtop and convertible. 6. Only the convertible cost more than a $2988 Hornet Hollywood hardtop. 7. Just 26 were produced, but few cars outdid the Hudson Italia's breathtaking styling—and it was loaded with innovations. Built in Italy, with an aluminum body atop a Jet chassis, the sporty coupe cost a whopping $4800.

1954 Nash

1. The Nash Statesman got its own twin-carb engine, dubbed Dual Powerflyte, rated at 110 horsepower. This Custom Country Club hardtop, on a 114.3-inch wheelbase, started at $2423. Front wheels still were semi-enclosed. Rear wheels on this car wear small skirts. 2. Custom two-door sedans were dropped, but a four-door Ambassador went for $2600. Super Ambassadors cost less. All full-size Nashes had a new "floating" grille. Note the accessory fog lights, headlight hoods, extra window trim, and dual mirrors. 3. Patrons of this Nash dealership might have been eligible to win a new Metropolitan, like the one parked along the curb. Note the Nash-Healey sports car poking its nose out the door. The Nash-Healey convertible was dropped, while the Le Mans coupe, wearing a new three-piece backlight, faded away in August. Total Nash production dropped below 78,000 cars (not including Metropolitans).

1

3

2

5

6

4

1. Cheerfully hued Metropolitans had enclosed front wheels resulting in a large turning radius—typical of Nashes— along with a jaunty spare tire out back. A hardtop coupe and convertible went on sale in March, priced at $1445 and $1469, respectively. 2. Metros rode an 85-inch wheelbase, and the ragtop weighed 1803 pounds. The 73-cid Austin A-40 engine made 42 horsepower. Three-passenger capacity was declared, but only two folks fit easily. 3. Nash claimed up to 40-mpg gas mileage for the Metropolitan. Because president Mason did not want a "cheap" car, standard equipment included a Weather-Eye heat/ vent system, radio, turn signals, and nylon/ leather interior. 4. Not all celebrities who touted cars were well-known. When this publicity photo for the Metropolitan was shot, actor John Bromfield was appearing in *The Big Bluff*. 5. In addition to the usual two-doors (shown), a top-of-the-line four-door Rambler Custom Cross Country station wagon went on sale, on a longer wheelbase. 6. Rambler convertibles kept their external spare tire—and cost less this year.

Chrysler Corporation

Final year for Chrysler and DeSoto six-cylinder engines

Chryslers show more brightwork, but change little . . . Hemi V-8 grows to 195/235 horsepower

DeSotos and Dodges available with PowerFlite, but three-speed stick remains standard

Luxury DeSoto Coronado sedan arrives in spring, with dressed-up interior and extra chrome

DeSoto output skids 41 percent; drops to 12th place

Dodge marks 40th anniversary . . . output drops by more than half

Dodges finish in five of top six positions in Medium Stock class at Carrera Panamericana

Dodges set 196 stock-car records at Bonneville

Dodge tops all Eights in Mobilgas Economy Run—25.4 mpg

Mildly facelifted Plymouths gain two-speed PowerFlite option

Chrysler road-tests gas turbine engine in Plymouth Belvedere

DeSoto Adventurer I show coupe carries outside exhausts—comes closer to production than most

Corporate sales drop below 800,000—down 40 percent . . . share dips near 13 percent

New proving grounds dedicated

1

2

3

1. In basic trim, a Chrysler New Yorker sedan cost $3229, but the better-selling DeLuxe version ran $3433. 2. Six-cylinder Chryslers were about to become extinct, but the top '54 seller was the Windsor DeLuxe sedan at $2562. PowerFlite was optional on sixes, but standard with the V-8. 3. The Hemi FirePower V-8 rose to 195 horsepower in New Yorkers, while a vigorous 235-horse version went into the New Yorker DeLuxe and long-wheelbase Custom and Crown Imperials. 4. TV Guide magazine sponsored "Hoppy Day" to honor movie cowboy Hopalong Cassidy, played by William Boyd. Hoppy's ride in this parade was a wire-wheeled New Yorker.

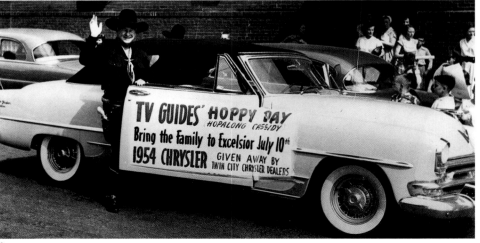

4

1

2

1. A castle-like home serves as a fitting backdrop for the Custom Imperial Newport hardtop. Just 1249 were produced, with a hefty $4560 price. 2. Custom Imperials looked more ordinary in sedan form, but affluent shoppers snapped up 4324 of them, paying $4260 for the privilege. 3. Chrysler once again helped to heat up the horsepower race. A New Yorker DeLuxe Newport mixed style and strength, though this example evidently had a hard day at the proving grounds. 4. On the show-car circuit, Chrysler's La Comtesse hardtop wore a transparent plastic top. Interior leather complemented the rose/gray body colors, with seatback inserts of platinum brocatelle fabric. 5. Modern at the time, this Shell outlet in Ohio was typical of Fifties gas-station architecture, with two service bays.

3

4

5

1954 DeSoto

1

1. Before Howard Johnson's turned into a motel chain, it was known nationwide for its road food. Top menu choices at this "landmark for hungry Americans" included baked beans and clam chowder. 2. DeSotos sported a massive new bumper and two fewer grille teeth, but otherwise showed little more than trim shuffling. 3. Top-selling DeSoto by far was the FireDome V-8 four-door sedan, with 45,095 built. 4. Interiors featured new solid-color moldings, and two-tone door panels to match seat colors. 5. Dealers typically sold and serviced both the DeSoto and Plymouth makes. 6. Town and Country DeSoto-Plymouth, on University Avenue in St. Paul, Minnesota, announces its grand opening in November of 1954.

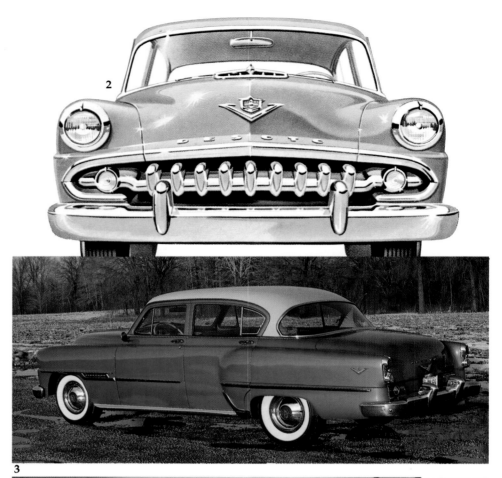

2

5

3

4

6

1. According to the sales brochure, DeSoto's $2923 FireDome V-8 Sportsman hardtop held a leather/fabric interior, featuring "gem-like chrome fittings." 2. Just over a thousand folks got a FireDome convertible, billed as a "powerful playmate" with the "sportiest look on the road." This season's line was promoted as "DeSoto Automatic," referring not only to newly available PowerFlite, but also to a host of options intended to ease driving. 3. Horsepower of the 276.1-cid Hemi V-8 grew by 10 to 170 bhp—resulting from a compression boost to 7.5:1—to deliver "greater power reserve on the road." 4. Offered for the last time, the L-head Powermaster six-cylinder engine yielded 116 bhp. 5. Once again, eight-passenger sedans kept the 1949-52 body with rear-hinged back doors. This is a Powermaster Six, but the eight-seater also came with a V-8. 6-7. Now that's one l-o-n-g fastback profile, culminating in huge round taillights. Like most DeSoto show cars, the Adventurer II was built by Ghia.

1954 Dodge

1

2

3

4

5

1. Spring brought a special-edition Dodge, the $2503 Royal hardtop, in fresh new colors. Note the innovative two-toning, suggestive of things to come in '55. 2. At the rear of a Royal, the outside spare tire swiveled to the side for trunk access. 3. Top-of-the-line Royals came in four body styles, with V-8 engines and fancy interiors. The four-door sold for $2373. 4. PowerFlite cost $189 in a Dodge, while power steering added $134—and Airtemp air conditioning demanded $643. 5. Dodge's Red Ram V-8 earned a boost to 150 horsepower, via increased compression—a typical way to add power. The Get-Away six delivered 110 bhp. 6. Sierra station wagon bodies, now with four doors on a 119-inch wheelbase, hailed from the Ionia Manufacturing Company in southern Michigan.

6

1

2

1. Dodge promoted the rich upholstery of its Royal series, done in textured Jacquard fabric, as used for furniture and draperies. Sedans, club coupes, and four-door wagons continued on a wheelbase five inches longer than on other models. 2. Dodge built 701 replicas of the yellow Royal 500 convertible that paced the Indianapolis 500 race on May 31, 1954. The $201 option package included Kelsey-Hayes wire wheels and a rear-mounted spare. The V-8 engine in the actual pace car—and several others—had a high-performance package. 3. In their film heyday, the comedy team of Jerry Lewis (*left*) and Dean Martin posed in a pace car. 4. Dodge's Firearrow Sport Coupe was the third in a series of concept cars of that name. Betty Skelton drove it to 143.4 mph, running a modified engine.

3

4

1954 Plymouth

1

2

3

4

1. Belvedere replaced Cranbrook as the top-of-the-line Plymouth series. A Belvedere convertible, shown in Santa Rosa Coral, cost $2301. 2. Four body styles made up the Belvedere line, with tiny chrome fins atop rear fenders. 3. "Color-Tuned" styling gave Belvederes an interior that matched body hues. 4. Plymouth described the upper dashboard panel's enameling as a "soft, leather-like, no-glare finish." 5. Dealers needed plenty of friends to counteract the slow sales year. For the first time since 1931, Plymouth dropped below third place in calendar-year production—though the model-year total was strong enough to retain a Number Three ranking.

PLYMOUTH
AUTHORIZED
SALES · SERVICE
THAT MAKES FRIENDS

5

186

1. Formerly named Cambridge, budget-priced Plymouths now wore Plaza badges. Bare-bones model was was the business coupe, with a minimal $1618 sticker. Stripped-down cars attracted a certain following—and not just for use by salesmen and business travelers. **2.** The Plaza four-door sedan cost $1765, versus $1873 for a Savoy and $1953 for a Belvedere. **3.** Savoy was Plymouth's new mid-range series, shown in club coupe guise. **4.** This is a Plaza station wagon, but two-door Suburbans came in all three Plymouth series. **5.** Plymouth continued to focus on value in its advertising—but also on comfort and color harmony. Note the contrasting-color panel on the upper door of the Belvedere hardtop—now called a Sport Coupe. Hy-Drive was optional at first, but PowerFlite became available at midyear. So did a new higher-powered (110-bhp), 230.2-cid PowerFlow engine. Power steering could be ordered for the first time, but like all Chrysler units, the system lacked much road "feel." **6.** Corporate president Lester L. "Tex" Colbert feels the exhaust of Chrysler's first turbine car—a Plymouth Belvedere. Exhaust heat was no longer an obstacle, as a regenerator recovered heat from exhaust gases, reducing fuel consumption as it improved cooling.

1954 Ford

Ford Motor Company

Y-Block overhead-valve V-8 replaces long-lived flathead under Ford and Mercury hoods

Y-Block engine is so named for its deep crankcase design

New V-8s are about the same displacement as departed flatheads, but considerably more powerful

Six-cylinder engine, standard in all Ford models, is bored to 223 cid, yielding 115 horsepower

Ford, Lincoln, and Mercury get mild facelifts in last year of '52 redesign

Ford is first low-priced car with ball-joint front suspension; Mercury gets it too, replacing old kingpins

Ford Skyliner and Mercury Sun Valley hardtops debut with tinted Plexiglas roof panels—idea borrowed from show cars

Other new Ford models include Customline Ranch Wagon and luxury Crestline four-door

In addition to Ford-O-Matic, Fords may have four optional power assists: steering, brakes, windows, and four-way seat

Model-year production of 1,165,942 Fords edges Chevrolet by 22,381—new V-8 engine gets the credit

Lincoln engine gets internal improvements; brakes are bigger

Half-year car/truck-sales total breaks record set in 1924

1

2

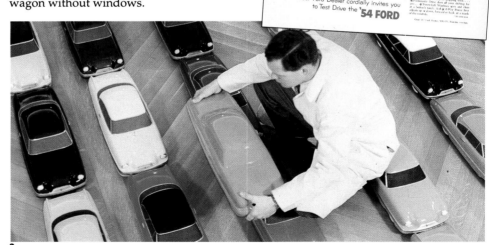

1. Ford's new Crestline Skyliner featured a tinted Plexiglas roof insert above the front seat. The hardtop began at $2164—same as the convertible. 2. Although the new 130-bhp V-8 got loads of publicity, Ford's six-cylinder engine grew and added 14 horses —now 115. The new ball-joint suspension offered longer wheel travel, "which smooths out even the roughest roads." 3. Color and style were becoming big selling points. Stylists used dozens of models to develop color selections for production automobiles. 4. Like other sedan delivery models, the Ford Courier was essentially a wagon without windows.

3

4

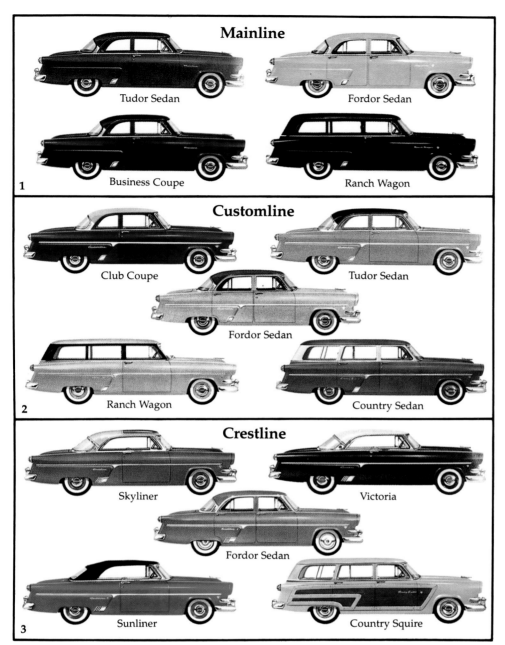

Mainline

Tudor Sedan

Fordor Sedan

Business Coupe

Ranch Wagon

1

Customline

Club Coupe

Tudor Sedan

Fordor Sedan

Ranch Wagon

Country Sedan

2

Crestline

Skyliner

Victoria

Fordor Sedan

Sunliner

Country Squire

3

There's always room for one more

in a FORD Ranch Wagon!

The Customline Ranch Wagon

Now **four** Ford quick-change artists...and each with the smooth, agile 'Go' of Ford's modern V-8 engine!

The Crestline Country Squire — The Customline Country Sedan — The Mainline Ranch Wagon

Worth More when you buy it . . . Worth More when you sell it!

4

1. Mainline Fords served as price leaders, starting at $1548 for a business coupe. **2.** Mid-range Customline models now came in five body styles. **3.** The more costly, richly fitted Crestline series added two models—Skyliner hardtop and posh sedan. **4.** Adding a Customline Ranch Wagon gave Ford four station wagons. Aiming at "young and rambling" families, Ranch Wagons could haul cargo by folding the stowaway seat into the floor. **5.** Ford was busy developing the two-seat Thunderbird—though the twin wind screens in this 1953 rendition would not be used. **6.** Henry Ford II shows off the soon-to-arrive "personal" T-Bird.

> ❝The Thunderbird will begin a new era in the automotive field.❞
>
> *Ford division general manager* **L. D. Crusoe**, *during unveiling of Ford's Thunderbird sports car; February 1954*

5

6

1954 Lincoln

1

1-2. Raising the price of a Lincoln Capri convertible by $332 doubtless didn't help sales. Only 1951 were built this year. Sheetmetal did not change, but the grille looked bolder, new full-length upper body-side chrome spears sat higher, and integrated tail/backup lights brought up the rear. 3. Instruments across the upper panel now sat against a gold background making them more difficult to read. All models had Hydra-Matic, with its shift quadrant in a band above the steering wheel hub. 4. Lincoln's V-8 engine still put out 205 horsepower—less than Cadillac or Chrysler—at a time when power boosted sales. 5. A total of 13,598 Capri four-door sedans rolled off the line—highest sedan production figure in the 1952–55 era. This year's cost: $3711. 6. Judging by sales figures, the "trend toward Lincoln" wasn't growing quite as quickly as heralded in this ad. Yet, Lincoln rose from 17th to 15th in model-year output.

2

3

4

6

5

190

Lincoln 1954

1. These Lincolns are on display at the 1954 Chicago Auto Show. Veteran road-tester Tom McCahill of *Mechanix Illustrated* still considered Lincoln "America's finest and safest automobile." More and brighter colors were offered, on both the Cosmopolitan and costlier Capri series. Under Lincoln hoods, the four-barrel carburetor was improved, hotter spark plugs helped prevent fouling, and a new distributor gave better spark advance control. Brakes grew an inch, to help shorten stopping distances.
2. Lincoln No. 103 ran second in the stock-car class at the 1954 *Carrera Panamericana* race, driven for the factory by Walt Faulkner. This is a replica of that competitor, complete with appropriate decals. Four factory-backed Lincolns dropped out of the race, but the winner was a privately run Lincoln.

Final Muntz Jets rolled out of the Illinois plant in 1954, with removable padded hardtops—no soft top at all. Late examples switched from a flathead Lincoln V-8 to the overhead-valve version, and adopted fiberglass fenders.

Big-grilled brainchild of sportsman Sterling Edwards, the $4995 Edwards America rode a Mercury chassis. Two of the six cars built had 205-bhp Lincoln engines; others carried Olds or Cadillac V-8s. High costs precluded volume production.

1954 Mercury

1

1. No Mercury beat the $2452 Monterey two-door hardtop in popularity; shoppers picked up 79,533 of them. 2. Four-door sedans came in Custom or Monterey guise, with only an $82 price differential. 3. Value leader was the two-door sedan, offered only as a Custom at $2194. This Merc has stick-shift, but shoppers turned eagerly to Merc-O-Matic. A modest facelift included neatly faired-in wraparound taillights. 4. Like other modern V-8s, the Merc's was over-square—bore larger than stroke. 5. Though festively colored, Mercury's Carnival show car didn't look much different from stock models. 6. The Carnival showed off a red/white interior with uniquely patterned seat and door-panel upholstery.

2

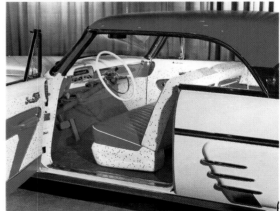

4

3

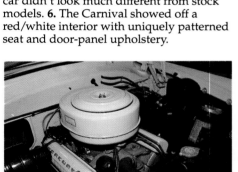

5   6

1. Like Ford's Skyliner, the Monterey Sun Valley had a transparent, green-tinted roof section of quarter-inch Plexiglas. Just 9761 were built, selling for $2582 ($130 more than a plain hardtop). **2.** Mercury claimed interior temperatures in a Sun Valley rose only five degrees in direct sunlight, but some disgruntled owners complained of stifling heat. A zip-in vinyl cover kept the sun out completely. Sun Valleys had special interior trim combinations and body color schemes. **3.** Dream cars had transparent roofs before, but the Sun Valley and Ford's Skyliner were the first to offer this feature to the public. In addition to making scenery more viewable, the see-through roof was good for overhead traffic lights—and provided the same weather protection as a solid-steel top. **4.** Naturally, those who craved full exposure to the elements could select a Monterey convertible for $28 more than a Sun Valley. Ragtops weren't quite as popular, but the plain hardtop coupe beat both by a mile. Engine output took a big leap with introduction of the 256-cid overhead-valve V-8: from a mere 125 horsepower in '53, all the way to 161 bhp.

1954 Buick

General Motors Corporation

Panoramic wraparound windshield is new trend, led by Buick, Cadillac, and Oldsmobile

Buicks earn moderate squared-up restyling . . . Oldsmobiles get new, more massive bodies

Buick Special abandons straight-eight, turns to 264-cid V-8

Buick launches hot Century, stuffing Roadmaster engine into lightweight Special body

Revamped Buick Skylark wears bold wheel cutouts, but lacks dramatic impact of '53 version

Buick beats Plymouth for third place in calendar-year output

Cadillacs longer, lower—first with standard power steering

Little-changed Cadillac V-8 now is rated 230 horsepower

Cadillac output totals 96,680 cars—as usual, far ahead of Lincoln or Packard

Ford builds more cars during the calendar year, but Chevrolet *sells* more; cars are pushed on dealers in no-holds-barred battle to be Number One

Oldsmobiles get bigger V-8 engine, longer wheelbases

Olds is the only make to post model-year output gain

Pontiac issues final L-head inline engines

1. In addition to a refined grille treatment, "beautiful buy" Buicks wore mini-finned rear fenders, more slab-sided bodies, a longer deck, and a shorter, lower hood. All Buicks now ran a V-8 engine, including the lowest-priced Special. 2. Roadmaster (shown) and Super shared Cadillac's C-body—more than 10 inches longer than a Special, and a quarter-ton heavier. Note the wire wheels on this Roadmaster sedan, built on a 127-inch wheelbase. The Roadmaster's V-8 got a hike to 200 horsepower. 3. For the first time since prewar days, Buick offered four series. Known as the "banker's hot rod," the sizzling Century melded Buick's hottest engine with a Special body, for an impressive power-to-weight ratio. Starting off in Low range with Dynaflow, a Century could hit 60 mph in as little as 10.6 seconds—and that was traveling in '54. Manual shift was available, too.

1. Super Riviera hardtops were the hottest sellers, but this Special came close. Ads pushed the fact that early sales totals topped every car except Ford and Chevrolet. 2. Buick issued a different sort of Skylark—a sporty variant of the Century. Despite a lower price than in 1953, just 836 were built. Note the wheel arch slashes and tacked-on taillight housings. 3. Convertibles came in each series, including the Special. 4. The aptly named Wildcat II, with exposed fender undersides, showed little kinship to production Buicks when it appeared at the Motorama. 5. Buick Super V-8s developed 177/182 bhp. 6. Buick fielded all-steel station wagons for the first time, in Special and Century (shown) series. 7. Station wagon bodies came from Ionia Manufacturing Company.

1954 Cadillac

1

1. Though attractive, Cadillac Eldorado convertibles were far less distinctive than in '53—but four times as many were sold, helped by a $2012 price cut. Note the ribbed bright metal lower quarter-panel trim.
2. Longer in wheelbase, more slab-sided in profile, Cadillacs looked heavier and more massive—including this Series 62 sedan.
3. Only the $4863 Fleetwood Sixty Special sedan occupied a 133-inch wheelbase. This car's emblems were redone in 24K gold. Features included wire wheels, automatic headlight dimmer, and air conditioning.
4. Series 62 convertibles shared their bodyshell with the Eldorado. Ads continued to appeal to well-off seekers after superior quality—male or female. Note that this woman was considered "fortunate" enough to be able to own a Caddy.

2

4

3

1. GM design chief Harley J. Earl directed restyling of the '54 Cadillacs, including the Eldorado (*left*). Scoops flanking the rear window of the Coupe de Ville reveal the presence of air conditioning—not available on Eldos. Two-door models had a long rear overhang and huge trunks. Note the bumper exhaust tips and the taller tailfins. **2.** Future President Ronald Reagan took the wheel of Cadillac's La Espada show car at the Chicago Auto Show. A companion El Camino wore a brushed aluminum roof. **3.** Cadillac's Series 75 Fleetwood Imperial eight-passenger sedan rode a monstrous 149.5-inch wheelbase. This year's bumper/grille had prominent guards. Panoramic windshields began with the '53 Eldorado, styled with vertical A-pillars and a visor above the glass.

1

2

3

Frank Kurtis created the predecessor to the Muntz, then left the business—until 1953. In '54, he brought out the fiberglass-bodied Kurtis 500-M. Some of the 20 built carried 230-bhp Cadillac V-8s. Priced at $5800, they were "guaranteed to outperform any other sports car or stock car on the road."

1954 Chevrolet

1. The "power features" promoted in this Bel Air ad included a more potent engine (125-horsepower with automatic, 115 with stickshift), plus optional power seat, windows, brakes, and steering. "Zippy thrifty Powerglide" added $178. **2.** Chevrolet's light facelift included a fresh grille with fluted headlight rings, plus revised taillights and hubcaps. **3-4.** Accessories on this $2185 Bel Air convertible include bumper guards, side shields, and fender skirts. Ragtop production fell to 19,383. **5.** Interiors of a Bel Air convertible matched the body colors. **6.** The 30-millionth Chevrolet was built on December 28, 1953. General manager T. H. Keating sits at the wheel, while chief engineer Edward N. Cole rides tall in the back seat.

198

1

2

3

4

5

1. Chevrolet's $1884 Bel Air four-door sedan ousted the Two-Ten as the most popular model, signaling an upscale trend. Bel Airs had dual rear fender chrome strips, Two-Tens wore a single bodyside spear, and One-Fifty models were nearly devoid of chrome. **2.** Now named Sport Coupe, the two-door hardtop came only in the Bel Air series, at $2061. Two-Ten convertibles and hardtops were gone. **3.** A Two-Ten two-door with standard blackwall tires ran $1717. **4.** Loading luggage into a Two-Ten Handyman station wagon was a snap. **5.** In its first full season, 3640 Corvettes were built, as production moved to St. Louis. For $3523, sports-car fans got plastic side curtains and no outside door handles. **6.** Showgoers got to see this Corvair fastback coupe, as well as a Corvette-based Nomad station wagon.

6

199

1954 Oldsmobile

1

1-2. Oldsmobiles gained new bodyshells, for the biggest change since their 1948-49 redesign. Many declared this year's Olds the best-looking of the decade. Note the flashy two-toning on this Series Ninety-Eight Holiday hardtop. **3.** Series Ninety-Eight Starfire convertibles weren't rare, with 6800 built on a 126-inch wheelbase. Engines were enlarged for the first time, to 324.3 cid. **4.** Oldsmobile touted the show-car origin of its Starfire, with "spectacular sweep-cut" fenders and the "surging might" of its 185-bhp Rocket engine.
5. Aunt Jemima (of pancake fame) rode in a Starfire convertible for a benefit supper at the factory.

2

4

OLDSMOBILE'S
FABULOUS NEW
Starfire

3

5

1. Oldsmobile's 88 four-door sedan, at $2337, was handily outsold by the Super 88, which cost just $140 more. Both had the new B-body, as on Buick's Special and Century: lower, blockier, more spacious. 2. A Holiday hardtop joined the base 88 line, but this Super 88 version proved more popular. 3. Dealers, including this one in Atlanta, had to find innovative ways to promote their trade-ins. This dealer's "reconditioned" used cars were touted as "real values." 4. Not only did tract homes in many of the growing suburbs look alike, some were ordered from catalogs and ads that promised more affordable prices. This company delivered wood homes, but some were metal—prefabricated partly or fully.

1954 Pontiac

1

1-2. Most costly Pontiac, at $2630, was the new Star Chief convertible, weighing a stout 3776 pounds. Bodies in this four-model series measured nearly 18 feet long—the biggest Pontiacs ever. The 11-inch stretch showed mainly in the rear deck, for monstrous trunk space. 3. In addition to the big Star Chief version, four-door sedans came in Chieftain Six or Eight guise, in either Special or DeLuxe trim level. This one looks fairly plain. Styling was little changed, but side trim was smoother and more graceful toward the rear. Pontiac claimed 109 new features, including the first air conditioner in its price range. 4. An elegant home warranted a sophisticated automobile—perhaps a $2394 Star Chief Custom sedan. A Star Chief promised "new heights of size and beauty and luxury," unrivaled in its class. 5. The five-millionth Pontiac, a Star Chief Custom Catalina, rolled off the assembly line on June 18. Here, general manager Robert M. Critchfield (*left*) releases the car to H.E. Crawford, general sales manager. It was estimated in '54 that 70 percent of all Pontiacs built were still on the road.

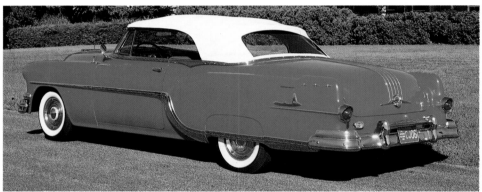

2

3

4

5

1. Big Pontiac Star Chiefs often were decked out with accessories. This Custom Catalina hardtop, which started at $2557, has a spotlight and six-way Comfort-Control front seat. New options also included electric front window lifts, power brakes ($35), and air conditioning ($594, for Eights only).
2. Full leather upholstery with Wilton wool carpeting was optional in a Star Chief. Leather came in three shades, each with ivory bolsters. Instrument panels showed little change. 3-4. A Chieftain DeLuxe two-door sedan cost $2072 with the six-cylinder engine, or $2148 with a straight-eight. A carburetor change gave the Eights 127 horsepower (122 with manual shift). Full wheel discs were standard. 5. Even in 1954, summer traffic on the Hollywood Freeway could get brutal as cars jockeyed for position following a merge.

1954 Kaiser

Kaiser-Willys Corporation

Willys Motors Inc. is wholly-owned subsidiary of Kaiser

Facelifted Kaiser Manhattan sedans offer supercharged engine, rated 140 horsepower . . . Special engine yields 118 bhp

Kaiser lineup is limited to Manhattan and Special sedans—no Dragons or Travelers

Kaiser passengers get crash padding in front and rear

Just over 1100 leftover '53 Henry J sedans are reserialed as 1954 models

Fiberglass-bodied Kaiser-Darrin sports car features sliding doors, landau top, and Willys' F-head engine

Seatbelts offered in Kaiser-Darrin; tachometer is standard

Kaiser-Darrin production lasts less than a full season, as company faces final days

Kaiser-Willys abandons U.S. market late in 1954, fielding modest number of final '55 models

Though extinct in domestic market, Kaisers will be sold in Latin America into the 1960s

Stylist "Dutch" Darrin later will buy 100 leftover Kaiser-Darrins, installing Cadillac V-8 engines

Kaiser engine available under Willys hoods late in season

Only 11,856 Willys models are built—good for 17th place

1

2

3

4

1-2. Two- and four-door Kaiser Special sedans made the lineup, priced at $2334 and $2389, respectively. Specials kept the 118-horsepower engine; Manhattans added a McCulloch supercharger that kicked in when the gas pedal was floored, boosting horsepower to 140. 3. Prototype Kaiser-Darrin carried a two-piece windshield incorporating a "Darrin dip" like other Kaisers. Production versions got a conventional one-piece windshield. 4. Kaiser's '54 facelift included unique Safety-Glo taillights that extended their lenses atop the fenders. Manhattans also got a wraparound rear window. The concave Jet-scoop grille and oval headlight nacelles were suggested by company president Edgar Kaiser, said to be inspired by Buick's XP-300 show car.

1

2

3

1. A fiberglass hardtop could be ordered with a Kaiser-Darrin, which cost $3668 in roadster form with a 90-bhp Willys engine. Though stylish, the sliding doors weren't so easy to slip past. 2. TV personality and car collector Dave Garroway took the wheel of a fiberglass-bodied Kaiser-Darrin. Only 435 were built. 3. An outside spare tire was available for the Willys Aero-Eagle. Changes in March included availability of Kaiser's 226-cid engine. 4. Beneath this Aero-Ace DeLuxe sedan's hood sits the 115-bhp Kaiser six. 5. Blackwall tires seemed fitting on the low-budget Willys Aero-Lark two-door sedan. 6-7. Camouflaged in olive drab, the Willys M-38 A1 quarter-ton military Jeep was officially known as a 4x4 utility truck. 8. The Jeep's F-head engine had 24-volt waterproof ignition.

4

5

6

7

8

1954 Packard

Studebaker-Packard Corporation

Studebaker and Packard meld into Studebaker-Packard Corporation late in year

Packard president James J. Nance takes charge of new company

First stockholders' report lists "loss before income tax credits" of $41.7 million—both Packard and Studebaker had been in poor financial health

Still lacking V-8, top Packards get huge straight-eight: 359-cid and 212 horsepower

Clipper line expands to Special, DeLuxe, and Super—with distinctive large-lensed taillights

Air conditioning available in Packards for first time since World War II

Packard adopts tubeless tires during year; other manufacturers will follow for 1955

Packard adds Panama hardtop in new Super Clipper series

Chauffeur-driven Packard formal sedan is gone

Studebakers get finned grille, larger brakes . . . engines gain compression

Studebaker adds a pair of Conestoga two-door station wagons—six or V-8

United Auto Workers union accepts wage cut in August to boost productivity and reduce costs . . . workers vote overwhelmingly in favor

1

2

3

1-2. Just 400 Packard Caribbean convertibles were built this year—no surprise, considering the $6100 tariff. Caribbeans rode a Clipper-size 122-inch wheelbase. 3. Final assembly on early Caribbeans was done at Ionia Manufacturing Company. Here, workers finish trimming the convertible top. The massive 359-cid engine had an aluminum cylinder head, 8.7:1 compression, and nine main bearings. 4. This Chicago dealership, called a "Retail Branch," was Packard's most successful store. Many Packard stockholders fought the merger with Studebaker, because Studebaker had been a big-money loser.

4

1

3

2

4

1. Like the costly Caribbean, Packard's $3827 Pacific hardtop had the big 359-cid engine. This one has dealer-installed air conditioning. During the year, Ultramatic was modified for low-gear start, and tubeless tires became standard. **2.** Cavaliers came only as four-door sedans, at $3344. Just 2580 were produced, on a 127-inch wheelbase, with a smaller (327-cid) L-head engine that yielded 185 horsepower. **3.** Edward Macauley, son of an early Packard chairman, served as vice president for design from 1932 to 1955. Responsible for fine custom bodies in the '30s, he also earned credit for the Panther-Daytona show car. **4.** Four prototype Panther-Daytonas were built, all carrying fiberglass bodies and super-charged engines. Note the stylized Packard grille, wraparound windshield, and Clipper taillights. Production was never really considered. **5-6.** Clippers, represented by this Super four-door sedan, rode a 122-inch wheelbase and carried either a 288- or 327-cid straight-eight engine, rated 150 or 165 horsepower.

5

6

1954 Studebaker

1

2

3

1. As many as five well-dressed folks could ease into a Commander Starliner hardtop. 2-3. Studebaker's Commander Starlight pillared coupe cost $2233 in DeLuxe trim, $2341 for the Regal—versus $2502 for the pillarless hardtop. Turn signals and automatic transmission cost extra. 4. Studebaker board chairman Paul G. Hoffman (*left*) and president Harold S. Vance posed with the new Conestoga station wagon. It was named for the wagon in which the company's founders trekked to South Bend, Indiana. 5-6. Conestogas came in Champion DeLuxe (shown) and Commander series. Note the accessory fog lights, luggage rack, and spotlight. Upper/lower tailgates made loading easy.

4

5

6

1

2

1. Six people fit easily into a $2438 Studebaker Land Cruiser four-door sedan. **2.** Running on higher compression this season, Studebaker's Commander V-8 engine claimed to be "packed with power that thrills, both on steep grades and in straight-away cruising." **3.** The Champion's six-cylinder engine also got a compression boost, to 7.5:1. **4.** Commander interiors had a livelier look this year, the work of decorating expert Eleanor Le Maire. **5.** Commander hardtops were upholstered in new two-tone vinyl and frieze nyle-tuft nylon. All-vinyl interiors were offered at no extra cost. Note supports for the rear seat's center armrest. **6.** In addition to the expected boasts of modern appearance and frugal operation, Studebaker continued to push its tie with famed stylist Raymond Loewy.

3

4

5

6

209

1955

F ew years rival 1955 as a boom season, or for signaling cultural shifts that were quickly taking place—in and out of the auto industry. American auto production jumped 44 percent in the model year, topping 7.9 million cars—a new record.

Close to seven out of 10 families had an automobile (or even two). The horsepower race was in full swing, led by the new Chrysler 300—so named for its engine output. Kaiser-Willys Corporation was now the only automaker without a V-8 engine—and the company was about to exit the business.

Six-cylinder engines remained available in lower-priced cars, but straight-eights were gone and fours limited to imports, such as Renaults and VWs, and the English-built Metropolitan sold by Hudson and Nash dealers. Those manufacturers that didn't offer a choice of V-8 displacements issued "power packs," typically including a four-barrel carburetor and dual exhausts, which offered a few extra horses. Chevrolet and Pontiac shared a new A-body, led by shapely Nomad and Safari wagons. Buick, Ford, and Mercury got different looks without enduring major structural change. Nearly everyone had a wraparound windshield. Chrysler's "Forward Look" ranked as most dramatic of all, helping that beleaguered company to hike its market share to a healthy 17 percent—up from 11 percent a year earlier.

Legislation was introduced to make seatbelts required. Ford and Chrysler announced dealer-installed belts. Dealers in 311 cities launched a free safety program, aiming at two million vehicles.

The American Automobile Association halted sanctioning of auto races, and urged manufacturers to emphasize safety, not speed. Michigan was the first state to require a driver's education course before issuing a license to youths under 18.

Not only did two-tone paint gain popularity, but three-tones hit the market—some in strange pastel shades. Color-coordinated interiors grew more lavish. Lincoln and Mercury offered push-button lubrication—an idea borrowed from the '30s. Chrysler moved its PowerFlite gear selector to the dashboard. New Variable-Pitch Dynaflow was a far cry from early droning Buick automatics, making this sedate cruiser a machine to be reckoned with. Tubeless tires became standard, and seven out of ten new cars had an automatic transmission.

In an effort to modify its image, the National Used Car Dealers Association voted to change its name to National Independent Automobile Dealers Association—the designation used today.

Even though today's enthusiasts can easily discern a Ford from a Chevrolet, a Buick from a DeSoto, experts at the time expressed dismay about the growing similarities among car models. The wrapped windshield, for one, suggested to some critics that automakers were merely following each other's lead—imitating rather than innovating.

In fact, each make had fewer unique mechanical features than in past seasons. Therefore, ads pushed styling, size, price, and power, along with less-tangible inducements such as status and comfort. Dealers began to decry the profusion of color and option possibilities, complaining that they couldn't stock enough cars to satisfy starry-eyed customers—who found it harder than ever to make up their minds.

Wages had been rising faster than car prices ever since the end of World War II. The average full-time worker now earned $76 a week, or $3851 per year—and the average car retailed for $2300.

More than half of families took in over $5000 yearly, up from one-third of families in 1950. Unemployment was no cause for concern, dipping below four percent.

A whopping 72 percent of car purchasers bought on time, versus 59 percent of those who signed on the dotted line in '53. Two-year payment periods were elbowed aside by longer-term schedules and low, low down payments. Auto contracts totaled $14 billion—more than half the total installment credit.

The National Automobile Dealers Association warned against "crazy credit terms." Repossessions were on the rise. Even General Motors Acceptance Corp. expressed concern that "some customers who should buy used cars are being induced through easy terms to take delivery of new cars."

Americans also tended to order their cars well-equipped, typically loaded down with options, shunning the price-leader specials that might have satisfied them a few years earlier.

The first McDonald's was erected in 1955—though few dared predict its eventual impact on American culture. Colonel Sanders had Kentucky Fried Chicken restaurants under way, and Disneyland opened in Anaheim, California. An LP (long-playing) record cost $3.98 or so, and GM stock split three for one. Shoppers could buy Crest toothpaste, and "Ann Landers" dispensed her first snippets of advice to newspaper readers. Kids wore Davy Crockett hats, in response to a TV series about the frontier hero. Male teens turned to pink shirts and charcoal gray suits with "pegged" (narrow) cuffs.

Some 4.5 million Americans read the scandal-riddled *Confidential* magazine, and President Eisenhower—affectionately known as Ike—gave his first televised presidential press conference. The minimum wage rose from 75 cents an hour to a dollar an hour.

Marty won the Oscar for best picture—and its star, Ernest Borgnine, took best-actor honors. James Dean starred in three films before his untimely death in an automobile accident on September 30. Meanwhile, Elizabeth Taylor married singer Eddie Fisher.

Fats Domino warbled "Ain't That a Shame," the Platters crooned "Only You," and Chuck Berry rocked his ode to "Maybelline." TV premieres included *The Honeymooners* with Jackie Gleason, and Bob Keeshin's *Captain Kangaroo*. Annette Funicello led *The Mickey Mouse Club*, and *Gunsmoke* debuted as the first "adult" western. A few critics condemned the jungle of TV antennas dotting rooftops, but most Americans eagerly sampled the latest video wares.

Best-selling books included Sloan Wilson's *Man in the Gray Flannel Suit*, an early warning of the conformity that was building fast in white-collar America. Housewives, not yet taking to the workforce in droves, were encouraged to own all the latest labor-saving gadgets, so families might have more leisure time—perhaps to tour the countryside in that dazzling new piece of Detroit iron. In fact, the Ethyl Corporation launched a "Drive More" campaign to encourage consumption of gasoline.

Auto dealers pushed hard to secure those record-breaking sales in '55, sometimes cutting their markups to the bone in a quest for volume. More than 61 million vehicles were on the road, eight million of them more than 15 years old. One-fourth of the American fleet had seen more than seven seasons, and were thus prime candidates for replacement with a spanking-new hardtop or sedan.

Detroit had another round of restylings in the wings to grab a few million more sales. But danger for dealers—and the industry—lay ahead. Not only did the Senate begin to probe merchandising techniques, led by subcommittee chairman Mike Monroney, but investigators alleged that GM might qualify as a monopoly—subject to forced breakup.

American Motors Corporation

Newly merged company launches crash program to update Nash—and create Nash-based Hudson

Sharing bodyshells and built on same assembly lines, Hudsons are viewed as Nashes in disguise—but differences exist

Full-size Nashes display inboard headlamps; Hudson's sit outboard . . . Hudsons have exposed front wheels, eggcrate grille, and different gauge cluster

AMC offers biggest wraparound windshield in the industry

Hornet continues with 308-cid Championship Six, but Packard V-8 available in Nash and Hudson

Use of Packard V-8 and Twin Ultramatic stems from short-lived step toward possible merger with Studebaker-Packard

Compact Hudson Jet dropped

Ramblers and Metropolitans wear both Nash and Hudson badges

Rambler line consists of a dozen models available in Nash and Hudson showrooms

Ramblers display exposed front wheels and eggcrate grille, and carry 90-horse-power engine

Shipments of Metropolitans to North America plunge nearly 54 percent to 6096 cars

1

2

3

4

Beautiful, new Hudsons by American Motors give you all these extras . . . at no extra cost!

5

1. Because facelifting the "Step-down" design was virtually impossible, AMC issued Nash-like Hudsons, including this $2460 Custom Wasp sedan. Note the distinctive two-tone paint. 2-3. Custom and Super Wasp sedans made the Hudson line-up. The bold crosshatch grille employed Hudson's familiar triangle badge. Hudsons also had their own taillight design. Wasps borrowed their 202-cid six-cylinder engine from the departed Jet. 4. Both compact (Rambler) and full-size Hudsons shared their basic structures with Nash equivalents, but the two makes differed more than many shoppers believed. 5. Priced only modestly higher than their Nash counterparts, Hudsons included a wealth of equipment, Deep Coil suspension, and big new wraparound windshield.

1

2

3

4

5

6

1. Gaudy colors made a Hudson noticeable, even if its link to Nash displeased some fans. Hornets rode a wheelbase seven inches longer than Wasps. 2. Hornets carried either the familiar 308-cid six (170 horsepower with Twin H-Power) or a 208-bhp, 320-cid V-8 driving Twin Ultramatic. Sedans came in Custom or Super trim. 3. A Wasp Custom Hollywood hardtop cost $2570. 4. Similar in appearance to a Wasp, the longer Hornet Hollywood hardtop went for $2880. 5. Hornets could now have the comfort of All Season air conditioning, the convenience of Airliner reclining seats and travel beds—plus Nash-style unit construction. 6. Fewer families took delivery of a Hudson than in '54, even though most automakers saw their output shoot skyward.

1955 Hudson

1

2

3

1-2. Rambler models cost the same whether they wore a Hudson or Nash badge. Two- and four-door wagons were sold. Note the unusual color scheme. 3. This is a Hudson Rambler Custom sedan, but four-doors also came in Super and budget-priced DeLuxe trim. 4. Not only was a Rambler cheap to buy and frugal with fuel, but AMC insisted a year-old model was worth more at resale time. 5. A Hudson Rambler assured "chaise lounge comfort" in Airliner reclining seats. Note the wheel spinner—nicknamed a "necker's knob" by young gents who felt they had more rewarding uses for their right arms than turning a steering wheel.

5

1

2

1-2. Starting at $1457, Hudson (shown) and Nash Ramblers lost their hidden front wheels. AMC claimed the "shortest turning radius of any family car in America." The cylindrical evaporative air cooler hanging out the passenger's window was a cheap—and less effective—aftermarket alternative to All Season air conditioning. **3.** Drivers waited politely for kids to cross a summertime street in 1955. Note the whitewalls on the girl's bike. **4.** This Mobil station in Illinois evidently sold outboard motors and guns, as well as gasoline. **5.** Hawaii was not yet a state when this photo of busy downtown traffic was shot.

3

4

5

1955 Nash

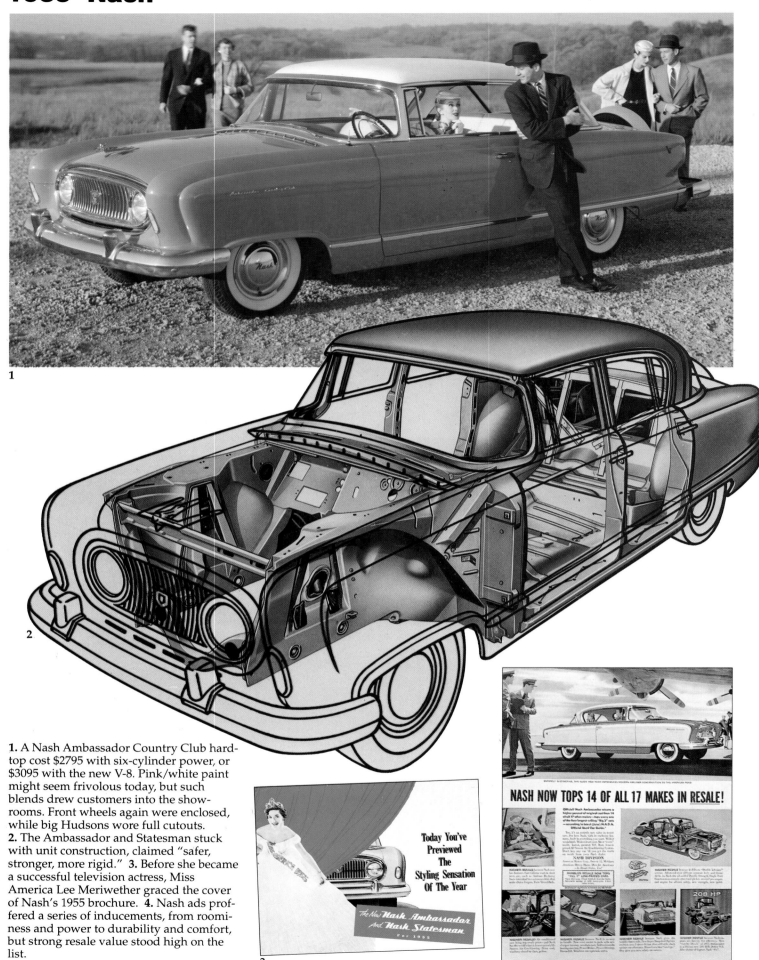

1. A Nash Ambassador Country Club hard-top cost $2795 with six-cylinder power, or $3095 with the new V-8. Pink/white paint might seem frivolous today, but such blends drew customers into the show-rooms. Front wheels again were enclosed, while big Hudsons wore full cutouts.
2. The Ambassador and Statesman stuck with unit construction, claimed "safer, stronger, more rigid." 3. Before she became a successful television actress, Miss America Lee Meriwether graced the cover of Nash's 1955 brochure. 4. Nash ads prof-fered a series of inducements, from roomi-ness and power to durability and comfort, but strong resale value stood high on the list.

1-2. Starting price for a Nash Statesman Custom Country Club hardtop was $2495, but this well-loaded example came to $3016. Unique two-toning imparted a four-layer look. The Statesman used Rambler's 195.6-cid six, while Ambassadors had a Clipper V-8 or Nash 252.6-cid six, rated 130 horsepower (140 with dual carburetion). 3. Nash's Safety-Vu headlights were joined by parking lights at the tips of its forward-thrusting fenders. 4. Like all big Nashes, the Ambassador Country Club hardtop had a Scena-Ramic wraparound windshield. The 208-bhp Jetfire V-8 came with Twin Ultramatic drive. 5-6. With the V-8, this Nash Ambassador Custom four-door sedan cost $2965 ($290 more than the six). 7. More new Nashes than Hudsons were seen on American streets, including this colorful Country Club hardtop.

Chrysler Corporation

Chrysler products wear "Forward Look" bodies, expertly styled by Virgil Exner

Three-tone color schemes appear, led by DeSoto Coronado and several Dodge models

Chrysler New Yorker's Hemi leaps from 195 to 250 horsepower

Chrysler Windsors get V-8

Chrysler 300 supercar debuts—dominates stock-car racing, earning 37 wins in NASCAR and AAA events of 100 miles or more

Firedome and Fireflite DeSotos get bigger (291-cid) V-8

Dodges come in four series: Coronet Six and V-8, Royal V-8, Custom Royal V-8

Dodge's La Femme hardtop contains pink leather interior, matching umbrella, and fitted purse—women fail to respond

Imperial now listed as separate make . . . some long-wheelbase Crown Imperials are built

V-8 engines go into Plymouths: first 241-cid, then 260-cid . . . L-head sixes remain available

Plymouth slips to fourth place in model-year production

Society of Illustrators names Plymouth "most beautiful car of the year"

Chrysler New Yorker wins class at Daytona Speed Weeks, reaching 114.6 mph

1

2

3

1. "The Power of Leadership is Yours," asserted Chrysler's promoters, when buying a New Yorker—whether a practical sedan or sharp $3924 convertible. 2. Most New Yorker DeLuxe models had twin full-length moldings with contrasting color between. A lush suburban backdrop seemed fitting for the dazzling design, dubbed "America's Most Smartly Different Car." 3. Styling evolved from the 1952 Imperial dual-cowl parade phaetons, with a broad, flat hood and deck. Hood lines were lower, too, behind a more intricate grille. The New Horizon Super-Scenic windshield had a built-in SunCap visor and rearward-slanting pillars. Shown is a New Yorker DeLuxe St. Regis—the fanciest and costliest hardtop at $3690, almost twice as popular as the regular Newport. Model-year output rose 45 percent, but Chrysler remained in ninth place.

1

2

3

4

5

7

6

8

1. Side-by-side views reveal that the new Chryslers were lower, with Twin-Tower taillamps. 2. All Windsors, including the convertible, were called DeLuxe this year. 3. The Windsor four-door sedan was top seller by far. 4. Most popular New Yorker was this $3494 DeLuxe four-door. 5. A Windsor DeLuxe Nassau hardtop was Chrysler's cheapest two-door model, now that club coupes were gone. 6. Chrysler issued a pair of "spring specials"—this Blue Heron and a green/white Green Falcon—in the Windsor series at just $65.80 extra. 7. Blue Heron interiors looked tempting. A safety padded top was available. 8. Beneath the Blue Heron's hood sat Windsor's 301-cid Spitfire V-8. 9. Chrysler's two-seat Falcon show car featured an outside exhaust system.

219

1955 Chrysler

1

2

1-2. Chrysler now had the most powerful production car in the world: the 300 hardtop. Fully loaded for $4110, the high-performance coupe's potent image lured shoppers into showrooms to scan the entire line. 3. The Chrysler 300 blended an Imperial's split grille with a New Yorker bodyshell and Windsor rear quarters. 4. A Chrysler 300 body meets its chassis at the Jefferson Avenue factory in Detroit. Only solid colors were offered. 5. From the start, the Chrysler 300 tore up stock-car tracks. Champion eagerly informed readers that some top stockers used its spark plugs—including the Chrysler 300s driven by Tim Flock and Lee Petty. 6. Tim Flock won the pole position in the 100-mile Grand National race at Asheville, North Carolina, in his Chrysler 300. No fancy grandstand here—just a hillside that gave a grand view of the raucous action.

3

4

220

6

1. Topping DeSoto's line of hardtop coupes was the $2939 Fireflite Sportsman. DeSotos rode the same 126-inch wheelbase as Chryslers, retaining the traditional toothy grille.
2. Bright hues translated to strong sales in '55, so this Fireflite Sportsman is decked out in Surf White and Emberglow. A huge sweepspear outlined a contrasting color area. **3.** Only 775 Fireflite convertibles were built, with a $3151 tag. **4.** Nothing timid about nylon upholstery in a Fireflite convertible. Hardtops wore leather. A dashboard lever changed ranges in the PowerFlite transmission.

221

1955 DeSoto

1

1-2. As in 1954, DeSoto fielded a fancy Coronado Fireflite to lure shoppers during the spring selling season. The limited-edition model had white/turquoise/black paint and a special interior. 3. DeSoto's gull-wing dashboard was a strong—even radical—design feature. Instruments sat under the left wing, matched by a radio speaker and glovebox. 4. Fireflites had a four-barrel version of the 291-cid V-8 with 200 horsepower. Five cheaper Firedome models made do with 185 bhp. 5. Sedans sold best in the Fireflite series—but lower-priced Firedomes found even more customers. 6. Ad copywriters stretched their wits to suggest that a person might want a Paper-Mate pen to match his or her automobile. Then again, color was a big sales point for all sorts of merchandise.

2

3

4

6

5

1

2

3

4

5

6

1. Flagship of the new Dodge fleet: the $2748 Custom Royal Lancer convertible.
2. Coronets could have six-cylinder or V-8 power, but other models all had the 270-cid V-8 engine—175, 183, or 193 bhp. 3. Three Lancer models were in the Custom Royal series: hardtop, convertible, sedan. 4. "Flair-Fashion" styling gave Dodge a fresh personality, "new as tomorrow's headlines." 5. Dodge's glitzy, aircraft-influenced dash put gauges squarely ahead of the driver—logical and easy to read. 6. Three-toning decorated everyday Dodges, not just limited-production models.

1955 Dodge

1. Many called three-toning a fad, but others loved the look of a Dodge Custom Royal Lancer hardtop, here enhanced by fender skirts. "Eyes widen, hearts quicken," said Dodge's sales brochure, "at this dream come true!" Only Custom Royals had small chrome fins atop rear fenders. **2.** A Royal Lancer hardtop sold for $2395, with 25,831 built—fewer than the Custom Royal equivalent. **3.** More subdued two-toning was used on this Royal four-door sedan, which sold for $2310 and held the mildest V-8 engine, yielding 175 horsepower. **4.** Though not quite as plush inside as a Custom Royal, the Dodge Royal's upholstery beckoned enticingly.

1

1. Now a separate division, Imperial shared its split grille with the Chrysler 300. **2.** Famed ventriloquist Edgar Bergen (father of Candice) and Mortimer Snerd—a country cousin of Charlie McCarthy—look pleased with an Imperial Newport. **3.** A sedan and hardtop made up the Imperial line. **4.** Chrysler shunned subtlety, asserting that an "Imperial bespeaks power, leadership, and good taste." **5.** In an Imperial, Chrysler suggested, one expected "glances of approval." **6.** "Gunsight" taillights stood free atop Imperial fenders. **7.** Exhaust from the 250-bhp V-8 exited from tips in the bumper.

3

4

5

6

7

1955 Plymouth

A WHOLE LOT OF PEOPLE WILL SEE IT THIS WAY

ALL-NEW PLYMOUTH '55

1. With Sportone body trim, a Plymouth Belvedere Sport Coupe looked dashing. Forward-lunging front fenders and reverse-angle taillights brought a fresh image. 2. Plymouth pushed the fact that its standard V-8 engine had more power than any rival's and that it was the biggest low-priced car. 3. Though it accomplished no more than a conventional column-mounted gearshift, the Flite Control selector for PowerFlite drew plenty of attention. 4. A Belvedere convertible cost $2351. Each had a 260-cid V-8 making 167 or 177 horsepower. 5. Belvederes with a V-8 easily outsold six-cylinder counterparts. 6. Lowest-priced Belvedere was the club coupe, starting at $1936. 7. Plushest—and costliest—wagon was the $2425 Belvedere Suburban. Loading a family's worth of cargo was easy. 8. Just $1837 bought a Savoy club coupe—provided you could resist the temptation to add options.

MAGIC!...AND ONLY PLYMOUTH HAS IT, OF THE LOW-PRICE 3!

ALL-NEW PLYMOUTH '55

1

2

4

1. Longer and more rakish, Plymouths remained conservative—more so if they skipped Sportone trim. 2. Belvederes suffered no shortage of chrome trim inside. Note the padded dash top. 3. Each series was available with the six-cylinder engine. 4. A PowerPak for the Hy-Fire 260-cid V-8 included a four-barrel carb and dual exhausts. 5. In addition to stylish lines, Plymouths were roomy. Note the "maze-patterned" seats of this Belvedere convertible. 6. Plymouths wouldn't become drag-race champions for a while, but this Plaza V-8 towed a headquarters trailer for the National Hot Rod Association.

3

5

6

Plymouth Turbine No. 2

Plymouth's 1955 Turbine Special, a modified red/white Belvedere, ran briefly down Detroit's busy Woodward Avenue. It was the second trial of the CR1 engine—and the first turbine-powered car driven on an American street. Note the central exhaust duct in the special back bumper. In most cities streetcars already were extinct, replaced by diesel buses.

Ford Motor Company

Three Ford series offered: Mainline, Customline, and glittery Fairlane

Ford touts Thunderbird-inspired styling and choice of engines

Five-model Ford station-wagon line is now a separate series

Rakish Ford Crown Victoria adopts "basket handle" roofline; transparent half-roof optional

Ford V-8 grows to 272 cid and 162 horsepower; 292-cid T-Bird engine optional

Automatic transmissions get new kickdown feature—start off in Low range

Fords and Mercurys can have factory air conditioning at midyear; cumbersome unit has evaporator mounted in trunk

Ford Thunderbird bows—16,155 sold in first year

Ford's model-year car output is highest since 1923—yet still a quarter million below Chevrolet

Ford launches biggest corporate expansion since 1920s

Lincoln's Fleet-Power V-8 grows to 341 cid and 225 horsepower

Lincolns drop Hydra-Matic, gain new three-speed Turbo-Drive

Three restyled Mercury series: Montclair, Monterey, Custom

1

2

1. Ford's experimental Mystere sported dramatic tailfins and a swing-up bubble canopy. Several Mystere styling features wound up on '57 models. Styling credit went to William P. Boyer, and the dream car was built by Creative Industries in Detroit. 2. Borrowing a touch or two from the Mystere, including the "basket handle" wrapover roof band, the new Fairlane Crown Victoria went on sale for $2202. 3. Colorful Crown Victorias came with or without a Plexiglas roof insert, which added $70 to the price. Just 1999 were built, versus 33,165 with solid top.

3

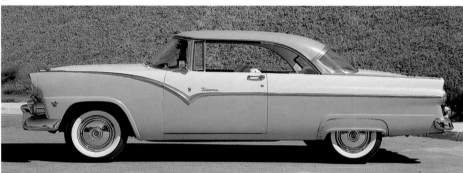

1. A Fairlane Sunliner convertible cost $2224, and sold better than the Crown Victoria. 2. A standard Victoria hardtop cost $107 less than a Crown Vic and proved far more popular, with 113,372 produced. Its roofline was rounder and taller. 3. Safety was gaining notice in Ford executive suites. Here, two dummy-equipped '55s are crash-tested. 4. Most Fairlanes had the darker color at the bottom, but not this Club Sedan—the lowest-priced model at $1914. 5. A Continental kit and skirts made the Crown Victoria look even longer and lower. Dual exhausts suggest this example has the most potent engine. 6. Ford's V-8 grew to 272 cid and 162 horsepower—boosted to 182 bhp with the Power Pack, which included a four-barrel carburetor and dual exhausts.

1955 Ford

1. Only 8 percent of families owned more than one car, but Ford wanted to provide a matched pair—say, a Ranch Wagon for utility and a Sunliner just for fun. 2. For those who couldn't buy a second car, Hertz had an answer. In Texas, Hertz cars rented for $7 per day plus 8 cents a mile. 3. Ford had plenty of two-car ideas. How about a wagon and a Town Sedan? 4. Potential freeway users saw dedication ceremonies of California's Bay Shore Expressway on June 14, 1955. 5. Will it all fit? Rather than promote the vastness of a Ford trunk, this photo showed why veteran travelers went "light." 6. Ford's Country Sedan was one of five wagons. Log houses weren't an everyday sight. 7. At $2392 the Country Squire—with simulated woodgraining—topped Ford's price scale.

1

3

4

FORD COLORS FOR 1955

Tropical Rose

Sea Sprite Green

Goldenrod Yellow

Thunderbird Blue

Neptune Green

Torch Red

Regency Purple Iridescent

Aquatone Blue

5

6

7

1. Stylists whipped out dozens of ideas, but this Thunderbird prototype looks close to production. Ford touted the two-seater as a high-performance "personal" car. **2.** Red paint notwithstanding, this T-Bird looks businesslike with blackwalls and a spotlight. The hood bulge was needed to clear the air cleaner. **3.** This hardtop prototype with rakish spare-tire mount served as a personal car for Lewis D. Crusoe, Ford Division's general manager. **4.** Many Thunderbirds came with both the soft top and a detachable hardtop. Prices began at $2944. **5.** A 292-cid V-8 gave 198 horsepower (193 bhp with manual shift). **6.** Exhaust outlets were built into the bumper guards. **7.** Dashboards were simple and functional. Note the tachometer at left.

1955 Lincoln

1

2

3

Ed Sullivan, M.C. of Toast of the Town, and Julia Meade introduce New Lincoln. Monitor sets show new rear deck, new longer body, new front assemble.

Camera one! Close up! Take the new Lincoln for 1955

FIRST you notice its unusual beauty: the dramatic new tail-lights, the sweep of chrome, the new front end treatment, the 11½ inch longer body, the lower, flowing look.

But perhaps even more exciting is the story on performance — further enhanced by new Turbo-Drive — biggest news in no-shift driving in almost 15 years. Here is no frustrating lag, no unpleasant jerk, but one unbroken sweep of silent power, from zero to superhighway speeds.

Turbo-Drive is especially designed and built to work in harmony with Lincoln's brand-new, high torque V-8 engine for 1955. But you must feel this action to believe it. Your Lincoln

dealer will be glad to let you drive a Lincoln or a Lincoln Capri. You'll know you've made a wonderful discovery the moment that Lincoln's wheels begin to turn.

LINCOLN DIVISION • FORD MOTOR COMPANY

NEW 1955

LINCOLN

for modern living
for magnificent driving

5

1. Lack of a wraparound windshield might have limited Lincoln sales, since even low-priced cars had one this year. This Capri hardtop, in popular Palomino Buff and White, has the optional Multi-Luber, which delivered grease to the chassis with the touch of a button. **2.** Rear-fender ducts reflect the presence of air conditioning in this Capri sedan. Lincolns got a minor grille touch-up. **3.** A Capri convertible commanded $4072. Only 1487 went to customers. **4.** Witty road-tester Tom McCahill of *Mechanix Illustrated* had kind words to say about Lincolns—and owned a '53 himself. **5.** Lincoln-Mercury continued to sponsor Ed Sullivan's *Toast of the Town* variety show. Lincolns measured nearly a foot longer overall, in the most extensive restyling since '52. The change failed to help sales, which even trailed Packard's.

1

2

3

4

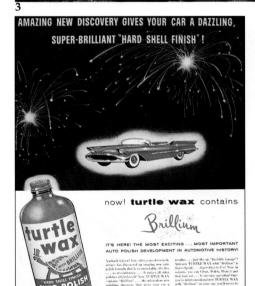

5

6

1. Longer Lincoln fenders held reverse-slant taillights. The Capri hardtop sold for $3910. 2. Lincoln's enlarged V-8 made 20 more horsepower than in '54. Dual exhausts were standard, exiting via bumper cutouts. 3. This display shows a Lincoln hardtop and convertible in the foreground, a Mercury wagon at right, and Lincoln's Futura show car in the background. 4. Women in evening dress heralded the virtues of '55 models at the Chicago Auto Show, including this Lincoln Capri convertible. 5. Ordinary waxes sounded feeble next to the "hard shell finish" promised by "miracle" Turtle Wax. 6. An Oregon dealer first owned this Capri, adding the non-factory paint job.

1955 Mercury

1. Air conditioning, power seat, and other extras quickly jacked up the $2631 base price of a Montclair hardtop—Mercury's most popular model. 2-3. Though only a hair longer than before, Mercurys looked much bigger. This Montclair convertible cost $2712. Montclairs had a 198-horsepower, 292-cid Super-Torque V-8 with four-barrel carburetion. Custom and Monterey models got a 188-bhp version, with the hotter version optional. 4. Once again, Mercury fielded a Sun Valley hardtop with transparent roof insert. Just 1787 were built. 5. Mercury styling now ran closer to Lincoln—and away from Ford's look. 6. A Monterey wagon seated eight and wore woodgrain bodysides.

1

2

3

4

1. The Montclair's V-8 came with dual exhausts. Bodies exhibited an abundance of chrome, with stainless steel rocker panels. Note the chunky taillights. **2.** Joining later in the season was a Montclair four-door sedan with chrome B-pillars, reverse-angle rear vents, and a flatter roof. **3.** Interiors were colorful and glitzy, but with well-designed dashboard layouts. Note the wide-sweeping three-tier fan-shaped gauge cluster. **4.** Portions of the Pennsylvania Turnpike were not yet complete. Here, the Lehigh Tunnel is under construction. **5.** Yes, the golden arches of McDonald's arrived on the American scene in 1955. The claim of having sold over a million burgers sounded quite impressive at the time.

MERCURY COLORS FOR 1955

Springdale Green	Biltmore Blue	Carmen Red	Yukon Yellow
Kingston Gray	Arbor Green	Tropic Blue	Sea Isle Green Iridescent

5

235

1955 Buick

General Motors Corporation

Four-door hardtop is trend of the year, led by Buick and Oldsmobile

V-8 engines are under Chevrolet and Pontiac hoods for first time

All GM makes now sport wraparound windshields

Hottest Buick engine jumps to 236 horsepower

Buick moves up to third spot in production

Buicks can have tri-tone paint

Cadillac Eldorado's V-8 delivers 270 horsepower; standard engine rated 250 bhp

Restyled Chevrolet offers 265-cid V-8 engine—first V-8 since 1917 . . . six-cylinder remains

Corvette also gets V-8 power; output sinks to 700 roadsters

Tachometer is standard in Corvettes; manual transmission available late in year

Nomad station wagon serves as Chevrolet's style leader; Safari is Pontiac's equivalent

Oldsmobile engines gain power—now 185 and 202 bhp

Oldsmobile production shoots up nearly 65 percent—finishes in fifth place again

Output nearly doubles, but Pontiac retains its sixth-place ranking

Cadillac offers remote trunk release—old idea to hot rodders

236

1

2

3

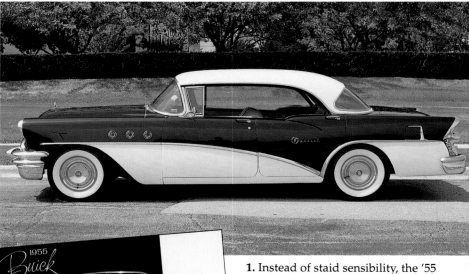

4

5

6

1. Instead of staid sensibility, the '55 model pledged to be the "Hottest Buick in History," and the "thrill of the year." Not only did the top V-8 produce 236 horsepower, but more efficient Variable-Pitch Dynaflow slashed acceleration times. 2. Most popular sedan was the $2291 Special, with a 188-bhp, 264-cid V-8 engine. Huge chrome housings circled tail and backup lights. 3. Only 4234 Century Estate Wagons were built, priced at $3175 with a new split rear seat, and carrying the bigger (322-cid) engine. 4. The new Riviera four-door hardtop came in the Special (shown) and Century series, with a $324 price differential. 5. All four series had a convertible. The Wide Screen grille incorporated a fine mesh background. 6. From Special to Roadmaster, Buicks covered a broad spectrum of the market.

Police Buick

A fleet of 270 Century two-door sedans saw use by the California Highway Patrol—the only year Buicks were employed. Even with automatic, a Century could accelerate to 60 mph in less than 10 seconds. Stator blades in the new Variable-Pitch Dynaflow swiveled in response to throttle position. Buicks earned two NASCAR victories this year.

1-2. Buick's heavyweight Roadmaster series included a sedan, convertible, and this $3453 Riviera two-door hardtop, of which 28,071 went to customers. Buick ended the season in the Number Three spot, far behind Chevrolet and Ford but ahead of lower-priced Plymouth. 3. This gent looks pleased with his Century Riviera hardtop sedan—or at least with the crowd it's attracting. 4. Convertibles had fancier interiors than other Special models—all-vinyl with a matching top boot. 5. Two-toned leather went into this racy $2991 Century convertible equipped with power windows and seats. Note the elegant ropes on front seatbacks—a touch of the classic '30s. 6. Mixing the 322-cid V-8 with the lightweight Special body again produced the sizzling Century, with 236 horses driving the improved Dynaflow.

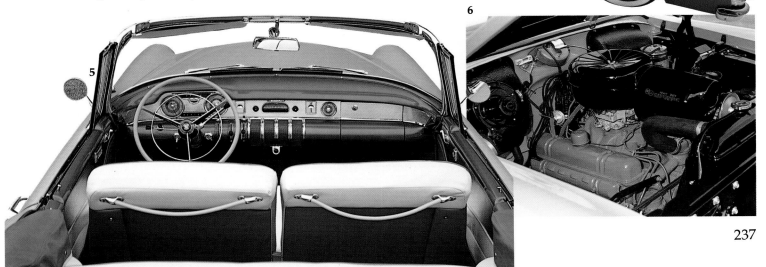

1955 Cadillac

CADILLAC FOR '55

1

2

3

4

1. Cadillac's front end featured bolder, pointed guards and outboard parking lights. New L-shaped trim decorated the bodysides. 2. Once again, the Series 62 four-door sedan ranked as top seller, with 45,300 built and a $3977 price. Sedans added a "Florentine curve" in the rear roofline. 3. Plushly upholstered in leather, the Series 62 convertible—sold in 19 colors—attracted 8150 customers despite a $4448 price. 4. Cadillac's Fleetwood Sixty Special sedan, with newly narrowed center pillars, again rode an exclusive 133-inch wheelbase. Note the air-conditioner duct on rear fender, near the back window. Factory air added $620 to the $4728 price, and production rose to an impressive 18,300 cars. Unchanged in displacement but running on tighter (8.5:1) compression, the standard V-8 gained 20 horsepower, now rated 250. Any Cadillac could have the Eldorado's more potent 270-horsepower engine for an extra $161.

238

1

2

3

4

5

6

1. The $4305 Series 62 Coupe de Ville looked particularly appealing in profile—and sold well, too. 2. Anyone investigating the "price on request" for a '55 Eldorado would find that it had escalated by $548—to an eye-popping $6286. 3. Eldorados featured an exclusive rear-end treatment with prominent "shark" fins and Sabre-Spoke wheels instead of wires. Under the hood sat a 270-bhp version of the V-8 breathing through twin four-barrel carbs. "Limited" production totaled 3950 cars. 4-5. Cadillac sanctioned production of seven Custom View Master station wagons by the Hess & Eisenhardt company. This prototype is painted Sea Island Green (a Chrysler color). 6. By 1955 every major automaker had followed Cadillac's lead in adopting an overhead-valve V-8.

1955 Chevrolet

1. Chevrolet's reliable but stodgy image slipped away in an instant when the "Motoramic" '55s debuted. 2. Brochures naturally boasted of Chevy's dramatic redesign and new-found power. 3. Sensibly stylish, the Bel Air Sport Coupe (hardtop) cost $2067. A whopping 185,562 were built. 4. What could be finer than a $2206 Bel Air convertible with all-vinyl interior? Extra-cost accessories on this example include grille and fender guards, skirts, and compass, plus Touch-Down overdrive. 5. Dealers had plenty to be enthused about when the '55 Chevrolets arrived. Note the new wagon at the curb, ahead of a rather tired old coupe. 6. Teens took eagerly to open Bel Airs, even when not towing a cheerleading float to a school parade.

1

2

3

4

1. Not only was Chevy longer, lower, and wider, it was remarkably free of the chrome-laden excesses that began to plague American cars. 2. Nearly finished cars await final attention. 3. The 265-cid Turbo-Fire V-8 made 162 horsepower in standard form, or 180 with the Power Pack, which included dual exhausts. 4. Sunoco advised motorists that one premium grade "could satisfy nearly all cars." Grease jobs were a part of regular maintenance. 5. Though teen idol James Dean tended to favor sports cars, here he is—toting an attaché case—getting into a grungy 1955 Chevrolet Two-Ten two-door. Dean was killed on September 30, 1955, when the Porsche he was driving collided with another car on a rural California highway.

5

1955 Chevrolet

1

2

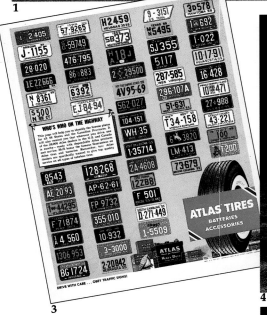

3

4

1. Chevrolets featured a Sweep Sight windshield and rakish beltline dip. 2. The twin-cove dashboard design held a central glovebox. 3. License plates still varied in size—as they would until 1957—and color schemes changed from year to year. This Atlas Tire ad also mentioned that dealers were equipped to repair the new tubeless tires. 4. Not many station wagons have achieved near-classic status, but Chevrolet's Nomad is the exception. 5. On November 23, 1954, a gold-trimmed Bel Air hardtop rolled off the line—the 50-millionth car produced by General Motors. 6. GM president Harlow H. Curtice poses with the 50-millionth car, at Flint, Michigan. 7. A Two-Ten Delray coupe cost $1835. 8. A pleated, all-vinyl interior distinguished the Delray, which was based on the two-door sedan.

5

6

7

8

1

2

3

4

5

1. Chevrolet's general manager, Thomas H. Keating, piloted the pace car, a Bel Air convertible, for the 39th Indianapolis 500 race. 2. Speedway board chairman A. C. Hulman directed activity from the pace car. A four-car tangle took the life of leader Bill Vukovich, who'd won the previous two Indy events. 3. No, this isn't a real police car. It's a converted Chevrolet One-Fifty. 4. DuPont polish promised to restore "weathered" paint "to new-car brilliance." 5. An adept do-it-yourselfer could install an aftermarket heater. 6. Final first-generation Corvettes kept their mesh-covered headlights. 7. Chevy's sports car could finally boast of V-8 power, but sales totaled less than one-fifth of the '54 tally, at 700. 8. The Corvette's 265-cid V-8 developed 195 horsepower.

7

8

6

1955 Oldsmobile

1

2

3

OLDSMOBILE COLORS FOR 1955

Burlingame Red	Turquoise Iridescent	Twilight Blue
Frost Blue	Chartreuse	Coral
Glen Green Iridescent	Bimini Blue Iridescent	Mist Gray Iridescent
Mint Green	Shell Beige	Regal Maroon

4

1. Oldsmobiles enjoyed a moderate facelift with "flying-colors" side trim. Like many Ninety-Eight Starfire convertibles, this one is loaded—with Autronic Eye, and power seats and windows. 2. Red/white upholstery gave the Starfire ragtop even greater flair. Note the sharp "dogleg" slant of the windshield pillars. 3. Simoniz gave away a Holiday Ninety-Eight hardtop, plus cash, to the person who wrote the best last line for a limerick about the new Simoniz Easy Method. 4. The Fire Chief of Newark, New Jersey, blazed to the scene in this 88 four-door sedan. At its base price of $2362 (not counting the accessory "gumball" light and fender-mounted bell and siren), the 88 was the only model to came standard with a 185-bhp version of Oldsmobile's 324.3-cid V-8.

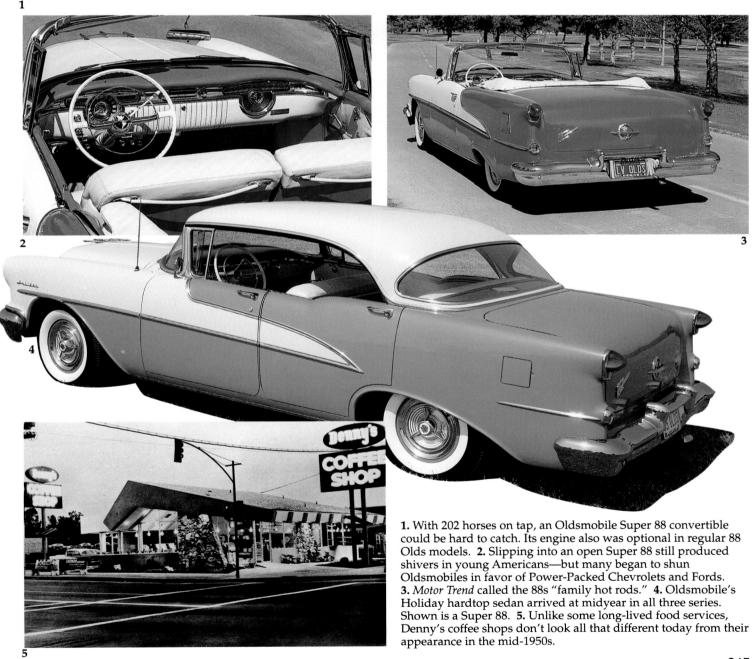

1. With 202 horses on tap, an Oldsmobile Super 88 convertible could be hard to catch. Its engine also was optional in regular 88 Olds models. 2. Slipping into an open Super 88 still produced shivers in young Americans—but many began to shun Oldsmobiles in favor of Power-Packed Chevrolets and Fords. 3. *Motor Trend* called the 88s "family hot rods." 4. Oldsmobile's Holiday hardtop sedan arrived at midyear in all three series. Shown is a Super 88. 5. Unlike some long-lived food services, Denny's coffee shops don't look all that different today from their appearance in the mid-1950s.

PONTIAC COLORS FOR 1955

Avalon Yellow	Marietta Blue	Valley Green	Bolero Red	Corsair Tan	Firegold "Metalli-Chrome"	Nautilus Blue

1. Pontiac's sole convertible was the Star Chief, priced at $2691, with a stronger frame this season. This one carries extra-cost wire wheel covers and spotlights. **2.** Then or now, few analysts would consider a new Pontiac—or any other new car—to be a "solid investment." Automotive fashions would keep changing, so Pontiac's set no more trends than other makes. The Strato-Streak V-8 helped change Pontiac's image from family traveler to snarling brawler. **3.** The Star Chief Custom Catalina hardtop turned out to be the top seller, with nearly a hundred thousand built. This one has many options, including power brakes and steering, $97 power windows, and air conditioning. **4.** No point in buying a sharp car unless you keep it shined.

1. Though shaped similarly to Chevy's Nomad, the Pontiac Safari wagon sold far fewer copies. **2.** The $2962 Safari rode a Chieftain-size wheelbase—two inches shorter than other Star Chiefs. **3.** In basic form, the 287.2-cid Strato-Streak V-8 engine developed 180 bhp—with automatic transmission. A $35 Power Pack added 20 extra horses. **4.** A two-door station wagon held six passengers, but four-doors seated eight. **5.** Chieftain two-door sedans came in two trim levels. **6.** A fleet of 150 trucks was needed to haul GM's Motorama display. **7.** The city-hopping Motorama featured dream cars and engineering exhibits. Five "flying turntables" whirled cars out of the wings, as part of the dramatic stage show. **8.** Pontiac's Strato Star was one of eight Motorama show cars.

Kaiser-Willys Corporation

Final Kaiser Manhattans and Willys sedans are sold before tooling for both goes to South America

Both Kaiser and Willys trim model offerings; Willys are given new names

Just 270 Kaisers go to U.S. customers this year, but Willys sales are respectable in number

Kaiser and Willys are the only American automobiles to lack an available V-8 engine

Willys hardtops get Bermuda badge and sharply reduced prices—but the marque is doomed despite impressive facelift

Both 161- and 226-cid engines are available in Willys models

Civilian Jeep is restyled—first time since World War II

Sales vice president Hickman Price, Jr., says Jeeps "offer a more dynamic and faster expanding market"

Willys ships 7500 tons of tooling to Buenos Aires—called one of largest movements of machinery ever

Kaiser Carabellas later will be produced in Argentina, for sale in South American market

Passenger cars will remain on sale in South American countries into the early '60s

Argentine firm is owned jointly by Kaiser, Argentine government, and private investors

1

2

1-2. A mere 270 final Kaiser Manhattans were sold before that nameplate entered the history books. More than a thousand were exported to Argentina, where production continued as late as 1962. Kaiser Carabellas were produced strictly for the South American market. 3. Willys promised a hardtop body style for fewer dollars than any other manufacturer. Willys passenger cars got a fairly ambitious facelift in their final season on the American market, losing the Aero designation. Tail and backup lights were modified. Ace, Custom, and Bermuda models were offered with either a 161-cid F-head or 226-cid L-head six-cylinder engine, and available Hydra-Matic. A total of 5986 were built, mainly with the larger engine. Economy, visibility, safety, and beauty of a Willys—as promised in advertising—failed to attract sufficient customers. Production ground to a halt in June, after which tooling was sent to Brazil.

3

1

3

2

1-2. Kaiser-Willys billed its newly renamed Willys Bermuda as the cheapest American-built hardtop, starting as low as $1895—far less than the previous Eagle hardtop. Only 2215 were produced, most of them carrying Kaiser's 115-horsepower Super Hurricane engine. Showy two-tone paint was available, too. No self-respecting manufacturer could think of surviving long without dazzling color choices on tap—but nothing could help Willys hang on any longer. **3.** Flashy upholstery choices even pervaded the low-priced market, including Willys. Note the aircraft-style slide-lever controls. **4.** A Willys Custom four-door sedan sold for $1795. A total of 2822 were built, plus a few two-doors.

4

Studebaker-Packard Corporation

Packards get heavy facelift with wraparound windshield on same basic bodyshell as '51 models

V-8 engines go into Packards

Packard fields three series: Clipper, Clipper Custom, and trio of big Packard models

Tech-oriented Packards feature Torsion-Level ride with motor-controlled torsion bars instead of the customary springs

Limited-production Caribbeans wear three-tone paint treatment

Packard's new Twin Ultramatic starts in Low, locks out at cruising speed—proves to be an unreliable transmission

Packard produces 55,247 cars for 14th place—up from 16th . . . lower-cost Clippers account for bulk of sales

Top-line President series, a name not used since 1942, replaces Studebaker Land Cruiser sedan; four models offered

Studebaker Speedster features wild two-tone paint, quilted-vinyl interior, tooled dashboard

Studebaker builds 116,333 cars for 12th place (up from 13th)

January sees start of 36-day strike

Studebaker-Packard firm reports profit in first quarter, but suffers $30 million net loss in first full year of operation

1

2

3

4

1-2. Packard Clipper Customs, including this $3076 Constellation hardtop, got a 245-horsepower version of the new 352-cid engine. Basic Clippers used a 225-bhp, 320-cid V-8. Accessories included a four-way power seat and Wonderbar radio. For their final serious stab at the market, Packards had to be fresh and innovative—and they were, with major advances in styling, engineering, and marketing. 3. Even apart from the hood script, the ship's wheel grille insignia reveals that this Packard is a Clipper—either Custom or basic.
4. Packard's intense redesign didn't overlook the interior, which featured glittery gauges and a central glovebox. 5. An ornate grille and "cathedral" taillights, hurriedly penned by Richard Teague, marked the big Packards, but lower-cost Clippers had 1954-style taillights and their own grille design.

5

1. The 352-cid V-8 in the $5932 Packard Caribbean was rated at 275 horsepower. Senior Packards' wheelbase remained 127 inches. 2. Tri-toning could also be ordered on a Four Hundred, which was priced $2000 below the Caribbean. 3. Ads boasted of Packard's new Torsion-Level suspension. 4. In a Four Hundred, the V-8 yielded 260 bhp. 5. More than 7200 Four Hundred hardtops were built. 6. Design chief Bill Schmidt studies Teague's taillight rendering. 7. Exhaust gases exited via neat outlets at the bumper tips. 8. Every detail on the Four Hundred clamored for attention.

251

1955 Studebaker

1

2

3

4

5

1. Lack of a wraparound windshield marks this Studebaker President sedan as an early production model. Fender skirts failed to assist the sedan's slightly awkward shaping. **2.** Studebaker-Packard executives show off a President sedan: (*left to right*) executive committee chairman Harold S. Vance, president James J. Nance, and board chairman Paul G. Hoffman. **3.** Plushest President four-door was the $2381 State Sedan, with gold-plated hardware. The President's 259-cid V-8 gave 175 horsepower initially, then 185 later in the season. **4.** Comfort wasn't ignored inside a DeLuxe President sedan, priced $70 below the State version. **5.** A pillared coupe with two-tone interior was part of the State President series. **6.** The five-model President lineup included a State hardtop coupe. **7.** Six-cylinder and V-8 engines grew. A 224.3-cid Pace-Setter V-8 went into early Commanders, later replaced by a 162-bhp edition of the 259-cid engine.

6

252

1

2

3

1-2. A stimulating addition to Studebaker's lineup appeared at midyear: the Speedster hardtop. Just 2215 were built—this year only—starting at $3253. Part of the President series, the coupes appeared first at auto shows; enthusiastic public response led to limited production. Standard two-tone paint came in flamboyant shades, such as pink-and-black or lemon/lime. Interiors were upholstered in custom-stitched "quilt-ed" leather. A racy "engine-turned" instrument panel held an 8000-rpm tachometer and 160-mph speedometer. **3.** The Speedster's 185-horsepower Passmaster V-8 engine came with either overdrive or an automatic transmission. Though no super-sturformer itself, aiming more at comfort and luxury than swiftness, the Speedster paved the way for a full line of rousing Hawks beginning in '56.

1956

Executive suites were full of gray flannel suits, as avid strivers began their ascensions up corporate ladders—seen as the only way to travel. Even in factories and clerical offices, though, the overall mood remained unabashedly optimistic.

Sure, an occasional critic unearthed a flaw or two in the national character. William Whyte, for one, questioned the drive toward corporate conformity in his book, *The Organization Man*. Still, despite an occasional setback, prosperity was obviously here to stay—wasn't it?

After all the automotive excitement of 1955, it was probably inevitable that the four-wheeled frenzy would calm down the next year. Indeed it did, but Detroit still had some tricks up its sleeve for 1956.

Lincoln led the way with a major revamp for its regular line—plus the rebirth of the Continental, a name unused since 1948. Thus, Lincoln mounted a strong challenge to Cadillac's well-deserved reputation for reliability and high resale value.

Rambler, too, was all-new, as it dropped its two-door models to concentrate on four-doors—including the industry's first hardtop station wagon. Otherwise, with the exception of Studebaker's Hawk series, other makes sported only the traditional facelift. But there was more than just fresh styling to tempt new-car buyers.

Once again, horsepower was big news, topped by Chrysler's second-edition supercar: the 300-B, blasting out an unheard-of "one horsepower per cubic inch" in its hottest form. DeSoto, Dodge, and Plymouth issued semi-supercars, and nearly every make advertised major power boosts. Many engines grew in displacement, but Packard's V-8 beat them all, reaching a then-whopping 374 cubic inches.

Four-fifths of new cars had a V-8 engine, and only seven makes offered a six at all. Comfort played an ever-larger role, and a dozen makes offered leather interiors. Transistor radios began to elbow aside the old vacuum-tube units. Ed Cole, soon to be named Chevrolet's general manager, predicted a trend toward fuel injection and lighter engines.

The 156-mile Indiana Toll Road opened, joining the Ohio Turnpike to create a Chicago-New York superhighway. Meanwhile, a 41,000-mile interstate highway system was approved, with the federal government prepared to pay 90 percent of the cost. A five-man team of legislators visited Detroit, hinting at the prospect of a safe-car law.

Industry output eased to 6.3 million cars. Even so, America now had as many registered cars as households—a figure predicted to rise steadily as the notion of a "second car" grabbed hold.

Imports continued their gradual influence on the market, but were barely noticed by Detroit executives. Volvo sent its PV544 from Sweden, Germany marketed a little Lloyd, unorthodox Citroëns began to arrive from France—and Volkswagen sales grew steadily.

Influence of young people also continued to spiral. Teenagers, having grown up in wartime and postwar prosperity, lacked their elders' firsthand experience with deprivation. More than a third of high-school graduates now went on to college.

For the first time, in fact, young folks foresaw a better life for themselves than their parents had enjoyed—or endured. And for better or worse, material goods—topped by a proper automobile—were a big part of that rosy picture for the future.

Car prices rose this year—some substantially. So despite continued wage increases, not everyone could come up with the cash—or secure sufficient credit—to drive home a spanking-new '56. Going secondhand was the only answer. Once considered a "problem" by franchised dealers, used cars were now a vital element of the auto trade, and a blessing to lower-income families in need of "cheap wheels."

The Eisenhower-Nixon ticket won reelection in a landslide. Democratic nominee Adlai Stevenson, still derided as an "egghead" intellectual, was defeated for the second time. His running mate, Tennessee Senator Estes Kefauver, had campaigned wearing a coonskin cap—echoing the faddish popularity of Davy Crockett.

On a lighter note, ads for Clairol hair coloring wondered: "Does she or doesn't she?" TV viewers could now see *As the World Turns* and *The Price is Right*. They also took a liking to such quiz shows as *The $64,000 Challenge* and *$64,000 Question*, which would blossom into scandal a few years later.

Out Hollywood way, Carroll Baker's sensual performance in *Baby Doll*—which would barely warrant a raised eyebrow today—startled '56 moviegoers. No less shocking was the steamy best-selling novel, *Peyton Place*.

Public tastes generally leaned toward far tamer fare, such as best-picture Oscar winner *Around the World in 80 Days*. Future president John F. Kennedy won a Pulitzer Prize for his collection of biographical essays, *Profiles in Courage*.

James Dean was gone, but his last movie, the epic *Giant*, earned a best-director award. Meanwhile, the eyes of the world focused on former actress Grace Kelly, as she exchanged storybook marital vows with Monaco's Prince Rainier. Playwright Arthur Miller took Marilyn Monroe as his lawful wife.

Elvis Presley recorded "Heartbreak Hotel," but when he appeared on Ed Sullivan's show for the third time, viewers saw his gyrations only from the waist up. Teens danced to everything from "Moonglow" and Doris Day favorite "Que Sera, Sera," to The Platters' soulful rendition of "The Great Pretender."

Mothers could now buy disposable diapers, owners of noisy cars could hit a Midas Muffler shop, and airlines carried as many passengers as railroads. Private cars remained king, and Detroit's designers were busy with some special treats for '57.

255

American Motors Corporation

Rambler earns complete redesign, wears Hudson or Nash badge

All Ramblers have four doors on 108-inch wheelbase

Rambler Cross Country debuts as the first four-door hardtop station wagon

Ramblers come in seven models and three trim levels (DeLuxe, Super, Custom); AMC pushes harder on "compact" designation

Rambler's engine is transformed from L-head to overhead-valve

Full-size models are facelifted, as AMC makes stronger effort to separate Nash and Hudson makes

Hudsons earn jeers for overblown styling; equivalent Nash models look somewhat more restrained

AMC-built V-8 replaces Packard engine in Hudson Hornet and Nash Ambassador at mid-season

Hudson Hornet Special arrives at midyear on Wasp chassis; Nash Ambassador also gets Special

Metropolitans get mid-season facelift and bigger engine

Rambler sets transcontinental economy record at 32.09 mpg—costs less than a penny a mile

Hudson again ranks 15th in production; Nash sinks to 12th

1

2

> 66 [AMC] has made itself not only lean and hard, but rock-hard during its reorganization of the past two years. The American Motors program has concentrated the facilities of two companies—Nash and Hudson—into a tightly integrated operation, with probably the lowest break-even point in the industry. 99
>
> *American Motors president* **George Romney**; *October 1956*

1-2. With Twin H-Power, the six-cylinder engine in a Hudson Hornet Custom four-door sedan produced 175 horsepower. A Continental-style outside spare remained available on full-size models. Styled by consultant Richard Arbib, the '56 Hudsons were viewed by many as excessive—or even bizarre, bordering on the grotesque. 3. In March, the Clipper V-8 (borrowed from Packard) was replaced by AMC's own V-8 engine: 250 cid and 190 horsepower, with new Flashaway Hydra-Matic optional. Compared to its 320-cid predecessor, though, the new motor lacked "go" power.

3

1

2

3

5

4

1-2. Hardtops never were a high-volume item at Hudson, so only 1640 Hornet Hollywoods were built this season. The huge eggcrate grille was interrupted by a "V" carrying the Hudson emblem at the top, dipping in another V-shape at the bottom. A small chrome fin topped each taillight. **3.** Designed in-house, Hudson's instrument cluster looked relatively plain for this gaudy period—especially when compared to the garish body. **4.** Ramblers had an all-new shape for 1956, as ads asked: "Why be satisfied with the 'All Three Look'?" Except for badging, a Hudson Rambler looked the same as a Nash version, featuring a box-section Fashion Safety Arch over the rear window. The four-door Custom Cross Country wagon cost $2329, but a Super wagon could be purchased for $96 less. Three-tone paint cost extra. Hydra-Matic was popular on top Ramblers. **5.** "V-Line" styling failed to send Hudson into the high-sales arena. Hudson promised a ride that was "3 times softer, smoother."

257

Nash 1956

1

2

3

1. Big Nashes earned a mild facelift, but looked more colorful. This Ambassador Custom Eight sedan cost $2939. 2. A four-door sedan was the only body style in the Ambassador Super Six series, priced at $2425. 3. Nash (and Hudson) continued as the only makes to offer reclining seats that converted into twin beds—popular with drive-in movie patrons and outdoor types. 4. Midyear brought an Ambassador Special series, including this $2462 Country Club hardtop. 5. Ambassador Specials held the new 250-cid Torque-Flo V-8. Improved Flashaway Hydra-Matic promised "whip-quick response."

5

66 Factory pressure? Are you kidding? They're romancing me. 99

Unidentified Massachusetts Nash dealer, *on the kid-glove treatment received by his and other "Little Three" new-car dealerships; February 1956*

4

258

1

4

2

3

5

6

8

7

9

1-2. Even compact AMC models went the four-door hardtop route, including this colorful Custom Nash Rambler at $2224. Converted to overhead-valve design, the 195.6-cid six-cylinder engine put out a third more horsepower, now 120. **3.** Only 2155 Rambler Custom hardtop sedans were produced. Note the duo-color roof band. **4.** Ads promised much that was new and different in a Rambler, from the Fashion Safety Arch to the Typhoon engine and enhanced visibility. Power steering was now optional. **5.** For $1939, Rambler's mid-range Super sedan had less brightwork and a plainer interior than the Custom. **6.** Cheery multi-coloring marked many Ramblers, including this Super. **7.** AMC issued an occasional show car, such as this little Rambler Palm Beach coupe with a gaping oval grille. **8-9.** Initial '56 Metropolitans stuck with the 1954-55 look. April brought a 1500 series wearing a mesh grille and no hood scoop. A larger (1500-cc) Austin A-50 engine made 52 horsepower.

259

Chrysler Corporation

Four-door hardtops arrive, offered by each Chrysler make

Pushbutton automatic transmission selectors installed

Displacements and outputs of V-8 engines grow

Highway Hi-Fi record players optional in Chrysler Corp. cars; gasoline heater also offered

Chrysler 300-B engine achieves "one horsepower per cubic inch"

Chrysler 300-B is billed—accurately—as "America's most powerful car"

At Daytona Speed Week, Chrysler 300-B sets unofficial flying-mile record of 142.914 mph

DeSoto launches Adventurer, Dodge has D-500, and Plymouth gains Fury—each a high-performance model

A DeSoto paces the Indianapolis 500 race, and approximately 400 Pacesetter convertibles go on sale

By start of 1956, Dodge D-500 has broken every U.S. closed-car speed record at Bonneville

Dodge ranks third—topping its class—in NASCAR racing . . . D-500 sets new track record at drag-race championship

Swift Plymouth Fury hardtop carries 240-bhp, 303-cid V-8

Three-speed TorqueFlite transmission arrives in spring, first installed in Imperials

1

2

3

1-2. "PowerStyle" Chrysler Windsors wore a new horizontal-bar grille, and modest Flight Sweep fins held revised Twin-Tower lights. Best-seller was the $2870 sedan. The poly-head Spitfire V-8 now measured 331-cid, delivering 225 horsepower. A Power Train option upped the ante to 250 horses. 3. Running for reelection as Vice President, Richard Nixon and wife Pat paraded in an open Chrysler. 4. An offer too good to refuse? Not only did you get "18 gleaming feet of power" in a Chrysler, but the adeptly facelifted Windsor was "eager to call you master."

Chrysler 1956

1. Well-detailed Chrysler New Yorkers showed a new mesh grille. 2. Only the $3995 St. Regis got three-tone paint—virtually guaranteed to turn heads. The Hemi V-8 grew to 354 cid and 280 bhp. 3. Only 921 New Yorker convertibles were built. 4. Dashboards held a cornucopia of round dials and knobs—plus the new pushbutton PowerFlite selector. New Yorkers used fine leather. 5. A roof rack added more utility to the New Yorker Town & Country wagon—costliest Chrysler at $4523, and a heavy 4460 pounds.

1

3

4

2

5

6

7

8

9

10

6. Despite a larger 354-cid Hemi that made 340 standard horse-power, or 355 optionally, 300-B output sunk to 1102 cars. 7. Just $2905 bought a Windsor Nassau hardtop. 8. Tim Flock flogged a Chrysler 300-B to record speeds at Daytona Beach. 9. Doris Day arrived at the premiere of her latest movie in a New Yorker. 10. The streamlined, experimental Dart had a retracting hardtop.

261

1956 DeSoto

1

2

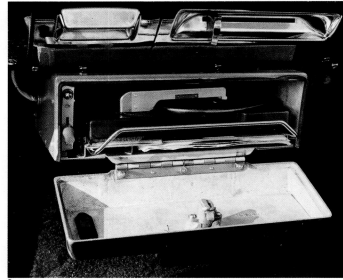

3

4

1. DeSotos lost their teeth, displaced by a mesh grille. 2. This Shell Pink-over-white hard-top contrasts nicely with the woman's purple dress. She looks ready to move into the DeSoto's huge trunk. 3. Highway Hi-Fi players were sold from 1956 to '61. Special 7-inch records spun at 16⅔ rpm. 4. DeSotos got showier two-toning, revealed by this Sportsman. The Hemi V-8 made 230 bhp in a Firedome, 255 in a Fireflite. 5. Not only would Flying A products protect your car—according to the refiner—but they could be bought on credit. Gasoline cards were not yet common, but "buy now, pay later" was becoming an anthem of American life.

1

2

3

1. At mid-season, DeSoto issued just under a thousand lavish, high-performance Adventurer hardtops, sporting gold-anodized trim. The 341-cid V-8 made 320 horsepower. 2. Dual exhausts were evident on this Sportsman hardtop. 3. An older Dodge and DeSoto, along with a '56 Fireflite, occupy this street in the Los Angeles area—prepped for Christmas. Note the Earl Scheib shop, with paint jobs starting at $29.95. 4. Motor scooters carried thousands of teens to school, but three-wheelers could perform delivery duties. Cushman was the big name in scooters, Whizzer in motorbikes. 5. Drivers got a free newspaper as well as full service at this gas station.

> 66 We're very enthusiastic about it. But it's new. Some people think it's just a gadget. The ones who have bought it are really enthusiastic about it. 99
>
> *Unidentified* **Chrysler-dealer-ship sales manager**, *on Chrysler Corporation's optional Highway Hi-Fi record player; February 1956*

4

5

1956 Dodge

1. Automobiles served as the most visible evidence of a person's status. Who could resist an opportunity to attain success—merely by buying a "dynamically powered" Dodge? Rear ends displayed Jet-Fins, and bodysides wore newly patterned two-toning. **2-3.** Dodge Royals were strongly identified with the concept of flamboyant three-tone paint. Trains still carried a large volume of long-distance travelers, but these passenger coaches are oldies. **4.** Like all Chrysler products, Dodge turned to push-button control for its PowerFlite transmissions. Edge-lit at night, the selector—mounted at the driver's left—contained no "park" button. **5.** Not often did the head styling honchos of the Big Three gather together to scan a design exercise. Here (*from left*), Virgil Exner of Chrysler, William Mitchell of GM, and George Walker of Ford, study an experimental scale model.

1. Marketers pushed the fashionable attributes of the Dodge line, including the Custom Royal Lancer. **2.** A Custom Sierra V-8 wagon seated up to eight. Lucille Ball and Desi Arnaz drove a Dodge in their movie comedy, *Forever, Darling*. **3.** Dodges could be flashy or practical. Four-door wagons began at $2716. **4.** Dodge reached the apex of misguided marketing to women with the La Femme—a daintily fancified Custom Royal Lancer. **5.** As a man hawked La Femme, an elegantly attired woman could point out the matching umbrella, rose leather shoulder bag, and gold-flecked pink upholstery. **6.** Any Dodge could have the D-500 package, but it was especially potent in a lighter-weight Coronet. With a four-barrel carb, big valves, and dual exhausts, the 315-cid V-8 yielded 260 horsepower, to take off "like a jackrabbit." Salesmen quickly learned to "talk car" with ardent young fellows.

1

2

6

3

4

5

5

1956 Imperial

1

3

1. Imperial wheelbases grew three inches. This luminous sedan has extra-cost wire wheels. 2. A rear-fender tip rotated to reveal an Imperial's gas filler. Mild but sweeping fins held "gunsight" lights. 3. Chances are, these newlyweds had more on their minds than Flying A's Ethyl gasoline. Ethyl additive turned fuel from regular into high-octane. 4. A row of round gauges and knobs dominated the dashboard of an Imperial Southampton. 5. Roll down the back window of an Imperial Southampton and the adjoining vent wing lowered at the same time. 6. The Imperial line expanded to include both two- and four-door Southampton hardtops.

2

4

5

6

1

2

3

4

5

1. Ghia, of Italy, did the bodywork for Crown Imperial sedans and limousines. Only 226 were built this year. 2. Crown Imperial limos had a rear jump seat for eight-passenger capacity. 3. Both Crown Imperial models rode an extended (149.5-inch) wheelbase. 4. Government dignitaries could parade in a specially built Imperial convertible sedan—a body style that never reached regular production. 5. There's some confusion as to whether the Norseman was to be a concept car or merely a test bed for its unique cantilevered roof, which was supported only by the rear pillars. In the end, it was neither; the Norseman was being transported from Italian builder Ghia aboard the *Andrea Doria* when the ship sank in July of 1956.

1956 Plymouth

1

2

4

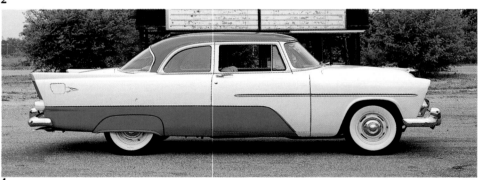

5

3

Leading designers agree that THE FLIGHT-SWEEP is the car style trend of the future!

CHRYSLER CORPORATION ➤ THE FORWARD LOOK
PLYMOUTH · DODGE · DE SOTO · CHRYSLER · IMPERIAL

1-2. Launched at mid-season, the Plymouth Fury begged to be noticed—and was, easily erasing the make's stodgy image. Each hardtop was Eggshell White, with gold-anodized accents. Other Plymouths got a 277-cid V-8 as top choice, but the Fury engine measured 303-cid, held twin four-barrel carburetors, and belted out 240 horsepower. A heavy-duty suspension, police brakes, and tachometer were included in the $2866 price. Only 4485 were built. This Fury wears dealer-installed wire wheels. **3.** In this ad, designers from other fields evidently approved of the Flight-Sweep Plymouths, now sporting an "upswept tail" (also known as fins). **4.** Once again, Plaza was the budget-priced series. This six-cylinder two-door club sedan started at $1883, but optional side trim and two-toning added dollars. **5.** This year's Turbine Special, a Belvedere sedan, made a historic four-day cross-country run, powered by a modestly modified CR1 turbine engine.

268

1. Newly shaped Sportone trim went on all Plymouth Belvederes, including the club sedan. This two-door holds a trusty six, but Belvederes could have a new 277-cid V-8, making 187 or 200 horsepower. 2. Makers of unrelated products sought tie-ins to the stylish cars. A narrow-brimmed Lee Flight Sweep hat, inspired by Plymouth's "forward-thrusting look," cost $10.95. Plymouths began at $1784. 3. A $2281 sport sedan, with two-section rear door glass, joined the Belvedere lineup. 4. Many wondered about the structural integrity of the no-pillar four-door hardtop body styles. 5. Steering wheels differed, but Plymouth dashes changed little from '55.

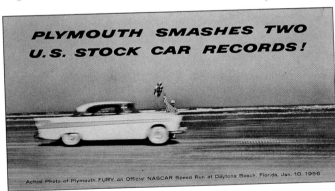

6. "Bigger is better" was becoming a rallying cry, and Plymouth Suburban wagons were ready, promising to be the "biggest, longest in the field." No telling exactly what sort of "better deal" retailers had in mind, but hard-sell tactics could be expected. 7. Who'd have believed, a year or two earlier, that a Plymouth would be smashing stock-car records? The Fury pictured made its official run at Daytona Beach, in January. 8. NASCAR officials, like founder Bill France, Sr. (left), must have been as surprised as anyone to see a Plymouth reach record-shattering velocities.

Ford Motor Company

Ford and Mercury offer four-door hardtop body style

Full-size Fords can have T-Bird's 292- or 312-cid V-8

Lincoln is sole make (apart from Rambler) with a major restyle . . . sales nearly double

Continental Mark II debuts, separate from Lincoln line, with 285-horsepower V-8 . . . the two divisions merge in July

Continentals are assembled and finished with far greater precision than other Ford products

Only 1325 Continentals are shipped, priced at $9695

Ford and Mercury may have seatbelts and other safety extras, but trend fails to take hold . . . dealers believe people hunger for style and power

A young Lee Iacocca comes up with the idea of offering a '56 Ford for $56 (a month)

Mercury comes in four series to better rival Pontiac

Mercury tops class at Daytona Speed Trials, breaks 20 world speed records at NASCAR events

Ford builds 1.4 million cars, but trails Chevrolet's 1.56 million

Ford company joins Automobile Manufacturers Association; Henry Ford II serves on AMA board

Ford stock goes on public sale for first time since 1919

1

2

3

4

1. Ford's Crown Victoria proved less popular in 1956. This transparent-top version has a 292-cid T-Bird V-8. A steel-roofed Crown Vic cost $70 less, and sold better. 2-3. One of the heaviest Fords, the new Fairlane Victoria four-door hardtop cost $45 more than its two-door mate. 4. Ads pushed Lifeguard design features: deep-dished steering wheel and double-grip door locks, plus optional seatbelts, padded dash and visors. 5. True top-down fun could be found in an open Sunliner, at $2359.

5

1

2

3

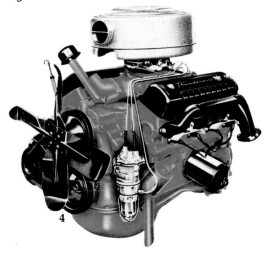

4

5

6

1. Styling similarities between a Thunderbird and full-size convertible—and even the Country Squire wagon—were evident on the banked turn at Ford's test track. 2. Thunderbirds added an outside spare tire, "flipper" vent windows, and vent doors in the front fenders. Complaints of poor visibility brought extra-cost portholes for the hardtop, but they didn't add a lot to the view. 3. Dashboards were unchanged, except for passenger-side padding and a deep-dish steering wheel. 4. T-Bird buyers got three engine choices. Standard was a 202-horsepower, 292-cid V-8. Ordering optional Overdrive or Ford-O-Matic brought a new 312-cid V-8, delivering 215 or 225 bhp, respectively. 5. Long before Big Macs made the scene, Richard's Drive-Ins offered delectable Twinburgers. This curb-service hangout in Massachusetts showcased several Fords—and plenty of litter. 6. Ever since 1916, this St. Louis dealership had been selling Fords.

1956 Lincoln

1

1-2. Not only did Lincoln finally have a wraparound windshield, it was the biggest in the industry—part of the massive redesign. Sales nearly doubled, as 19,619 Premiere two-door hardtops were built. Note the rear-bumper exhaust tips. Capris cost $482 less. 3. Lincoln's new chassis had full box-section rails. The V-8 engine grew to 368 cid and 285 horsepower, with dual exhausts. 4. A wedge-shaped dashboard held its instruments high, with aircraft lever-type heat/vent controls and a horizontal speedometer. Drivers faced a dished safety-type steering wheel. Note the unusual door handle.

2

3

4

1

4

5

2

3

1. Production of Lincoln Premiere sedans almost matched the two-door hardtop—the only body styles, apart from the Premiere convertible. This sedan started at $4601 (same as the hardtop coupe), but has fog lights and power extras. 2. To catch up with Cadillac, Lincoln had to instill pride of ownership. That meant promoting the all-new Premiere as "the longest, lowest, most powerful, most wanted Lincoln of all time." This ad also claimed that women considered Lincoln "easier to drive than even a small car." 3. Copywriters weren't shy about calling the '56 Lincoln the "most beautiful car in the world," lauding its "beauty of motion [and] power." 4. George Walker (*second from right*) led Ford's design staff. 5. Top management included, in front row, (*third from left*) president Ernest Breech and (*fourth from left*) chairman Henry Ford II.

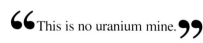

❝This is no uranium mine.❞

Ford Motor Company chairman **Ernest R. Breech**, *reassuring representatives of firms ready to underwrite more than 10 million new shares of FoMoCo stock; January 1956*

1956 Continental

1. A classic long-hood/short-deck profile marked the Continental Mark II—Ford's brighter idea, attempting to recapture a major share of the high-end market. Their immodest goal: to create America's most luxurious, carefully crafted production car. Mechanical components were shared with Lincoln, but Continental began as a Ford division unto itself. **2.** Champion jumped on the Continental bandwagon, noting that its Turbo-Action spark plugs were installed in this latest luxury machine. **3.** Tacky if installed on a lesser car, the simulated spare-tire bulge looked just right on a Continental coupe—reminiscent of 1940–48 ancestors.

1

2

3

4

1. Continental Mark II bodies demanded 60 hours for metal finishing alone—five times the effort on a "normal" automobile. Drivetrain components were machined to high tolerances. The 368-cid V-8 sent 285 horsepower to Turbo-Drive automatic. **2.** Interiors were fitted with old-fashioned broadcloth and nylon, or fine leather could be ordered. Round gauges included a tachometer and chronometer. A "cowbelly" frame resulted in a recessed floor, not unlike the old "Step-down" Hudsons. Each chassis was tuned and tested before mounting the body. **3.** Understated elegance was the byword, promising a lasting "experience" rather than a mere adventure. To help attain "ride control," Continentals had temperature-sensitive shock absorbers. **4.** After exhaustive testing and inspection, Continentals were shipped in a fleece-lined cloth cover—wrapped in a plastic bag.

1956 Mercury

1

1. At the low end of Mercury's range, a Medalist hardtop coupe cost $2398. Early models lacked part of the "lightning bolt" side trim. 2. Most popular Mercury was the $2765 Montclair hardtop coupe. 3. Mercury dubbed its Montclair four-door hardtop a "Phaeton," borrowing a name from prewar days to identify convertible sedans. 4. All hardtops adopted the Montclair's roofline (shown). Each Merc held a 312-cid V-8. 5. In many states, turning sixteen meant you could get a driver's license—and haul over to the local Dairy Queen for those soft-frozen sundaes.

5

2

3

4

276

1

1. Carousel Red paint on this Mercury Custom convertible was "flo-toned" with Classic White to emulate Montclair trim. 2. Monterey stood just below Montclair in Mercury's hierarchy. This $2555 sedan sold better than mates in other series. 3. Six- and eight-passenger wagons came in Custom (shown) and Monterey form. 4. A two-door Custom started at $2351. 5. The experimental XM-Turnpike Cruiser debuted at the Chicago Auto Show, "designed to take full advantage of the nation's budding new improved highway system." Transparent "butterfly" roof inserts lifted as doors opened. Concave channels ended in huge vee'd taillights.

2

3

4

5

1956 Buick

General Motors Corporation

Four-door Cadillac, Chevrolet, and Pontiac hardtops debut

Mildly facelifted Buick stays in third place in industry

Improved Buick Dynaflow runs with two stator wheels

All Buicks, including Special series, have 322-cid V-8

Cadillac engine is bored to 365 cid—285 or 305 horsepower

Cadillac Eldorado buyers get two posh choices: Biarritz convertible or Seville hardtop

Unlike most makes, Cadillac enjoys increase in model-year output—up nearly 10 percent

Chevrolet earns modest restyle and stronger engine selection

Corvettes get "second generation" restyling

Oldsmobile engines gain power . . . Pontiac's V-8 is bored to 316.6 cubic inches

Lightweight Pontiac Chieftain two-door sedan with 285-bhp engine sets world record, traveling 2841 miles in 24 hours

A Pontiac beats all Eights in the Mobilgas Economy Run

Alfred P. Sloan steps down as GM's chairman in April

Semon E. "Bunkie" Knudsen, Pontiac's new general manager, vows to beat Olds in sales

1

2

3

1. Front sheetmetal for Buicks was new, with a vee'd grille and teardrop-shaped Ventiports. All models now had rounded rear wheel wells. The Riviera name was used solely for hardtops—both two-door and the new four-door, offered in each of the four series. 2. Roadmaster (shown) and Super four-door sedans were six-window designs, while Special and Century had a four-window profile. 3. Then, as now, oil companies concocted impressive claims for their products, and fancy names for additives—like the protective Petrox that went into Sky Chief gasoline. Increasingly powerful V-8s demanded more from fuels. Unless octane ratings kept pace, engine knock could be a problem as compression ratios approached 10:1.

1

2

3

4

5

6

7

8

1. Each Buick series had a convertible. Wire wheels added dash—and dollars—to a radiant Roadmaster. Specials got a 220-bhp engine; others, a 255-bhp version of the 322-cid V-8. **2.** Of Buick's 21,676 ragtops, 22 percent wore a Century badge. **3.** A Century Riviera hardtop cost $343 less than the convertible. **4.** Just $2457 bought a Special Riviera hardtop—the top-selling Buick. **5.** A $3256 Century Estate wagon flaunted its three-toning. **6.** Only the Special series included both two- and four-door pillared sedans. **7.** Station wagon bodies get final attention at Ionia Manufacturing Company—GM's only outside body supplier. **8.** Buick's fiberglass-bodied Centurion appeared at the GM Motorama. A TV camera substituted for the rearview mirror. **9.** "Big Bill" Gardner claimed to have a used car "corral" in every corner of Milwaukee, Wisconsin.

9

1956 Cadillac

1. Cadillac renamed its Eldorado convertible Biarritz, to distinguish it from the new Seville hardtop. Both kept the "shark fin" rear end, skirtless rear wheel openings, and chrome door-top trim. Front-bumper protrusions sat taller, and a twin-blade hood ornament was installed. **2.** In '56, at least, the Eldorado hardtop sold twice as many copies as its open mate. Cadillac's V-8 grew to 365 cid—first enlargement since its 1949 debut. Eldo engines whipped out 305 horsepower—20 more than other Caddies—due to twin four-barrel carburetion. **3.** Like other regular Cadillacs, the Series 62 Coupe de Ville got a new rear bumper with higher oval exhaust outlets, plus squared-off fins. Coupe de Villes jumped to $4624, but Cadillac also offered a cheaper, less-posh hardtop. Note the "jet-tube" bodyside sculpturing. **4.** GM's Technical Center was dedicated on May 16, 1956, before 5000 distinguished guests in a program carried nationwide over closed-circuit TV. The 330-acre facility in Warren, Michigan, would house GM's styling, research, engineering, and process development staffs.

280

1. Compared to the $6556 Eldorado, this Series 62 convertible was a veritable bargain at $4766, and sold four times as well. 2. Cadillac called its new four-door hardtop the Sedan de Ville. Priced $457 above a pillared sedan, it became the top seller. 3. Despite a $5047 tag, 17,000 buyers turned to the thin-pillared Fleetwood Sixty Special sedan—again the sole model in that series. An optional air conditioning unit sat in the trunk. 4. Albert Bradley served as GM's fifth chairman from April 1956 through August 1958. 5. Cadillac's experimental fiberglass-bodied Eldorado Brougham Town Car, with leather landau roof, drew crowds at the GM Motorama. Doors could not be opened from outside when the transmission was in Drive. 6. Actress Natalie Wood posed with her poodle, but auto fans also enjoyed the sight of a Corvette and the latest Coupe de Ville.

1

2

3

4

5

6

1956 Chevrolet

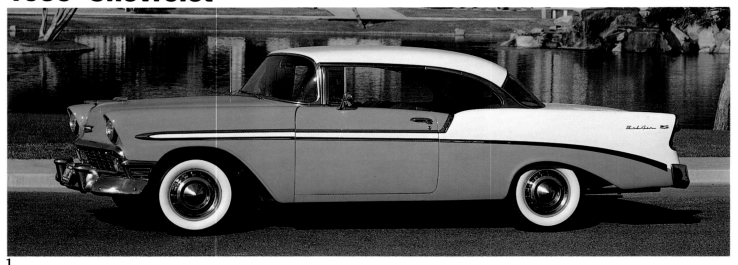

1

2 3

5 6

7

1. "The Hot One's Even Hotter," Chevrolet said of its facelifted models. **2.** Wire wheel covers cost extra on a Bel Air ragtop. One taillight held the gas filler. **3.** Dashboards repeated the symmetrical look from '55. **4.** Even a looks-tame Two-Ten sedan promised "quick and nimble ways," with up to 205 horsepower available. Later in the year, Corvette's 225-bhp engine was offered. **5.** Least costly Bel Air, at $2025, was the two-door sedan. **6.** A chrome "V" on the hood revealed the presence of V-8 power in a Bel Air. **7.** Only 7886 Nomads went on sale, with the same rear wheel opening as other Bel Airs. **8.** Stainless steel decorated the Impala show car, which included a speed warning system.

1

2

3

4

1. Mesh headlight covers were gone as Corvettes adopted concave bodyside coves, which permitted neat two-toning. 2. Enthusiasts picked up 3467 Corvettes in '56, with or without a removable hardtop. Moving ahead of European-made sports cars, Corvettes got real roll-up windows, replacing the side curtains—and could even have a power-operated fabric top. 3. Basic Corvette V-8 engines made 210 horsepower, but the twin-carburetor edition, with high-lift cam and dual exhausts, yielded an extra 15 horses. A close-ratio three-speed gearbox helped perk up performance, but boulevard cruisers could pick Powerglide instead. 4. Why wait for a driver's license to take advantage of Corvette fervor? With the hottest V-8 instead of pedal-power, a full-size 'Vette could reach 60 mph in 7.5 seconds. 5. Chief engineer Zora Arkus-Duntov took the wheel of a disguised '56 Bel Air four-door hardtop to storm up Pikes Peak, leaving a broad trail of dust in his wake. 6. Arkus-Duntov set a new American Stock Sedan record for the 12.5-mile Pikes Peak Run, finishing in 17 minutes, 24.05 seconds.

5

6

1956 Oldsmobile

1

2

1. "More power" is what customers were presumed to be calling for. Oldsmobile, like most automakers, was eager to oblige. The 324-cid Rocket V-8 in an 88 Holiday hardtop put out 230 horsepower—up from just 185 a year earlier. Like most performance-oriented cars, this ebony beauty has dual exhausts. **2.** Careful facelifting gave Oldsmobiles a stout, more substantial demeanor. Like the Ninety-Eight series, this Super 88 Holiday coupe enjoyed the benefits of 240 horsepower. Engine revisions included 9.25:1 compression, larger exhaust valves, and a reprofiled cam. **3.** A stylish Super 88 convertible cost $3031, versus $2808 for the Holiday hardtop coupe. All three series included both two- and four-door hardtops. Oldsmobile held on to fifth place in a sagging year for the industry as a whole.

3

1. Far from cheap at $3740, Oldsmobile's Starfire Ninety-Eight convertible nevertheless found 8581 buyers. Flair-away fenders ended in new projectile taillights. 2. Jetaway Hydra-Matic promised smoother upshifts via the addition of a second fluid coupling. A foot-operated parking brake replaced the old pull-handle unit. 3. Pop singer Patti Page visited the Olds plant to pose with workers and a Holiday sedan. 4. Actress Shirley Jones appeared at the GM Motorama with the dramatic Golden Rocket show car. Roof panels rose as the door opened, and the seat lifted and turned. 5. After lending his talents to GM cars since the '30s, William L. Mitchell was poised to take over as styling director, succeeding legendary Harley Earl.

1956 Pontiac

1

2

presenting the **STAR CHIEF** *Custom Convertible*

A Very Special Car for a Very Special Person!

PONTIAC
PONTIAC MOTOR DIVISION OF GENERAL MOTORS CORPORATION

3

4

1. Not every Pontiac was two-toned, as this Star Chief convertible reveals. Its hood ornament lit at night, though. No ragtops were offered in the lower-cost Chieftain series. **2.** With twin four-barrel carburetion, the newly enlarged 316.6-cid V-8 in a Star Chief convertible developed 216 or 227 horsepower. Rear-mounted spare tires weren't exactly common add-ons. **3.** As the "first word in glamour and the last word in go," Pontiac promised a dozen extra horses from the Strato-Streak V-8, via extra-cost dual exhausts. Performance zealots got another choice in January: a 285-bhp version with 10:1 compression, hot cam, and special lifters. **4.** Catalina hardtops came in both Chieftain series: the 870 (shown) and detrimmed 860, which cost $470 less.

1

2

3

4

1. A Pontiac Chieftain 870 sedan cost $2413, versus $2298 for its lesser-trimmed 860 counterpart **2.** Interiors were fancier in a Chieftain 870 than in an 860. New Strato-Flight Hydra-Matic assured smoother upshifts. **3.** Pontiac tried to appeal to both high-performance fans and family folks. The stylish Catalina hardtop sedan came in all three series. **4.** Denver's Mayor Nicholson officially snips the ribbon to open one of 15 Sinclair stations in the area. **5.** Dealers applauded Pontiac's emphasis on performance, but were less ecstatic about sales totals off by about 150,000 cars from '55. Like other retailers, this New Jersey dealership needed strong sales of "Goodwill" used cars to round out the year's profits. **6.** Only 4042 shoppers got a Safari wagon—the Star Chief equivalent of Chevrolet's shapely Nomad.

5

6

Studebaker-Packard Corporation

Last "true" Packards go on sale

Ads dub '56 models "The Greatest Packard of Them All"

Packards employ pushbutton automatic transmission selector

Shorter-wheelbase Clipper now listed as separate make

Executive series fits between Clipper and upper Packards

Senior Packards get 374-cid V-8, biggest in the industry

Packard Caribbean features reversible leather/fabric seat cushions

Packard offers electrically controlled door latches and non-slip differential

Studebaker launches quartet of sporty Hawks, led by Golden Hawk with 352-cid Packard V-8

Studebaker sedans and wagons get more upright profile

Final '56 Packards are built in May; future is uncertain

Attempting to keep company afloat, chairman James Nance searches frantically for merger prospects—turned down by AMC and Big Three automakers

Curtiss-Wright firm takes over Studebaker-Packard management in August, with engineer Harold E. Churchill as president, in a three-year contract

66 We know the comeback trail is tough and uphill, but we believe we're tough enough to keep taking those upward steps. 99

Packard-Clipper-division manager **Robert Laughna**, *on Studebaker-Packard's resolve to reclaim market share; April 1956*

1. Marketed as a separate make, Clippers came in five models: a pair of hardtops and three sedans. 2. The Clipper Custom Constellation hardtop had a standard 275-horsepower, 352-cid V-8 engine. 3. Packard's Torsion-Level suspension also went into the medium-priced Clippers. 4. Packard president James J. Nance stands beside the company's Predictor show car at the Chicago Auto Show. Described as "sculptured in steel," the four-seat hardtop hoped to be "forerunner of a styling direction which will be followed by future American automobiles." As it happened, no real Packards at all would be built after this year, and the 1956 models were branded gaudier and brasher than most.

Packard 1956

1. Multi-color paint jobs drew stares, but solid colors showed off the elegance of a $4160 Packard Patrician sedan to its best advantage. The senior-Packard series also included a Four Hundred hardtop.
2. Launching of the Executive series—hardtop and sedan, on a Clipper-sized wheelbase—tended to dilute the image of senior Packards. 3. Only 2815 Executives were produced, all carrying the Clipper's 352-cid engine. Note the subtle dual exhaust tips at the bumper's base. 4. No production Packard ever looked remotely like the Predictor show car. Built on a Clipper chassis, with a 374-cid V-8, it stood 54 inches high. Roof doors rolled back, the back window could be lowered, and seats swiveled. The Predictor's wraparound windshield curved into the roof. Note the lack of belt or window moldings.

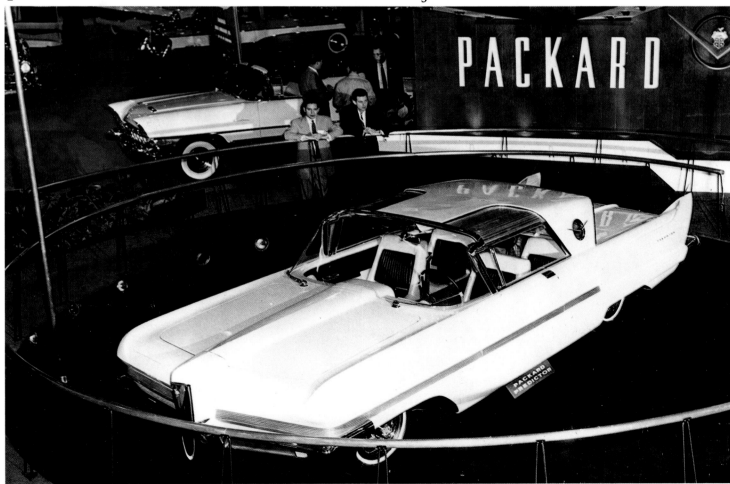

1956 Packard

1. Packard issued twin Caribbeans: the $5995 convertible, and a hardtop for $500 less. Styling changed little. 2. Tri-toning was almost expected in the open Caribbean, which carried a 310-horsepower version of Packard's 374-cid engine. 3. Dashboards were laden with round dials and knobs. Seat cushions had reversible covers—pleated leather or bouclé cloth. A six-button pod alongside the steering wheel controlled Twin Ultramatic—electrically. 4. Only 263 Caribbean hardtops were built, versus 276 ragtops. Wire wheels, air, and Twin-Traction were the only options. 5. Studebaker-Packard had a car for nearly every price class, yet the company was faltering fast.

Studebaker 1956

1. Studebaker's glorious Golden Hawk held a 352-cid V-8, borrowed from Packard, whipping up 275 horsepower. Just 4071 were produced, with a $3061 price tag. A large square grille ahead of an elevated hood helped conceal its 1953-55 coupe origin. **2.** Unlike modern sport coupes, the Golden Hawk really did have room for five. Promoted as "family sports cars," Hawks appealed more to enthusiasts. **3.** Dashboards contained tooled metal, as in the '55 Speedster, declared ideal "for sports car pilots." **4.** A 289-cid V-8 went into Sky Hawks, rated at 210 or 225 horsepower. **5.** Ordering a Power Hawk brought a 259-cid V-8 making 170/185 bhp. **6.** Rounding out the coupe lineup was the Flight Hawk, with a Champion six-cylinder engine, priced just below $2000.

> **"** There is absolutely no place for political bickering or a scramble for credit in the essential job to be done. **"**
>
> *New Mexico senator* **Dennis Chavez,** *on the need for a strong U.S. highway-improvement bill; January 1956*

1956 Studebaker

1

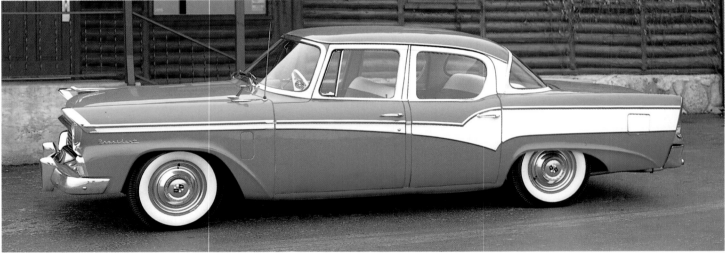

2

1. Studebaker Presidents shifted to a shorter wheelbase, except for the fancy new Classic sedan—priced $254 above an ordinary President four-door. Designers sought a more massive look for the sedans and wagons, resulting in a squared-off profile and large mesh grille, which helped disguise the carryover bodyshell. Studebaker-Packard's financial woes precluded a major redesign at this time. **2.** Each President model carried a 289-cid V-8, rated 195, 210, or 225 horsepower. Studebakers might have a conventional column three-speed, overdrive, or Flight-O-Matic. **3.** Only the President Classic sedan (shown) and the Hawk coupes rode a 120.5-inch wheelbase. Meanwhile, low-budget two-door sedanets joined the Champion and Commander series. Studebaker issued more than 85,400 cars in the '56 model year, including 19,165 Hawks.

3

1

2

1. Each Studebaker series had a station wagon, topped by the $2529 President Pinehurst. Note the oddly patterned two-toning. 2. Four small round gauges sat in a panel ahead of the driver of a sedan or wagon. Optional air conditioning went below the dashboard. 3. Studebaker prices ranged from $1844 to $2529—similar to Chevrolet's. 4. A Pinehurst's 289-cid V-8 made 195 or 225 horsepower.

Can this be a low price car?

Yes! Studebaker has brought *Craftsmanship with a Flair* to the low price field ... that's why it's the big *new choice* among low price cars!

Studebaker

The big new choice in the low price field—Studebaker

3

4

1957

Following 1956 sales that were off somewhat from record-setting 1955, the auto industry managed a modest rebound for '57. But disaster loomed by year's end, as economic recession knocked at the nation's door.

In this season of the tailfin, those oh-so-American rear-end appendages soared taller, but had not yet reached their zenith. American cars also began a switch to quad headlamps, but they were ruled illegal (temporarily) in several states. For that reason, several '57 makes can be found with either single or twin lights on each side.

Chevrolet cleverly facelifted its cars to a shape destined for near-classic status—as close as any postwar car has come to that exalted level, at any rate. At the time, however, the restyled Fords drew just as much attention. Years passed before the '57 Chevy turned into the crown jewel of the Fifties.

Few realized its significance, but AMC was about to lead the way into the compact era, killing off its big cars in mid-season to concentrate solely on Ramblers. Chrysler products, meanwhile, drew raves for their overwhelming "Forward Look" shapes as well as new Torsion-Aire Ride.

Most domestic cars switched to 14-inch wheels, several offered six-way power seats, and luxury models came with electric door locks. In some cars, speedometer buzzers sounded when a preset speed was reached. Several had nonslip differentials.

Studebaker-Packard plopped a supercharger atop its V-8 engine—a hop-up device unseen since the final Kaisers, and far more potent this time around. Pontiac unleashed a Bonneville convertible, named for the desolate Utah salt flats where so many land-speed records were set and broken. Plusher and more powerful than any prior model, it helped set the stage for Pontiac's transformation into a performance-oriented marque.

Both Chevrolet and Pontiac adopted fuel injection for their hottest engines, while Pontiac also used triple carburetion, as did Oldsmobile.

Stung by criticism of Detroit's escalating emphasis on horsepower and performance, the Automobile Manufacturers Association banned factory-sponsored racing. The AMA also resolved to eliminate a focus on speed from auto advertising.

The 42nd National Automobile Show, the first since 1940, was held at New York's new Coliseum in late 1956 to showcase the longer, lower '57 models. Vice President Nixon spoke at a banquet during the show—the first one to be televised.

An average car sold for $2749, whereas the average worker now earned $4230 yearly, and median family income neared $5000. Physicians topped $22,000, while teachers stood a little below the overall average. Factory workers might expect to pull in about $2.08 an hour.

Economic inflation rose a bit, but unemployment remained stable—above four percent. Some churchgoers were attending services at drive-in facilities. The Soviet Union launched Sputnik, the first space satellite, into orbit, followed by Sputnik II, which carried a dog. America's Viking satellite, meanwhile, exploded prior to takeoff at Cape Canaveral, Florida.

Despite popular acclaim for unceasing prosperity, a few critics had harsh words to say about the burgeoning consumer society. Director Martin Ritt made caustic observations of the suburban lifestyle in a little-noticed movie, No Down Payment. Joanne Woodward and Pat Hingle had major roles, but Tony Randall nearly stole the show with his portrayal of a desperate-for-cash used-car salesman.

All told, it was a fine year for Hollywood, with such critically acclaimed (and popular) features as Twelve Angry Men, The Bridge on the River Kwai, and Gunfight at the O.K. Corral. On a darker note, Andy Griffith shined as A Face in the Crowd, portraying a wastrel-turned-celebrity in this searing exposé of media-induced publicity.

Raymond Burr's Perry Mason appeared on TV for the first time. So did Wagon Train and Leave It to Beaver, along with James Garner in Maverick. Dick Clark launched American Bandstand to capture the attention of teenagers after school. Half of the top shows were westerns. Studios could now use videotape, heralding the demise of live television. The Everly Brothers sang "Bye, Bye Love," but their humorous ditty "Wake Up Little Susie" was banned in Boston. Jerry Lee Lewis noted that there was a "Whole Lot of Shaking Going On," as Little Richard belted out his tribute to "Lucille." Debbie Reynolds hit the pop charts with her rendition of "Tammy," and Harry Belafonte scored with the "Banana Boat Song."

Charles Van Doren won $129,000 on TV's Twenty-One quiz show, attracting a flurry of public adoration that would ordinarily be limited to movie stars and sports figures. Elizabeth Taylor, then 24, took her next husband, producer Mike Todd (age 54). Both the Brooklyn Dodgers and New York Giants moved to California, to the distress of their zealous fans.

Parents worried about Asian Flu, while kids played with Slinky and Hula Hoops, and Sony issued a pocket-size transistor radio. Ford's director of engineering research warned that production of natural petroleum might "peak out" in the next two decades, but few believed that fuel supplies would ever be threatened.

One-third of new cars, according to a new study, were purchased by middle-class families, earning $5000 to $7500 per year. More than two-thirds of them were bought on credit. After all, an older car didn't look proper in the driveway of a neat suburban house. Not when every other home on the block flaunted a late-model sedan or station wagon.

To no one's surprise, moderate-income families were even more likely to buy cars on time—as did nearly 90 percent of young shoppers. Not even the prospect of increased credit, though, would help the auto industry through the rocky economic seas that lay immediately ahead.

1957 Hudson

American Motors Corporation

Nash and Hudson names used for last time, as full-size models face final season in lineup

Nash Ambassador gets rather extensive restyling; Hudson Hornet changes less

Full-size cars hold new 327-cid V-8 engine

Ramblers gain mild facelift, can have V-8 engine for first time

Rambler is now a separate make, with no Nash or Hudson badge

Super-swift Rambler Rebel four-door hardtop arrives at midyear, powered by 327-cid V-8

Fuel injection is planned for Rebel, but no production models are so equipped . . . was to be "the compact car with LIGHTNING under the hood"

Overdrive-equipped Rambler Cross Country wagon goes on coast-to-coast economy run—gets 32.09 mpg, consuming only five tankfuls

By year-end, Metropolitans wear their own badges; sales pick up sharply, to 15,317 cars (13,425 for U.S., the rest to Canada)

President George Romney orders big cars dropped at midyear, after only 3876 Hudson Hornets and 3561 Nash Ambassadors are built; company will focus on Ramblers

1

2

3

> " This is legally and economically absurd. "
>
> *American Motors president* **George Romney**, *on the disparity between restrictions on auto prices and theoretically unlimited wages for auto workers; March 1957*

1-2. Mild trim shuffling improved the look of final Hudsons, but they still ranked as garish. Wasps were gone, leaving only a Hornet sedan and hardtop. **3.** Tacked-on tailfins were body-colored. **4.** Three-tone paint remained common on Hornets, including this Hollywood hardtop. All Hudsons had a 255-horsepower, 327-cid V-8.

4

1

2

4

1-2. A relatively radical facelift graced the big Nashes. The Statesman departed, leaving only Ambassadors, like this $2847 Custom Country Club hardtop. **3-4.** Headlights returned to the fenders, and Nash was one of the first makes with standard dual lights (except where the four-headlight setup remained illegal). Front wheels were fully exposed for the first time since 1948. Enlarged to 327 cid, the V-8 made 255 bhp.

3

1957 Nash

1

2

3

4

1. Custom Ambassadors wore extra side trim for three-toning, and featured posher interiors. 2. AMC gambled its future on the proposition that Americans didn't want a "big, over-chromiumed rolling cabana" but would accept a frugal car if it were sufficiently roomy. 3-4. To demonstrate its reliance upon Rambler for the future, AMC launched the Rebel. This limited-edition four-door hardtop held AMC's four-barrel 255-horsepower V-8 engine—borrowed from the big cars. That was sufficient to propel a Rebel to 60 mph in as little as 7.2 seconds. Painted light silver metallic, Rebels had a gold anodized aluminum sidespear.

1

1-2. Altered only in detail, a Rambler Custom Cross Country station wagon cost $2500. The 195.6-cid six-cylinder engine got a boost to 125 horsepower (135-bhp optional). On Custom models, the upper bodyside chrome strip ran straight back to the taillights. The new 250-cid, 190-horse-power V-8 engine option included dual exhausts. 3. Little-changed and no longer badged as Nash or Hudson, a Metropolitan hardtop cost $1567. 4. The Metro convert-ible ran $24 more than a hardtop. Both retained the little rear-mounted spare tire, and typically sported colorful two-toning.

2

" There's a certain romance for people in buying a car imported from Europe. "

American Motors automotive distribution vice-president **Roy Abernethy**, *on the success of AMC's imported Metropolitan, and other European automobiles; March 1957*

4

3

Chrysler Corporation

All Chrysler products feature Virgil Exner's second-generation "Forward Look"

Exner, known for stunning show cars, spends $300 million for this year's redesign

Each make is long, low, sleek—with soaring, flamboyant fins

Torsion-bar suspensions replace conventional front springs on all Chrysler Corporation cars

Three-speed TorqueFlite automatic transmission, introduced on '56 Imperials, is available on all makes

Most V-8 engines gain in displacement and power, following industry trend

Rear-facing seats available in station wagons . . . transistor radios are installed . . . cars ride new 14-inch wheels

Chrysler offers four models: Windsor, Saratoga, New Yorker, and bold 300-C, the last adding a convertible

DeSoto adds lower-cost Firesweep series and open Adventurer

Imperials get a bodyshell of their own and display curved side window glass

Plymouth returns to Number Three ranking for first time since '54, ahead of Buick and Oldsmobile by a wide margin

Chrysler products suffer rattles, leaks, premature rust

66At the moment, we are embarrassed—and seriously—by a shortage of automobiles.**99**

Chrysler Corporation president **L. L. "Tex" Colbert,** *on Chrysler's inability to meet dealer demand for the all-new 1957 models; December 1956*

1. A broadened Chrysler lineup brought back the Saratoga as middle member, between the Windsor and New Yorker. Each rode a 126-inch wheelbase, including this skirted New Yorker two-door hardtop, which started at $4202. A total of 8863 were built. **2.** Fins soared tall on New Yorkers and all Chrysler products, part of the "Forward Look" that helped the company grab styling leadership from GM. **3.** With 10,948 built, Chrysler's $4259 New Yorker four-door hardtop outsold the two-door version. Output slipped a bit, but Chrysler stayed in 10th place, behind the perennial luxury favorite—Cadillac.

1. Chrysler New Yorkers wore the new look particularly well. New Torsion-Aire suspension aimed to boost handling, not just ride quality. **2.** Windsor convertibles were dropped, but the New Yorker ragtop carried on with a 325-horsepower rendition of the 392-cid Hemi V-8. This example has Highway Hi-Fi. Just 1049 were built. **3.** At the supercar level, a 300-C convertible joined the hardtop coupe.

66 You can look for it in body panels, bumpers, more aluminum roofs, fender panels, decklids, and hoods. 99

Reynolds Metals Company spokesman, *on future automotive applications of aluminum; March 1957*

1957 Chrysler

1

2

1. Chrysler's 300-C had a distinct grille for the first time. Its Hemi grew to 392 cid and 375 or 390 bhp. **2.** A round badge identified the 300-C, colored to suggest its U.S. origin. **3.** A 300-C convertible cost $5359. Five colors were available, all monotones, with minimal trim. Manual shift now was available, but seldom ordered. **4.** Chrysler called the 300-C "America's greatest performing car," proven by speed runs at Daytona. A total of 2402 were built, 484 of them convertibles.

3

> **"** The board wishes to encourage owners and drivers to evaluate passenger cars in terms of useful power and ability to afford safe, reliable, and comfortable transportation, rather than in terms of capacity for speed. **"**
>
> *Official statement of the board of directors, **Automobile Manufacturers Assn.**, on its decision to impose a racing ban on member companies; June 1957*

4

1

2

3

4

1-2. DeSoto's Adventurer became a two-model series, as a convertible joined the hardtop. This one holds a Highway Hi-Fi record player and Benrus steering wheel watch. Breathing through twin four-barrel carburetors, the Hemi V-8 engine now measured 345 cid and yielded 345 horses—one per cubic inch. Only 300 convertibles were built, priced at $4272. **3-4.** An Adventurer hardtop went for $3997, with 1650 produced. Torsion-Aire suspension helped reduce tilt and sway in hard cornering, and also eased the ride.

303

1957 DeSoto

1

1. A new, cheaper DeSoto Firesweep series debuted, basically a Dodge Royal with DeSoto trim. Its 325-cid wedge V-8 made 245/260 bhp. This Firesweep hardtop cost $2836. 2-3. DeSoto's Firesweep station wagon could have six or nine seats, dubbed Shopper or Explorer, respectively. Firedomes and Fireflites had a 341-cid Hemi V-8, rated 270 or 290 horsepower. TorqueFlite was standard in Fireflites, a $220 option in others. 4. Every make and model exemplified Chrysler's "Forward Look." Shown are a Plymouth Belvedere sport sedan, Dodge Sierra wagon, DeSoto Firedome convertible, Chrysler Windsor hardtop sedan, and Imperial Southampton hardtop. Customers really did take kindly to the new design, as the ads insisted.

2

4

3

1

2

3

4

5

1-2. Close to five percent of Dodges had a D-500 engine, including this Coronet Lancer hardtop—the second most popular Dodge model. Wedge-shaped fins perched atop rear quarter panels. **3.** Interiors held a pushbutton TorqueFlite selector, dashboard-mounted mirror, pull-handle parking brake, and Scope-Sight speedometer above a full bank of gauges. **4.** Dodge's 325-cid D-500 V-8 yielded 285 horsepower with a single carburetor or 310 with dual carbs. A 245-horse Red Ram version was standard issue. A few Coronets were fitted with the D-501 option, a 340-horsepower, 354-cid Hemi left over from the prior year's Chrysler 300-B. **5.** Dodge issued two convertibles: a $2842 Coronet Lancer (shown) and $3146 Custom Royal Lancer. **6.** The Tek company gave away two Dodge wagons to folks who composed the best reason for taking pleasure in a De Luxe toothbrush.

6

1957 Dodge

Dual Motors Corp., based in Detroit, blended a Ghia-built body and a Dodge chassis to create the flashy $7600 Dual-Ghia convertible—a favorite with celebrities. Only 117 were produced (including prototypes), powered by 315-cid Dodge V-8s from '56. Bare chassis were shipped to Italy, where hand-formed steel bodies were mounted. Drivetrains and interiors were installed back in Detroit. Just two Dual-Ghia coupes were built, with fiberglass roofs.

1. The $2920 Dodge Custom Royal Lancer two-door hardtop enticed 17,629 buyers. This one has the D-500 engine. Hoods were 3.4 inches lower than in '56, roofs as much as 5.5 inches lower. Customers could get PowerFlite or new TorqueFlite automatic. **2.** Like passenger cars, some pickup trucks grew fancier in the Fifties. Dodge's sharp Sweptside pickup could have a six-cylinder or V-8 engine. **3.** Car fans across the country pored through catalogs from Chicago's J. C. Whitney company (also known as Warshawsky's), to pick out hot aftermarket goodies—for dress-up or soup-up. Dodge owners might order non-stock fender skirts, wheel covers, or assertive car "club" plates.

1

> **❝**It is the most popular styling option on any 1957 automobile.**❞**
>
> *Chrysler division sales vice-president* **Clare E. Briggs**, *on the popularity of Imperial's embossed-wheel decklid; August 1957*

2

3

4

5

1-2. Imperials adopted their own bodyshell, featuring curved side glass—a "first" for American cars. Ten models went on sale, including this $5406 Crown Southampton four-door hardtop. 3. An optional simulated spare-tire cover on the decklid proved popular among Imperial buyers. Enlarged fins held the integrated "gunsight" taillights. 4. Two large round dials faced the driver, who wielded a padded steering-wheel rim and viewed the road through a wrap-over windshield. 5. Though posher than most, an Imperial's back seat was typical of the Fifties. 6. Long before his election to the vice presidency in 1960, Texas senator Lyndon Baines Johnson was photographed with this Imperial. A huge output boost, to 37,593 cars, brought Imperial into 15th place in the industry.

6

1957 Imperial

1. An expanded lineup included the Imperial, Imperial Crown, and Imperial LeBaron. Hardtop sedans came in each series, and a gorgeous Crown convertible debuted. 2. Imperial wheelbases shrank to 129 inches. The V-8 engine now measured 392 cid and 325 horsepower—again shared with New Yorkers. Torsion-Aire front suspension gave Imperials a strong selling point. 3. Texaco had quite a list of maintenance steps for dealer service shops—22 shown here, from checking ignition points to adjusting belts. Then as now, service work helped the dealer's bottom line, so it was essential to convince customers that each mechanic was a "trained specialist" and "the best friend your car has ever had." 4. Movie/TV cowboy Roy Rogers waves from behind the wheel of a four-door Imperial.

1

2

3

1. Again painted off-white and gold, Plymouth's $2925 Fury hardtop got a brand-new engine—biggest in the low-priced field. Production rose to 7438 cars. More than three inches lower and four inches wider, with the industry's lowest beltline and towering "shark" fins out back, Plymouths ranked among the best looking '57 cars. They appeared to be longer than ever, but actually measured slightly shorter overall. **2.** Plymouth wheelbases, including Fury's, grew to 118 inches (122 inches for wagons). **3.** Even the air-cleaner housings were gold-colored on the new V-800 dual-quad 318-cid Fury engine, which developed 290 horsepower and 325 pound-feet of torque, running on 9.25:1 compression. The engine was optional in any Plymouth model. Dealer-installed safety belts were available, but not widely advertised.

1957 Plymouth

1

2

3

4

1-2. A Plymouth Belvedere sport sedan (four-door hardtop) sold for $2419.
3. Plymouth wasn't so far off the mark in claiming that its '57 models were three years ahead of their time. A new Fury 301-cid V-8 yielded 215 horsepower (235 with PowerPak), promising "tremendous power for safety." 4. Close to 10,000 Belvedere convertibles were built, at $2638. 5. Gauges sat in a large upright pod on the low-profile dashboard, which held the mirror. Five buttons operated the TorqueFlite transmission. 6. A mid-level Savoy two-door went for just $2147.

6   5

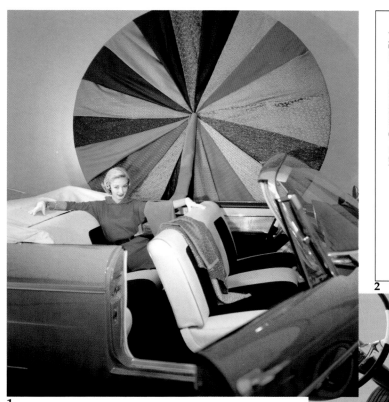

1

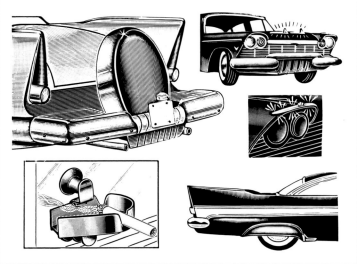

2

1. Dealers still had to push hard to move cars, despite all the flamboyant styling touches. At Plymouth and every other manufacturer, interior fabric choices were assuming crucial importance. **2.** Plymouth owners had a long list of aftermarket accessories to choose from in the J. C. Whitney catalog, including a Continental kit, double hood ornament, headlight trim, fender skirts, and handy suction-cup ashtray. **3.** Plymouth's new 318-cid V-800 engine was destined to see long life. Torsion-Aire Ride dispensed with customary coil springs in favor of long front torsion bars. In Plaza models, the Hy-Fire 277-cid V-8 delivered 197 horsepower, while the L-head six got a hike to 132 bhp. **4.** Could Plymouth have issued a Belvedere four-door convertible? This designer's rendering looks workable and tempting, at least in theory.

3

4

Ford Motor Company

Fords show sculptured-look restyle—Fairlane trim is inspired by Mystere show car

Four Ford series go on sale: Custom, Custom 300, Fairlane, and posh Fairlane 500

Ford Skyliner coupe has retractable steel hardtop

Fords come on 116- or 118-inch wheelbase, with choice of five V-8s or six-cylinder engine

Ford launches Ranchero car-pickup—first such body style since World War II

Supercharged 312-cid Thunderbird V-8 thunders out as much as 340 horsepower

Ford outsells Chevrolet for model year, with record 1.67 million cars built

Lincoln fields Premiere and cheaper Capri series, including new Landau four-door hardtop

Lincoln's V-8 now develops 300 horsepower and 415 pound-feet of torque

Output drops to 41,123, but Lincoln clings to 14th place

Mercury gets its own body structure, with distinctive concave rear panels . . . wheelbases stretch to 122 inches, bodies are lower by four inches

Gadget-laden Mercury Turnpike Cruiser features retractable, reverse-slanted back window and 49-position driver's seat

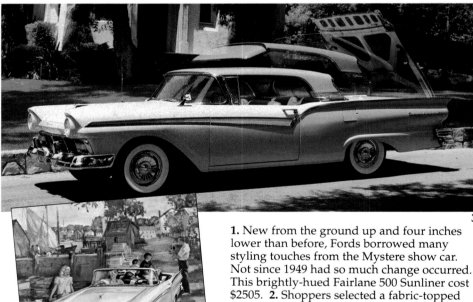

1. New from the ground up and four inches lower than before, Fords borrowed many styling touches from the Mystere show car. Not since 1949 had so much change occurred. This brightly-hued Fairlane 500 Sunliner cost $2505. 2. Shoppers selected a fabric-topped convertible over the new Skyliner coupe by nearly a 4-to-1 margin. 3. First production car with a retractable steel top was Ford's Fairlane 500 Skyliner. In this complex system, the roof's forward section tucked under so it would fit into the trunk area. Despite a hefty price (starting at $2942), 20,766 Skyliners were built this year. 4. Tie-in ads promoted both Fords and vacation destinations. Ford's V-8 engine marked its 25th anniversary in 1957.

1

1. Slowest-selling Fairlane was the Victoria hardtop sedan. 2. In the plush Fairlane 500 series, four-door hardtops were outsold by two-door mates. 3. Because of new thin-pillar styling, the Fairlane 500 club sedan looked almost like a hardtop. 4. A new Custom 300 sedan series replaced the Customline. 5. Lowest-cost Fords were in the Custom series. This practical Tudor sedan cost $1991. 6. Automakers tested cars in extreme temperatures, as evidenced by this frozen Ford wagon. 7. J. C. Whitney catalogs tempted Ford owners with an outside spare tire, wheel covers, and a conversion kit for the new quad headlights.

> ❝It's a husky youngster, and like most other new parents, we are proud enough to pop our buttons.❞
>
> *Ford Motor Co. chairman*
> **Ernest R. Breech,** *on the new Edsel; August 1957*

2

3

7

6

4

5

313

1

2

4

3

5

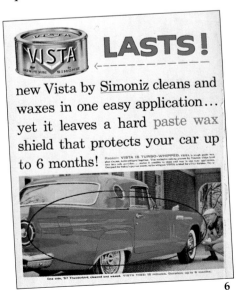
1. New Thunderbird styling included a combination bumper/grille. **2.** Three-speed T-Birds carried a 292-cid V-8, but others held the 312-cid engine (shown), rated 245 to 285 horsepower. **3.** Canted tailfins highlighted this year's Thunderbirds. A portholed hardtop remained optional. So did the outside tire, as the standard spare moved into the trunk, within longer rear fenders. **4.** Breathing via a Paxton-McCulloch supercharger, the 312-cid V-8 produced 300 or 340 horsepower. The blower cost $500 and delivered a 6-psi boost. Only 208 blown T-Birds were produced (13 for NASCAR competition), capable of 0–60 acceleration in under seven seconds. Regular passenger cars could get the supercharged V-8, but few were so equipped. **5.** With 21,380 produced, this year's T-Bird was the most popular of the 1955-57 two-seater generation. **6.** No point owning a sharp T-Bird unless you kept it sparkling.

1

3

4

2

5

6

7

8

1. Ford's woody-look Country Squire was the top-priced station wagon. A roof rack cost extra. 2. Ads continued to push for ownership of twin Fords—and claimed that more than 300,000 families already fit that category. Today's Mom might dispute the claim that she "looks and feels as young as the fresh new lines of her new kind of Ford." 3. Country Sedan wagons contained Fairlane 500 appointments. 4. Six-passenger Country Sedans sold far better than eight-seaters. 5. For $2301, Ranch Wagons were trimmed like the Custom sedan, but $96 more bought a fancier Del Rio. 6. A Ranchero car-pickup, shown with fancy trim, was essentially a Ranch Wagon with integral cargo bed. 7. Mid-level Rancheros lacked a colored trim strip. 8. Plain-bodied Rancheros could haul nearly three-quarters of a ton.

1

2

3

4

5

6

7

8

> **❝**It is the fair, fair lady of our family. **❞**
>
> **Ford Motor Company** *public relations description of the 1957 Lincoln; October 1956*

1-2. Priced at $5149, Lincoln's Premiere two-door hardtop accounted for one-third of total production. Quadra-Lite front ends held regular headlights and smaller road lamps with a separate switch. **3.** A padded dash was standard in sumptuous—even colorful—interiors. **4.** Courtesy lights and distinctive hardware marked rear compartments. Air conditioners still sat in trunks. **5.** A new Premiere Landau four-door hardtop looked similar to the sedan and cost the same ($5294). **6.** Only the Premiere line included a convertible, yet ragtop output rose by half. **7.** Voluptuous actress Jayne Mansfield is shown perched on the deck of an open Premiere. **8.** Lincoln was hardly alone in pushing its cars' massive length and low profile.

1

2

3

1. Only 444 Mark II Continental hardtops were built before production halted in May. Bodies showed little change, but the fuel filler sat in the left taillight. **2.** Interiors held a dished steering wheel and padded dashboard. Three out of four Continentals had air conditioning. **3.** The 368-cid V-8 rose from 285 to 300 horsepower, via 10:1 compression. **4.** Ford never issued a Mark II convertible, but Derham Coachworks built one prototype, and another was fabricated from a coupe. **5.** Head designer George W. Walker (*left*) and Lincoln-Mercury styling chief John Najjar study a Premiere front end. **6.** Canted fins were chosen early in the design process for '57 Lincolns.

4

5

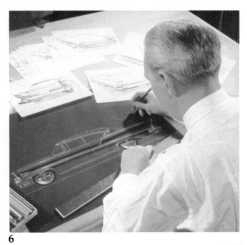

6

1957 Mercury

1. Daringly rebodied, Mercury rode a frame much like Ford's. This open Montclair cost $3430. Base engine was a 255-bhp, 312-cid V-8, with the Turnpike Cruiser's 368-cid V-8 optional. **2.** With such extras as skirts, spotlights, and factory air, this Montclair cost somewhat more than the $3236 base price. **3.** A lower floorpan gave Mercs more room inside. **4.** Adding a Continental kit made a Montclair look even more massive.

1

2

3

4

5

6

1. An open Turnpike Cruiser paced the Indianapolis 500 race. In addition to four original pace cars, Mercury issued a batch of replicas. **2.** Dramatic Turnpike Cruisers arrived late in the season, in convertible, hardtop sedan, and hardtop coupe body styles. **3.** "Cruiser" skirts help give this loaded Turnpike Cruiser a sassy stance. The 368-cid V-8 cranked out 290 horsepower. **4.** Gadget-packed Cruisers had keyboard-controlled Merc-O-Matic, a Monitor Control Panel with tachometer, Average-Speed Computer Clock, and Seat-O-Matic. A retracting rear window delivered Breezeway ventilation. **5.** One of six wagons, a six-seat Commuter cost $2973. **6.** Monterey served as bargain-level Merc.

1957 Buick

General Motors Corporation

Oldsmobile marks its 60th anniversary; all 88s add "Golden Rocket" nomenclature

Buicks earn ambitious restyle and bigger V-8 engine

Reworked Cadillac is inspired by Eldorado Brougham and Park Avenue show cars

Fuel-injected V-8 engines optional in Chevrolet, Pontiac

Restyled Chevrolet lags Ford in production, but will become far more prized as time goes by

Chevrolet's V-8 grows to 283 cid, developing up to one horsepower per cubic inch (with fuel injection)

Fuel-injected Corvette can do 0–60 mph in just 5.7 seconds

Heavy-duty racing suspension available for Corvettes

Three-speed triple-turbine Turboglide, with hill retarder, is available in Chevrolets

Station wagons return to Oldsmobile lineup

Triple-carburetor J-2 option gives Oldsmobiles 300 horsepower

Fast, flashy Pontiac Bonneville comes with fuel-injected V-8

Tri-Power (three-carburetor) engines available in Pontiacs, mainly for stock-car racing

Pillared sedans depart from Cadillac line

1

2

3

1. Though all-new in structure, Buick's restyling was evolutionary. Roadmasters now came in two series: 70 and an upmarket 75 (shown), with custom interiors and scads of extras. This hardtop sedan cost $4483. 2. Only 2065 folks got their hands on a $3981 Super convertible. All Buicks got a bored/stroked 364-cid V-8, yielding 300 horsepower in all models except the Special. 3. Top executives met at the GM styling studios in the Technical Center: (*from left*) chairman Albert Bradley, former president C. E. Wilson, president Harlow H. Curtice, and design chief Harley J. Earl. GM promoted the close tie between company officers and the styling staff.

> 66 We are testing these cars under the toughest conditions in the world insofar as brakes are concerned. 99
>
> *Buick chief engineer* **Verner P. Mathews**, *on Buick's 196-mile brake-test course on streets in and around Los Angeles; April 1957*

1. This gracious home welcomes a pair of Buicks, led by a Super Riviera four-door hardtop. 2. Most popular Century was the hardtop sedan. Despite added weight, this year's Century was the fastest yet. 3. Two-door Century hardtops sold slower than their four-door cousins. 4. New this year was the Century Caballero station wagon, a four-door hardtop style. 5. Ads continued to suggest an experience akin to aircraft, referring to Buick's "flight deck of a hood." 6. This Super convertible shows off its two-tone interior, padded dash, and diamond-tooled instrument panel.

1

2

3

4

5

1-2. Super-luxury shoppers had a new choice: Cadillac's Eldorado Brougham hardtop sedan. Only 400 were virtually hand-built, with air suspension, a stainless-steel roof—and a whopping $13,074 price tag. Note the rear-hinged back doors. 3. Eldorados earned a full restyling with inboard, sharply pointed fins. Cadillac issued 1800 Biarritz convertibles. 4. An Eldorado Seville hardtop cost exactly the same ($7286) as an open Biarritz. 5. Dual carburetion boosted the Eldo's V-8 to 325 horsepower, versus 300 for ordinary Cadillacs.

5

1

2

3

4

1. All Cadillac Series 62 sedans were now pillarless. A base hardtop (shown) cost $4781, versus $5256 for the plusher Sedan de Ville. A new tubular-center X-member chassis enhanced rigidity. 2. Coupe de Villes sold almost as well as the less-costly Series 62 hardtop. Cadillacs sat two inches lower, with forward-slanting A-pillars and reworked fins. 3. Now hardtop-styled, the plush Fleetwood Sixty Special sedan continued to sell well, with 24,000 produced. 4. Series 75 limos cost $7678, but an eight-passenger sedan went for $238 less. Note how doors are cut into the roof. 5. Marilyn Monroe waves from a Cadillac convertible to open a soccer game at Ebbets Field in Brooklyn, New York.

5

1957 Chevrolet

1. If any car defines the Fifties, it has to be the amply facelifted '57 Chevy. Chevrolet issued 166,426 Bel Air sport coupes, typically loaded with extra-cost goodies. 2. The sport sedan never held quite the allure of its two-door sibling, especially as a Two-Ten. Seven engine choices ranged from the 140-horsepower six all the way to a fuel-injected 283-cid V-8, cranking out as much as 283 horsepower. 3. Turquoise was an enticing color choice for a Bel Air convertible. A total of 47,562 were built, starting at $2511. 4. Detroit industrialist Ruben Allender produced a handful of El Moroccos in 1956-57, with Cadillac-like styling touches built around a Chevrolet body and chassis. Taking the Eldorado Brougham as a guide, R. Allender & Co. issued hardtops as well as convertibles, priced less than $500 above a stock Bel Air. Under the hood sat the 220-bhp version of Chevrolet's 283-cid V-8, and a Powerglide transmission. 5. DuPont wax doubtlessly helped bring out the lustrous sheen of some of those turquoise ragtops.

5

4

1. Another 6103 Nomad wagons went on sale before Chevy killed this exciting body style. 2. For every Nomad, more than four times as many Bel Air Townsman four-door wagons were built. 3. Best-selling Bel Air was a practical pillared four-door sedan. 4. Millions of drivers had never rented a car, but Hertz had Chevrolets waiting. 5. Any Chevrolet might be fuel-injected, but the $484 tariff helped limit sales. 6. With Ramjet injection and 10.5:1 compression, the top V-8 made 283 bhp. 7. Who'd have guessed that this bland One-Fifty utility sedan held a fuelie? 8. Corvette output almost doubled, to 6339 cars. 9. Corvettes could have a 250- or 283-bhp fuel-injected engine. A four-speed gearbox arrived in April. 10. Styling chief Bill Mitchell poses with the racing SR-2. 11. Chevrolet built the SS (Super Sport) to race at Sebring, but it lasted only four hours.

1957 Oldsmobile

1

1. Oldsmobiles gained an all-new body, and a far different look. Upper-level Ninety-Eight models added a Starfire prefix. This Starfire Ninety-Eight Holiday coupe cost $457 more than its predecessor. 2. Like so many makes, Oldsmobiles got a larger engine; in this case, a 371-cid Rocket V-8 with a 277-horsepower rating. 3. Olds drivers faced a large oval gauge panel. 4. Startling colors helped give the latest Starfire Ninety-Eight models a fresh personality. 5. Starfire Ninety-Eight convertibles began at $4217, but ragtops also came in the Golden Rocket 88 and Super 88 series. 6-7. For a mere $83, any Olds could have a Rocket J-2 engine. Breathing through triple carburetors, with 10:1 compression, the hopped-up V-8 yielded 300 horsepower. In normal driving, only the center carb operated.

2

3

7

6

4

5

1

2

3

1. For the first time since 1950, the lowest-priced Oldsmobile line included a convertible. An 88 cost $3182, versus $3447 for its Super 88 mate. **2.** A Super 88 hardtop, with skirts and outside spare, could still turn heads down at the drive-in. Sedans and hardtops adopted a three-section rear window. **3.** Ads continued to target younger drivers. Popular singer Perry Como announced a jingle contest for Noxzema, with 10 Super 88 Holiday sedans as prizes. **4.** Not only did Oldsmobile issue 88 and Super 88 station wagons, but the new four-door Fiestas were hardtop-styled. **5.** Only 18,477 base 88 two-door sedans went to customers, but that was six times the amount of similar Super 88s. **6.** An assertive grille opening highlighted Oldsmobile's F-88 show car.

5

6

1957 Pontiac

1-2. Pontiac went all-out with its new Bonneville convertible. Rochester fuel injection pumped the 370-cid V-8 to 310 horsepower, triggering Pontiac's performance image. No cheapie at $5782, it was the most potent Pontiac to date. Only 630 were built. **3.** Ads pushed Bonneville's "hand-crafted luxury" and "dream car" lineage. **4.** Star Chiefs again topped the regular line. **5.** Best-selling Star Chief was the Custom Catalina hardtop sedan. **6.** All wagons got a Safari name, but the dazzling two-door faced extinction.

Pontiac 1957

1. Tri-Power engines were optional in any Pontiac, including this Chieftain sedan, rated 290 horsepower for street use. 2. If NASCAR-certified, the triple-carb V-8 delivered 317 horses. Cars so equipped got a heavy-duty suspension. As promoted in this ad, a strict-production Chieftain broke a track record in Grand National competition. Note the appearance of Pontiac general manager S. E. Knudsen, and styling director Harley J. Earl. 3. Two-door sedans, like this Chieftain, were prime candidates for the hottest V-8 engines. 4. Six- and nine-passenger Chieftain Safari station wagons went on sale. 5. Pontiac called its four-door Safari "a custom creation inside and out," with "man-sized comfort" and "barrel-chested Strato-Streak V-8." 6. Station wagons could be converted for ambulance and other commercial duty.

Studebaker-Packard Corporation

Packards now are built in South Bend, Indiana, alongside similar Studebakers

Designer Richard Teague turns ordinary Studebaker into patrician "Packardbaker," in hurry-up project

Supercharged V-8 engine goes into Packards—and Studebaker Golden Hawk . . . Packard's own engines are history

Clipper station wagon debuts—first Packard wagon since 1950

Packard lineup cut to just two offerings . . . sales plunge to only 4809

Studebaker Hawks adopt sweeping concave tailfins

Golden Hawk engine, force-fed by Paxton supercharger, makes 275 horsepower

Studebaker sedans/wagons get garish facelift

May brings budget-priced, no-frills Studebaker Scotsman—9300 built in just three months

Curtiss-Wright management agreement ends in October; Studebaker-Packard has had $85 million loss over three years

Studebaker-Packard loses $11 million this year, despite revived military production

Studebaker-Packard becomes North American distributor for Mercedes-Benz automobiles

1-2. Although the revered Packard name lingered on, it now identified a Studebaker clone. Only two models made the lineup: a Clipper four-door sedan (shown) selling for $3212, and a Country Sedan wagon. 3. Clippers, like their Studebaker first cousins, wore flamboyant fins. Taillights came from the '56 Clipper, grafted onto Studebaker fenders. Twin rear antennas were a styling touch from the departed Caribbean. Only 3940 sedans were produced. 4. Announcement of the Clipper was delayed until January. Planned as a stopgap, the move was supposed to "buy time" until a true Packard could be produced again—which never happened.

1

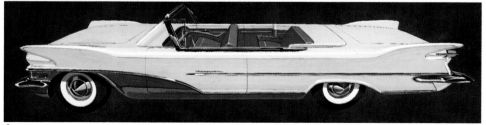

2

1. A mere 869 Clipper wagons were built, on a shorter wheelbase than the sedan.
2. A luggage rack cost $60 on a Country Sedan. Both body styles employed a Studebaker President chassis with a "proud Packard grille" and Caribbean-style trim.
3. Studebaker's new 275-horsepower, supercharged V-8 powered all Packards. Flight-O-Matic was standard and Twin Traction optional. 4. Packards moved quickly from drawing board to production, but stylists had ideas for a new Caribbean. 5. A "real" senior coupe might have looked like this.
6. A Clipper *not* based on the Studebaker would have had its own identity—perhaps even a convertible.

3

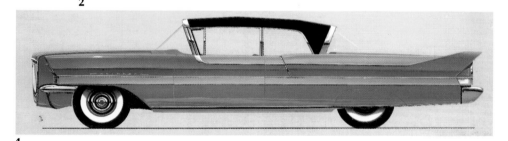

4

5

6

> 66 We are going to have a car. It may not be quite the car we hoped for, but it will be a lot better than what we feared. We'll go along. 99
>
> **Unidentified Packard dealer**, *on Studebaker-Packard's decision to bring out a Packard line for 1957; September 1956*

331

1957 Studebaker

1-2. Tailfins soared outward on the $3182 Golden Hawk. A fiberglass hood overlay hid a hole to clear the new supercharger. Just 4356 were built. 3. With the new engine, a Hawk's front end was 100 pounds lighter. The blower gave five-psi boost, "for extra power the instant you need it." 4. Studebaker planned to devote 25 percent of output to coupes. A Golden Hawk 400, added in spring, cost nearly $500 extra but held hand-buffed leather. 5. Golden Hawks had tooled instrument panels. 6. Only two Hawk models were built, including the pillared Silver Hawk (either six-cylinder or V-8).

1

2

> ❝When you walked into that room full of cars, you walked into a new era of Studebaker-Packard progress—an era of profit for you and for us.❞
>
> *Studebaker-Packard president* **Harold E. Churchill**, *at S-P's annual stockholders' meeting; May 1957*

3

1. Studebaker sedans and wagons again came in three levels, topped by the President. **2.** The $2666 Broadmoor station wagon was part of the President series. Its 289-cid V-8 yielded 210 or 225 horsepower. **3.** Commander club sedans came in Custom or DeLuxe trim, with a 259-cid V-8. **4.** This Parkview wagon served on police duty in South Bend, Indiana—Studebaker's home. **5.** Studebaker had a full range, from low-budget Scotsman and Champion to hot Golden Hawk—one car that really was "unmistakably ahead of the rest." Scotsman models started at $1776, with miserly gearing and manual-shift only.

4

5

1958

Recession arrived with a vengeance to the shock and dismay of Americans who'd grown accustomed to prosperity. Inflation dipped below two percent, but unemployment approached and passed the seven-percent barrier. By June, 5,437,000 Americans were out of work—the highest figure since 1941.

Not that *everyone* was suffering. Those fortunate enough to have a full-time job might expect average earnings of $3851 per year. College teachers averaged $6015, and factory workers approached the $5000 mark. Dentists averaged more than $14,000, and the median family income reached $5087. Car prices rose 3.3 percent as the model year began, but the average amount paid for a new car actually dropped—to $2990, from $3230 a year earlier.

In the wake of Congressional hearings, the Automobile Information Disclosure Act was passed. From now on, window stickers would have to display every new vehicle's serial number and suggested retail price. Ever since, these documents have been known informally as "Monroney" stickers, after the U.S. senator largely responsible for the new law.

Nearly all cars were bigger and heavier (though use of aluminum grew 13 percent). Chrysler adopted compound-curve windshields that reached into the roofline. That worked fine, but their new fuel-injected engines did not. Practically all makes adopted quad-headlamp setups, and horsepower ratings rose an average of seven percent (20 bhp).

The biggest news of the year was the arrival of the Edsel, Ford's great hope for the mid-price field. The excitement, however, would be short-lived; in this recession era, yet another rather costly car—especially one whose styling drew as many guffaws as plaudits—just couldn't attract enough customers to survive.

Over at General Motors, this year's Buicks and Oldsmobiles were branded the most gaudy and garish vehicles of the year—if not the decade or the century. Chevrolets, on the other hand, exhibited a graceful restyling, led by the posh Impala—with an available hot new Turbo Thrust engine.

Packard departed after a last-ditch attempt to stay afloat by gussying up their Studebaker-based bodies even further. Henceforth, Studebaker would focus mainly on its compact Lark, ready for market ahead of shrunken rivals from the Big Three.

Imports took 8.1 percent of new-car sales—up more than tenfold since 1951—as the first Datsuns and Toyopets (Toyotas) arrived on the West Coast. George Romney turned AMC's full attention to compacts, including a revived reduced-size American. Still, many industry leaders echoed the thoughts of an anonymous GM executive: "If the public wants to lower its standard of living by driving a cheap crowded car, we'll make it."

In this worst economic setback of the postwar era, car sales dropped 31.4 percent for the model year. The influence of teenagers as car buyers was being noticed at last. A credit executive explained that at high schools, "far more students are car owners than most persons realize."

Alaska became the forty-ninth state. America's first satellite was launched from Cape Canaveral, and the Soviets countered with *Sputnik III*.

Economist John Kenneth Galbraith, in *The Affluent Society*, criticized the conformity and materialism of Americans. He also warned of decaying cities, driven through by gadget-laden autos. John Keats published *The Insolent Chariots*, a devastating but comic critique of the auto trade and car culture, featuring Tom Wretch doing battle with dealers.

Jack Kerouac's *On the Road*, first published a year earlier as a "beat generation" chronicle, began to attract more readers. Best-selling books ranged from *Anatomy of a Murder* and *Doctor Zhivago* to Art Linkletter's *Kids Say the Darndest Things!*

Elvis Presley was drafted into the U.S. Army. Folk music, after trailing far behind rock 'n' roll and jazz in popularity, began a resurgence, led by the Kingston Trio's recording of "Tom Dooley."

The Donna Reed Show appeared on TV, along with Chuck Connors in *The Rifleman*. So did *77 Sunset Strip* (co-starring Edd "Kookie" Byrnes, adored by female viewers more for his pompadour hairstyle than his acting skills). In a major scandal, quiz-show contestants pleaded guilty to having received answers ahead of time.

Moviegoers could see everything from Alfred Hitchcock's *Vertigo* to *Auntie Mame* and *Cat on a Hot Tin Roof*. Kim Stanley turned in a devastating performance as a movie queen in *The Goddess*, while Robert Mitchum drove hard through mountain roads as a whiskey runner in *Thunder Road*. Weekly movie admissions dipped below 40 million, the lowest figure since 1922—evidence of TV's impact.

Connie Francis sang "Who's Sorry Now," Peggy Lee belted out "Fever," and records could be played in stereo. Van Cliburn became the first American to win the top classical-music competition in Moscow.

Even though compacts were in the works at each Big Three auto company, the threat from such *sub*compacts as the Volkswagen Beetle and Renault Dauphine was deemed insignificant. The era of big barges had a few more years to go, and Detroit had another season of excess on the drawing board.

American Motors Corporation

All models now grouped under Rambler nameplate (except Metropolitans)

Short-wheelbase Ramblers return, called American

Nearly 31,000 Americans are built in short model year

Regular Ramblers earn heavy facelift and sprout modest blade fins

All V-8s take Rebel nameplate; their 250-cid engine yields 215 horsepower

New Ambassador series debuts—it's actually an extended version of Rambler

Ambassador's V-8 engine is borrowed from departed full-size Nash/Hudson

Bigger model is called "Ambassador by Rambler," striving for separate identity

AMC touts '58s as the "world's finest travel cars"

New "deep-dip" rustproofing process sends unibodies into 15,000-gallon primer tank

Rambler reaches seventh spot in model-year production race—up from 12th in 1957

Metropolitan sales slip slightly to 13,128 units

AMC's new-car registrations more than double this year

Corporation earns $25.5 million profit

Ads claim that "no car is as strong—as safe—as quiet"

1

2

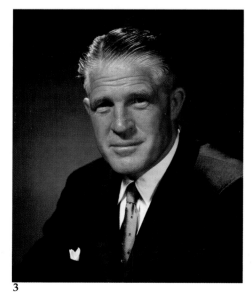

1. At mid-season, AMC revived its 100-inch-wheelbase model, now called American. Prices started at $1775 for a business sedan, but this Super went for $1874. A 90-horsepower six-cylinder engine promised up to 30 mpg. **2.** Americans came only in two-door form, topped by this Super. Few options were offered beyond overdrive, Flash-O-Matic, radio, and heater. **3.** AMC president George Romney earned credit for the daring revival of the small Rambler, unseen for three years. Except for a new grille and enlarged rear wheel openings, it looked similar to the '55 model. Romney had neither time nor money to come up with an all-new design, but Americans arrived at an opportune moment: during a recession, as imports were capturing serious sales.

3

1

3

4

5

6

7

> 66 Auto buyers are getting choosy, backing away from dreamboats to look for something more practical. 99

Consumers Union head of automobile testing **Laurence E. Crooks**, *on the changing tastes of new-car buyers; April 1958*

1. American interiors were simple, but not stark. **2.** The American got its own brochure, where it claimed to "put real fun back into motoring." **3.** AMC stretched the Rambler nine inches ahead of the cowl to create a new Ambassador. **4.** Called a "living room" on wheels, an Ambassador Custom could get 20 trim combinations. **5.** AMC's four-door models included the Rambler Six, Rebel V-8, and new Ambassador V-8. **6.** Only 1340 Ambassador Custom Country Club hardtop sedans were sold. **7.** Metropolitans continued with few changes, but prices rose by $59 to $1626 for the coupe, $1650 for the convertible.

1958 Rambler

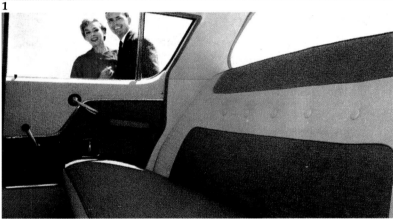

1. Rarest and most expensive Rambler Ambassador was the Custom Cross Country four-door hardtop station wagon. Only 294 were built, with a $3116 sticker price. **2.** No bigger inside than a standard Rambler, Ambassadors sported fancier trim. Both seats were described as "extremely wide and comfortable." All Ambassadors were four-doors. **3.** Tire makers had to rely on replacement sales. A *Look* magazine survey found that 61 percent of motorists bought a different tire brand after the originals wore out. **4.** Ambassadors used the same 327-cid V-8 as final Nash/Hudson models, making 270 horsepower. This Super sedan ran $2587.

338

1. Ambassadors rode a 117-inch wheelbase, versus 108 inches for regular Ramblers. Stretching the body helped enhance the car's proportions. 2. Pillarless styling of the Ambassador wagon was most striking when the doors stood open. Both the front and rear doors held vent panes. 3. The tailgate flipped open to reveal a carpeted, padded cargo compartment. 4. Ambassadors got a two-tone steering wheel. Note the pushbutton control panel at left for the Flight-O-Matic transmission. 5. Despite the company's "economy" image, Rambler pushed the Ambassador as a luxury model.

1958 Rambler

1

1-2. All Rebels, including this four-door hardtop, were V-8 powered. AMC's 250-cid engine made 215 horsepower. Ramblers wore a low grille and quad headlights in the normal position. The side trim on upscale models was reminiscent of final Hudsons. 3. This cutaway demonstrates how six people fit inside a Rambler. Single Unit Construction, ads stated, was "pioneered by American Motors—and now copied by others in the very highest price car lines." AMC claimed that it "offers the greatest strength, durability and safety ever known," because huge box girders completely surrounded the occupants. During manufacturing, 9000 electric welds replaced the old-fashioned body bolts to eliminate squeaks and rattles.

2

3

1

1. Station wagons were always crucial to the Rambler lineup. This pointy-finned Rebel four-door wagon came in Super or Custom trim.
2. AMC promoted the fact that its Economy six-cylinder engine held official NASCAR border-to-border and coast-to-coast economy records—33.93 and 32.09 mpg, respectively. The six made 127 horsepower, but optional dual-throat carburetion hiked output to 138 horses. Ads insisted a Rebel would mix "Rambler handling and parking ease with smooth, economical V-8 performance," branded "velvety" at cruising speeds. 3-4. Ads promised that Ramblers delivered an appetizing blend of big-car comfort and roominess, plus imported-car economy. The compacts could also "turn on a dime," unlike typical American sedans and wagons, and appealed to the "little woman."

2

3

4

> **❝**I'd just as soon see the public educated as to the actual cost price of a new car so that we could get the confusion out of the selling price. The way it is now, most buyers have a fantastic idea of how much money a dealer can make from selling a car. **❞**
>
> **Unidentified Missouri new-car dealer;** *September 1958*

1958 Chrysler

Chrysler Corporation

Chrysler products begin to abandon Hemi V-8s, turning to simpler—and cheaper—wedge-head configuration

Double compound, triple-curve Control-Tower windshields extend into roofline

Chrysler 300-D engine delivers 380 or 390 horsepower; hardtop and convertible offered

Bendix fuel injection offered—briefly—on 300-D engine, but complex unit proves troublesome

Privately-owned 300-D sets new Class E speed record at Bonneville, running 156.387 mph

Automatic speed control offered on Chrysler and Imperial

Chrysler Division dips to 11th place in the industry as output drops by nearly half

DeSoto output shrinks below 50,000—lowest since 1938

Nearly all fuel-injected engines are later fitted with carburetors

Imperial output drops to 16,113 cars—down by more than half

Any Plymouth may have the new Golden Commando 350-cid engine

Plymouth ends year in third place again, ahead of Oldsmobile and Buick

Experimental Plymouth Cabana hardtop features sliding sunroof

1. Little-changed overall, Chrysler New Yorkers wore new bodyside trim. This sedan cost $4295. The 392-cid V-8 produced 345 horsepower. Chryslers exemplified "the bold new look of success," according to the brochure. **2.** Saratogas carried a 310-horsepower, 354-cid engine. The sedan cost $3818. **3.** A 290-bhp version of the 354-cid V-8 went into Windsors, including this $3214 hardtop, which dropped to the 122-inch Dodge wheelbase. **4.** The most popular Chrysler was the $3129 Windsor four-door sedan, with 12,861 produced. **5.** As part of its push in the spring selling season, Chrysler issued Windsors with Dartline styling, "bright and cheerful as spring itself." Three gold crowns embellished a brushed aluminum insert.

> " The really modern automobile should convey an eager, poised-for-action look. "
>
> *Chrysler Corp. styling vice-president* **Virgil Exner**, *on the corporation's "Forward Look" design philosophy; December 1958*

1-2. Tall fins dominated the profile of the Chrysler New Yorker hardtop, which cost $4347. **3.** Oddly shrunken taillights no longer filled the big tailfin cavities. **4.** All entrants in this Gleem toothpaste contest had to do to win a new Chrysler was to estimate the total retail price of all items pictured. **5.** The 392-cid V-8 in a Chrysler 300-D put out 380 or 390 bhp. A hardtop sold for $5173, the convertible for $5603. Only 809 were built. **6.** Drivers faced large round gauges with a clock between. Round control knobs ran along the bottom, and TorqueFlite buttons were at the left. **7.** Chrysler promoted the glamorous aspects of its "mighty" models.

THE MIGHTY CHRYSLER FOR 1958

1958 DeSoto

1. DeSoto's lineup included the Fireflite (*foreground*), Firedome (*upper left*), and budget-priced Firesweep (*upper right*).
2. Stacked taillights made DeSotos easy to spot. Only 3243 Fireflite Sportsman four-door hardtops were built, starting at $3731. The 361-cid V-8 developed 305 horsepower. Note the curiously pinched exhaust outlets.
3. A Fireflite ragtop went for $3972, but only 474 folks got one. 4. Just $3219 bought a Firesweep convertible, new this season.
5. Can these Goodyears both be 14-inch tires? The new 11.00x14 luxury tire and 7.50x14 size represented the extremes on 1958 cars. The 11.00x14 tire ran at only 14–17 pounds of air pressure.

1

2

3

5

4

1. A DeSoto Adventurer two-door hardtop started at $4071, but the convertible commanded $298 more. This hardtop has rare spinner hubcaps and gold-fleck carpeting. All DeSotos got a more complex grille.
2. Under an Adventurer hood, DeSoto's 361-cid V-8 yielded 345 or 355 horsepower—the latter via complex (and finicky) Bendix fuel injection, which cost $637 extra. Most of the few fuel-injected models sold were later converted to dual carburetors, signaling the end of that experiment.
3. Only 350 Adventurer hardtops and a mere 82 ragtops were produced.
4. DeSotos had long been popular for use as commercial vehicles, so specialty manufacturers converted an ordinary sedan into an eight-door stretch limo. Note the extra-long roof luggage rack.

2

1

3

4

1958 Dodge

1. Dodge's mild facelift included a fresh grille and simplified side trim. At midyear came a new top-of-the-line model, the specially trimmed $3245 Regal Lancer two-door hardtop. 2. The Regal Lancer's plush, color-keyed interior sported a selection of notable touches, including ribbed door trim panels with molded-in armrests, bronze instrument cluster, and glovebox trim bevels. 3-4. Regal Lancers came only in metallic bronze with contrasting black roof, fins, and color sweep; or in a blend of bronze and white. Just 1163 were produced. The 350-cid engine made 285 horsepower. 5. A Custom Royal Lancer convertible cost $3298.

1

2

3

4

5

1. Dodge's open Custom Royal Lancer sold slowly, as only 1139 rolled off the line. **2.** Instrument panels held a horizontal-sweep speedometer and dash-mounted mirror. **3.** Dual exhausts were fitted to the $3142 four-door Custom Royal Lancer. Red Ram and Super Red Ram V-8s grew to 252 and 265 horsepower. New Ram-Fire V-8s came in 350-cid size, or 361 cid in the D-500 and Super D-500 options. **4.** Not too many shoppers got a "spring edition" of the Coronet Lancer, sporting a textured-insert chrome spear. This one has a six-cylinder engine with stickshift. **5.** Dodge's most popular wagon was the Sierra. **6.** New "knockout" colors, special trim, and "bewitching" interiors marked "Spring Swept-Wing" models. **7.** Celebrities such as actress/singer Debbie Reynolds liked the Italian-bodied, Dodge-powered Dual-Ghia. **8.** Strong engines made Coronets the choice of the Missouri State Highway Patrol.

6

7

8

1958 Imperial

1

1. Ten mildly facelifted Imperial models were issued, from base sedan and hardtops to the seldom-seen Crown Imperial limo. This Southampton Crown hardtop coupe cost $5388. **2.** Imperials, including this Crown convertible, were two inches longer and held a 345-horsepower, 392-cid V-8. **3.** Touch-up work included a fresh six-section grille below quad headlights. **4.** The most popular Imperial was the Crown four-door hardtop, with 4146 built. Note the unique landau roof section. Options included electric door locks, Auto-Pilot automatic driver assist (an early cruise control), and Super Soft Cushion tires. **5.** With the exception of the limo, LeBaron served as the top-rung Imperial. It was offered as a pillared or hardtop sedan for $5969. **6.** Like all luxury makes, Imperials had to be leakproof.

2

3

6

4

5

1

6

2

3

4

5

7

1. A simplified front end led Plymouth's detail changes. This Belvedere Sport Sedan has a PowerPak V-8. **2.** A Belvedere Sport Coupe cost $2457. **3.** Belvedere four-door sedans sold best. **4.** Only 4229 Belvedere Club Sedans went to customers. **5.** Belvedere convertibles came standard with V-8 power. **6.** Another Fury stormed in, aiming at "the man who really loves cars." **7.** Fury promised a blend of "family car comfort" and "capabilities of a true competition car."

1958 Plymouth

1

3

4

6

5

7

1-2. Sportone trim with anodized aluminum inserts decorates this Plymouth Belvedere Sport Coupe. 3. Dashboards showed little change, with four round gauges flanking the large speedometer. Note the two-tone upholstery and top-of-dash mirror. 4. The 318-cid V-8 developed 225 horsepower in standard form, or 250 with a four-barrel carburetor. 5. Low price sold many a Plymouth, but the new Golden Commando engine attracted a different breed of customer. Sales dropped 42 percent, but Plymouth remained in third place—not quite "ahead for keeps," as ads suggested. 6. The top-selling Plymouth was the Savoy four-door sedan, with 67,933 built. This one has the 132-horsepower six-cylinder engine and stickshift, as well as standard bodyside chrome. 7. Nearly as dashing as a Belvedere, especially with Sportone trim, the Savoy Sport Coupe cost $128 less.

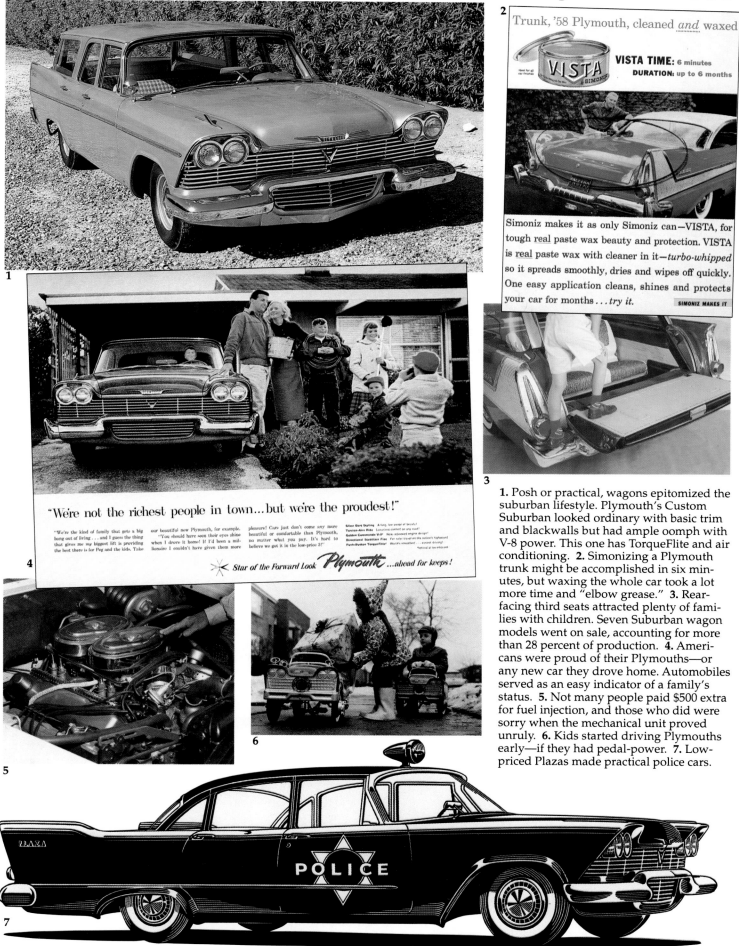

Trunk, '58 Plymouth, cleaned *and* waxed

VISTA

VISTA TIME: 6 minutes
DURATION: up to 6 months

Simoniz makes it as only Simoniz can—VISTA, for tough real paste wax beauty and protection. VISTA is real paste wax with cleaner in it—*turbo-whipped* so it spreads smoothly, dries and wipes off quickly. One easy application cleans, shines and protects your car for months...*try it.* **SIMONIZ MAKES IT**

"We're not the richest people in town...but we're the proudest!"

"We're the kind of family that gets a big bang out of living...and I guess the thing that gives me my biggest lift is providing the best there is for Peg and the kids. Take our beautiful new Plymouth, for example. "You should have seen their eyes shine when I drove it home! If I'd been a millionaire I couldn't have given them more pleasure! Cars just don't come any more beautiful or comfortable than Plymouth, no matter what you pay. It's hard to believe we got it in the low-price 3!"

Silver Dart Styling A long, low center of beauty!
Torsion-Aire Ride Luxurious comfort on any road!
Golden Commando V-8 New, advanced engine design!
Directional Stabilizer Fins For safer travel at this nation's highways!
Push-Button TorqueFlite World's smoothest...easiest driving!
optional at low extra cost

✳ *Star of the Forward Look* **Plymouth** ...*ahead for keeps!*

1. Posh or practical, wagons epitomized the suburban lifestyle. Plymouth's Custom Suburban looked ordinary with basic trim and blackwalls but had ample oomph with V-8 power. This one has TorqueFlite and air conditioning. 2. Simonizing a Plymouth trunk might be accomplished in six minutes, but waxing the whole car took a lot more time and "elbow grease." 3. Rear-facing third seats attracted plenty of families with children. Seven Suburban wagon models went on sale, accounting for more than 28 percent of production. 4. Americans were proud of their Plymouths—or any new car they drove home. Automobiles served as an easy indicator of a family's status. 5. Not many people paid $500 extra for fuel injection, and those who did were sorry when the mechanical unit proved unruly. 6. Kids started driving Plymouths early—if they had pedal-power. 7. Low-priced Plazas made practical police cars.

POLICE

PLAZA

351

1958 Edsel

Ford Motor Company

Long-rumored mid-price Edsel debuts amid a hail of publicity

Ford now has a five-model lineup, comparable to GM's

Edsel is positioned between Ford and Mercury

22,000 Edsels ready at launch—20 per dealer— "priced where you want it"

Edsels feature pushbutton automatic transmission in steering wheel

Edsel sales fail to take off— launch takes place just as national recession begins and mid-price market has sagged

Ford issues unibodied four-passenger Thunderbird

New "Squarebird" pioneers personal-luxury concept, and outsells original two-seater

Facelifted Ford offers new three-speed Cruise-O-Matic transmission, plus FE-series big-block V-8s

Lincoln adopts unibody construction, but weight goes up instead of down

Mark III Continental is Lincoln-based

Lincoln's 430-cid V-8 is biggest U.S. engine; also available in Mercury

About 100 Fords have optional air suspension— units prove to be problematic

Mercury offers three-speed Multi-Drive transmission

The EDSEL LOOK is here to stay
—and 1959 cars will prove it!

All Detroit knows it—next year's big style change is the fresh, distinctive styling that Edsel has right now! So step into the car that has future written all over it. And discover how the future is also *built into* it! Only Edsel Teletouch Drive puts the shift buttons where they belong, on the steering-wheel hub. Only Edsel gives you high-economy 303 and 345 hp V-8 engines. Only Edsel gives you comfort-shaped contour seats, Dial-temp heating, self-adjusting brakes, along with many other exclusive advances. So get the car with the advanced design that makes it worth more now —worth more when you finally trade it in. And get the magnificent Edsel at a surprisingly low price. There's less than fifty dollars difference between Edsel and V-8's in the Low-Priced Three.* See your Edsel Dealer. EDSEL DIVISION • FORD MOTOR COMPANY

Less than fifty dollars difference between Edsel and V-8's in the Low-Priced Three

Based on comparison of manufacturers' suggested retail delivered prices.

1

1. During the design process, there was reason to believe that Edsel styling was "here to stay." Mid-price sales had been booming, but by the time Edsels debuted, that market had shrunk substantially. Ford hoped to sell 100,000 in the first year, but built just over 63,000. 2. Rumored for two years, the Edsel turned out less radical than expected—but critics found amusing (and crude) words to describe the "horse-collar" grille. 3. Vice President Richard Nixon greets the crowd from an Edsel in Lima, Peru.

2

3

1. Company president Henry Ford II had reason to smile when he first took the wheel of an Edsel, but hope turned to disaster as the car failed to attract buyers. Benson and William Clay Ford ride along on this publicity trip. **2.** Edsel's 18-model lineup included three top-rung Citations, twin Corsairs, four Pacers, and four budget-priced Rangers—plus station wagons. **3.** More than most '58 cars, the Edsel's "distinctive" appearance was indeed recognizable from a distance, as this ad claimed. **4.** After pondering 6000 possible names for the new make, Ford chose to honor Edsel Ford, who'd passed on in 1943. Edsel was the only son of the company's founder, and the father of Henry Ford II. **5.** Basic engineering followed corporate trends, but the cars could be packed with gadgets. Once on sale, Edsels were actually faulted for being over-powered, especially with the bigger engine. **6.** Ford design chief George Walker (*left*) and Benson Ford posed in the design studio with Edsel manager Richard Krafve (standing). Note the work being done on a full-size clay model, which looks close to final form.

1

2

3

4

5

6

1-2. An Edsel Citation convertible sold for $3801, but only 930 were built. Like most upper models, this one is loaded, including the 410-cid V-8 and Teletouch automatic. Note the slim, wide horizontal taillights. **3.** J. C. Whitney, the Chicago parts supplier, soon added Edsel extras to its catalog. **4.** A Corsair hardtop is pictured at the Proving Grounds prior to launch date. **5.** The cheapest Edsel, at $2519, was the Ranger two-door sedan. **6.** In publicity photos, at least, engineers wore serious-looking white coats. Here, a pack of Pacers takes to the test track.

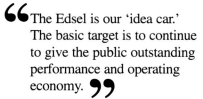

66 The Edsel is our 'idea car.' The basic target is to continue to give the public outstanding performance and operating economy. 99

Mercury-Edsel-Lincoln general manager **James J. Nance***; March 1958*

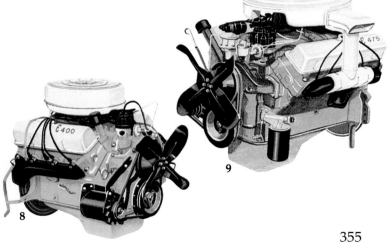

1. An Edsel Pacer convertible went for $773 less than the Citation version, and sold twice as well. **2.** Teletouch Drive put transmission pushbuttons in the steering wheel. **3.** Dashboards followed aircraft practice, with instruments, controls, and warning lights in three horizontal rows. Edsels used a "cyclops eye" rotating-drum speedometer. **4.** It's true that "Edsel dared to break out of the lookalike rut," but the new look wouldn't last nearly as long as Ford expected—and "next year's cars" wouldn't be copying its stylistic touches. **5.** Part of the Pacer series, the Bermuda wagon could be fitted for six or nine passengers. **6.** Kids could slip easily into the rear of a Bermuda wagon. **7.** The E-196X was supposed to illustrate a possible evolution of the 1958 Edsel's front-end theme. Here, Edsel executive stylist I. B. Kaufman (*left*) explains the potential of the vertical-grille design to styling director George Walker. **8:** Edsel's E-400 engine, used in the Pacer and Ranger series (and all wagons), delivered 303 horsepower. **9.** Citations and Corsairs used the 345-horsepower, 410-cid E-475 engine.

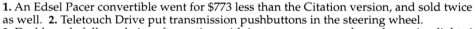

1958 Ford

1

2

3

1-2. Ford's fully facelifted Fairlane 500 Club Victoria cost $2435. Oval taillights sat in a newly sculpted deck. Grooves went into roof panels, and hoods held a fake scoop. **3.** A Fairlane 500 Sunliner convertible cost $2650. Several features of this year's restyle were done not with beauty in mind, but to increase body-panel strength. **4.** Fender skirts and a Continental kit added extra flash to the Ford Fairlane's shape. **5.** Naturally, the J. C. Whitney catalog held temptations for Ford owners. Thousands of car fans pored through the small-print pages of each catalog as it arrived in the mail.

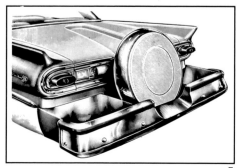

4

5

1

2

3

1. Production of Ford's Fairlane 500 Skyliner retractable hardtop coupe dropped to 14,713 cars, priced at $3163. **2.** More than 135,000 Custom 300 Fordor sedans went on sale. The popular model started at $2159. **3.** Custom 300, Ford's second-cheapest series, included only Tudor and Fordor sedans. **4.** Styled earlier in the decade, the experimental FX Atmos looked more at home in a sci-fi movie than on any street—especially with those protruding spears. **5.** This scene in Oak Park, Illinois, is typical of suburban business streets in the late '50s. Note '58 Fairlane at right.

4

> **66** Ford surveys find only a limited place for the little car and no evidence that the American public is interested in lowering its standard of living by buying an economy car on a large scale. **99**
>
> *Mercury-Edsel-Lincoln general manager* **James J. Nance**, *justifying Detroit's reluctance to aggressively enter the small-car market; April 1958*

5

1958 Ford

1

3

4

1. Ford had a new breed of Thunderbird ready, seating four instead of two. The stylish hardtop cost $3631, and 35,758 buyers drove one home. The 352-cid V-8 engine developed 300 horsepower. **2.** With a back seat now installed, a whole family could drive to fancy spots in the latest Thunderbird, hauling luggage in a full-size trunk. Though one of the lowest cars around, the T-Bird had plenty of interior space.

3-4. Debuting late in the season, only 2134 Thunderbird convertibles were produced, starting at $3929. The new wheelbase stretched a foot longer than the old two-seater's, and the new cars weighed 800 pounds more. Bodysides were amply sculpted.

1

1. Ford's Ranchero Custom car-pickup adopted this year's styling changes. This one has stickshift and the 292-cid V-8.
2. Six-passenger Country Sedans outsold their nine-seat mates by more than three to one. 3. There's no telling how many youngsters developed a liking—or distaste—for Fords after waxing the family wagon. Ranch Wagons now had either two or four doors. 4. Three-seat station wagon interiors might be washable pleated vinyl or woven plastic/vinyl. 5. Looks like an ambitious project, trying to load that big boat inside a Country Sedan. Note the wagon's amply sized roof rack.

2

4

5

1958 Lincoln

1

2

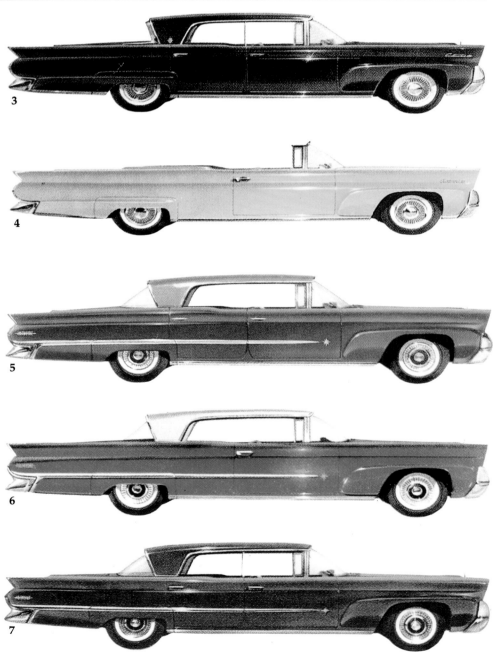

3

4

5

6

7

1. Bearing no resemblance to the graceful Mark II, the heavily sculpted Continental Mark III came in four body styles. This Landau hardtop sedan cost $6072.
2. Lincolns and Mercurys took their turns for testing at the Proving Grounds. 3. A pillared Continental Mark III sedan cost the same as the hardtop, but only 1283 were built. 4. Just over 3000 customers paid $6283 to grab an open Continental. 5. A Lincoln Premiere Landau hardtop cost $5505. To cope with heavier structures, Lincoln enlarged its V-8 to 430 cid—the biggest in America—making 375 bhp. 6. A Lincoln Premiere looked little different than costlier Continentals. 7. Premiere four-door sedans failed to sell well.

> **❝**Domestic cars are awful, particularly the styling. **❞**
>
> **Unidentified Los Angeles import-car dealer**, *on why he chose to sell imports instead of a domestic make; September 1958*

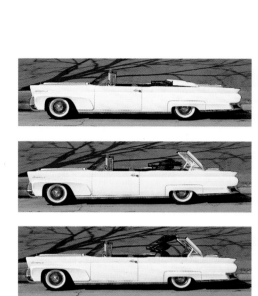

1. The new Continental's top-stowage setup borrowed ideas from Ford's retractable hard-top. A metal panel raised out of the way, allowing the top to raise or lower. Lack of a pro-truding boot accentuated the long lines. Soon dubbed "land yachts," these were the biggest Continentals ever. **2.** Slanted housings held quad headlights. Structurally identical to Lincolns, Continentals had their own grille and reverse-slant rear window. **3.** Conti-nentals carried fine fabrics or Bridge of Weir leather from Scotland. **4.** Lincoln's Capri series cost about $500 less than the Premiere. **5.** Not quite a superstar just yet, Elvis Presley took the wheel of a Mark III. **6.** Vice President Richard M. Nixon served as Grand Marshal of this Aquatennial parade, riding in a Continental convertible with wife Pat.

1958 Mercury

1. Only 844 Mercury Montclair Phaeton convertibles were built, starting at $3536, but extra-cost accessories could easily send the price skyward. This car has the 383-cid engine, Multi-Drive, and factory air conditioning. 2. Riding a new 125-inch wheelbase, the Park Lane replaced the Turnpike Cruiser as the top-of-the-line Merc, promising "impressive size, performance and luxury." Its 430-cid Marauder V-8 engine yielded 360 horsepower. 3. Montclairs cost about $600 less than equivalent Park Lanes but could get the latter's 430-cid engine. 4. Montereys came in five body styles, including this Phaeton sedan. Mercury's two new hard-driving big-block V-8s ran on 10.5:1 compression and demanded premium fuel. The 383-cid version put out 312 horsepower in the Monterey, 330 in Montclairs. Mercury's brochure claimed a "sports car spirit and limousine ride."

1

3

4

2

5

6

1. Monterey was Mercury's best-selling series. A Phaeton hardtop cost $2769. **2.** "Cruiser" skirts aren't the only extras on this Montclair, which holds the rare triple-carb Super Marauder engine, belting out 400 horses. **3.** Automatic-equipped Mercs got Keyboard Control. Multi-Drive split the Drive bar into High Performance and Cruising buttons. **4.** J. C. Whitney's catalog offered a Continental kit for Mercurys. **5.** The 400-bhp Super Marauder V-8 was optional in all models. **6.** Station wagons were popular, whether in Ford, Edsel, or Mercury form.

General Motors Corporation

GM celebrates 50th anniversary

Buick revives Limited series—a badge unused since the 1940s

Flight Pitch triple-turbine Dynaflow debuts in Buicks

Buick sinks to fifth place in production, behind Oldsmobile, as output drops 40 percent

Buick dealers now sell German-built Opel; Pontiac dealers get British Vauxhall

Chevrolets and Pontiacs adopt all-coil suspensions

Chevrolet adds luxury Impala

Full-size Chevrolets may have Turbo Thrust 348-cid V-8

Chevrolet captures 30 percent of market—a record figure

Demand for restyled Corvette sports cars rises smartly—to 9168 cars

Each make offers air suspension; unit proves troublesome, and many are converted to springs

Garishly reworked Oldsmobiles look bigger and heavier

Triple-carb J-2 option boosts Oldsmobile's V-8 to 312 bhp

All Pontiacs hold Bonneville-sized 370-cid V-8

Buicks and Oldsmobiles get new one-piece rear windows

1

2

3

4

1. Buick's Limited Riviera hardtop sedan listed at $5112 ($33 higher than a Series 62 Cadillac). Though two inches shorter in wheelbase than a Caddy, the Buick was longer overall. **2.** Limiteds wore more brightwork than other Buicks, but all flaunted a studded Dynastar grille. **3.** Twin-Tower taillights helped give the Limited convertible a distinctive stance. **4.** This special "Wells Fargo" Limited was built for Dale Robertson, star of the Buick-sponsored *Tales of Wells Fargo* TV show. **5.** Ads lauded visibility through the huge wraparound back window.

5

It's the "HIS" and "HER" car

—first big car that's light on its feet

Big·Bold·Buoyant
the AIR BORN B-58 BUICK

1. Overwrought and overchromed, Buick's open Century epitomized the age of excess.
2. Hardtop station wagons came in the Century (shown) and Special series.
3. Buick promised glamour and easy handling for her, robust behavior for him.
4. A Special Riviera hardtop sedan cost $2820, but this body style was issued in all five series. 5. Buick and Olds bodyshells leave the welding jig at Ionia Manufacturing Co., the supplier of station wagon bodies. 6. General manager Edward T. Ragsdale displays the *Sports Car Illustrated* Award for safety. Buick was first to employ aluminum brake drums.

1958 Cadillac

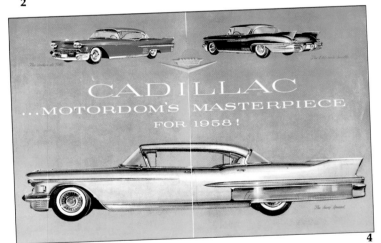

1

2

3

1. Again priced at $13,074, the Eldorado Brougham showed little change apart from new wheel covers. **2.** Only 304 Broughams were built. This car spent its early life in Holland. **3.** Brougham door panels switched from metal finish to leather.

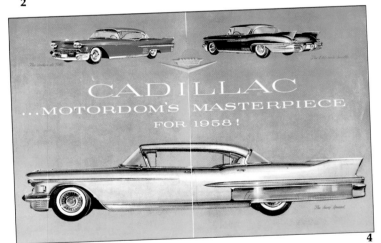

4

5

6

4. Not everyone dubbed the '58 Cadillac a "masterpiece." Sheetmetal got only minor reshaping with spiked fins, but these were the most flamboyant Cadillacs yet, gushing with chrome. Shown: a Sedan de Ville, Eldorado Seville, and Sixty Special. **5.** Rather than issue special editions to mark its Golden Anniversary, GM merely promoted a typical example from each of the five makes. **6.** Portraying a raucous-living rancher with a stupefying lack of scruples, Paul Newman drove his Cadillac convertible hard in the 1962 movie *Hud*. In one scene, the car nearly leaps into the air as it crosses a railroad track at breakneck speed.

1. Few convertibles had air conditioning in 1958, not to mention walrus-hide upholstery. This Eldorado Biarritz has both. 2. A Biarritz brought an even $7500 this season—same price as the Seville hardtop coupe. Eldorado engines adopted triple two-barrel carburetors, boosting output to 335 horsepower. Other models made do with a single four-barrel carb and 310 bhp. 3. Sedan de Villes ranked as the top Cadillac sellers. Series 62 added a hardtop sedan with an extended rear deck, which sold almost as well. 4. Tradition still played a major role in attracting customers to Cadillac. Ads implied that arrival at a classy resort or restaurant was best accomplished in a fancy automobile. 5. Even Cadillacs had to have their oil checked periodically. Visitors to this gas station near Pensacola, Florida, got a free beverage while they waited.

1

2

3

4

IT OUTSTEPS ITS OWN GREAT TRADITIONS!

Cadillac

5

1

2

3

4

5

1. GM's Biscayne show car of 1955 (*rear*) influenced styling of this year's full-size Chevrolets, including the new Impala (*foreground*). Even Corvettes benefited from show-car ideas. 2. Chevy drivers who yearned to be "the boss" had a new engine option: a big-block 348-cid Turbo-Thrust V-8 tossing out 250, 280, or 315 horsepower. The tasteful new body—longer, lower, wider, and heavier—lasted only one year. A new, low-slung X-member frame contained all-coil suspension, displacing the old rear leaf springs. 3. Shoppers had five wagons to choose from in the Yeoman, Brookwood, and Nomad series. Larger liftgates, curved at the corners, hinged into the roof and raised out of the way. 4. Ads pushed the beauty and "low, thrusting silhouette" of full-size models—up to nine inches longer and five inches lower, on a 2.5-inch-longer wheelbase than before. Weights escalated by 200 to 300 pounds. 5. As usual, the J. C. Whitney catalog featured a Continental kit, plus trunk and hood ornamentation.

1

SWEET
SEVENTEEN—
AND NOT
TO BE
MISSED!

CHEVROLET

IMPALA SPORT COUPE—super-special hardtop of the Bel Air Series! No mistaking its fine Fisher Body. Like other Chevrolets, it has Safety Plate Glass all around for sharper seeing.

BEL AIR SPORT COUPE—it's easy to see why this one's so popular. Here's dashing hardtop styling with a colorful, comfortable interior!

BEL AIR 4-DOOR SEDAN—looks big and roomy, and it is! All new Chevrolets are nine lively inches longer, four inches wider. All are lower, too.

BEL AIR 2-DOOR SEDAN—a beauty, all right, and built solidly. New Safety-Girder frame (X-built) accounts for that firm feeling on the road.

BROOKWOOD 4-DOOR 6-PASSENGER—you get bigger tires and springs in Chevy wagons, and 88 cubic feet of load space with the rear seat folded!

DELRAY 4-DOOR SEDAN—the beautiful way to be extra thrifty. There's fresh styling and fine appointments, too, in this lowest priced series!

DELRAY UTILITY SEDAN—and here's the beautiful way to be businesslike. This Delray's rear compartment was made for salesmen's samples!

IMPALA CONVERTIBLE—another new luxury model in the Bel Air Series. How about those long, low lines! And colors—wait till you see the samples!

CORVETTE—America's only authentic sports car! Offers five spirited V8's, two with Fuel Injection;* three transmissions, including 4-speed manual shift.*

BEL AIR SPORT SEDAN—imagine getting this one with Turbo-Thrust V8* and Turboglide!* You'd have the smoothest power combination in Chevrolet's class.

NOMAD—star of a high-styled five-wagon lineup for '58! Seats for six in this one—and it surrounds you with luxury. Choose any Chevy engine; up to 280 h.p. in V8's.

BISCAYNE 4-DOOR SEDAN—in Chevrolet's middle priced series. Biscaynes, you'll notice, have a bright look of beauty that's all their own!

BISCAYNE 2-DOOR SEDAN—ready to take you for a super-smooth ride with Full Coil suspension at all 4 wheels! New air ride* is also offered.

BROOKWOOD 4-DOOR 9-PASSENGER—you can take half the neighborhood to school in this one! Upholstery is easy to keep clean; wears well, too.

DELRAY 2-DOOR SEDAN—you'll save with a Delray and still get everything Chevy's famous for: smooth ride, easy handling, real performance!

YEOMAN 4-DOOR 6-PASSENGER—comes with any one of Chevrolet's superb new engines. For biggest savings, choose the new 145-h.p. Blue-Flame 6.

YEOMAN 2-DOOR 6-PASSENGER—pile the family in this one for a good time; put in a cargo (up to a ½ ton of it) and you've got a willing worker!

Optional at extra cost.

THE BEAUTIFULLY MOVING '58 CHEVROLETS

Here's Chevrolet's whole happy family. Here's styling that sets a new style—new developments in riding comfort that make the high-priced cars jealous—new peaks of performance (V8 or 6) in every model. Don't miss seeing and driving a '58 Chevrolet before you buy that new car. It's a beautiful way to be thrifty! ... Chevrolet Division of General Motors, Detroit 2, Michigan.

2

3

> 66 Cleanup is when the family boys come in for bargains on the four-door cheapie sedans. 99
>
> **Unidentified Chevrolet dealer,** *on what dealers expect during end-of-model-year sales; June 1958*

1. Chevrolet's "happy family" consisted of 17 models. Delray replaced the One-Fifty series, Biscayne edged aside the Two-Ten, and Bel Air/Impala topped the line. Virtually new from the ground up, this year's models were better as well as bigger, though leaning more toward luxury than roadability. **2-3.** More than a trim option, Impala differed structurally from garden-variety Chevys. It was offered only as a Sport Coupe and convertible. The Impala started at $2586 with a six-cylinder engine, while $2693 bought a V-8 version. Impalas had a slightly shorter greenhouse and longer rear deck than other hardtops, plus bright rocker moldings and dummy rear-fender scoops. A total of 55,989 ragtops and 125,480 Sport Coupes were built—15 percent of production.

1958 Chevrolet

1

1. Impala served as Chevrolet's sole convertible. This loaded example has power windows and seats and Autronic Eye. 2. With Ramjet fuel injection, the 283-cid V-8 whipped up 290 horses. 3. Now an exclusive model marked by a distinctive badge, the Impala name would soon become almost synonymous with Chevy. 4. This Impala ragtop is dressed to kill with fender skirts and Continental kit. 5. Impala interiors held a competition-inspired steering wheel and color-keyed door panels with brushed aluminum trim. 6. A low-budget Delray sedan might have any engine—six or V-8.

2

3

> **"**We don't like it but we have to write it when the buyer asks for it. Otherwise, he'll go down the street. **"**
>
> **Unidentified new car dealer**, *on the increasing popularity of 36-month new-car loans; March 1958*

4

6

5

1

2

3

1. With a V-8, Chevrolet's Delray sedan was a fine choice for the Michigan State Police. 2. A V-8 edges into place at the engine drop site. 3. A finished Fisher-built body meets its chassis. 4. Chevrolets were popular as urban police cars, as shown by this lineup in Cicero, Illinois. 5. A Yeoman station wagon served police ambulance duty. 6. Ten inches longer overall, Corvettes had a choice of five ratings for their 283-cid V-8 engine. This one has the 270-horse version with a four-speed gearbox. 7. Now priced at $3631, Corvette was still America's only production sports car. 8. Corvettes got sturdier bumpers and dummy air scoops. 9. All gauges now sat ahead of the driver in a cockpit that added a passenger grab bar and locking glovebox.

4

5

6

WHEREVER THE WORLD'S BEST SPORTS CARS GATHER

CORVETTE DOES AMERICA PROUD!

7

8

9

371

1958 Oldsmobile

1

2

4

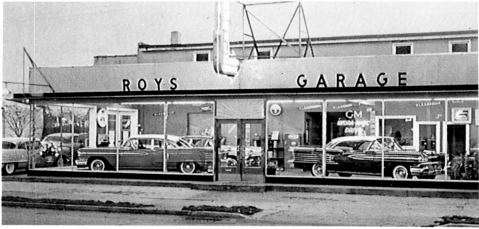

5

Off to a Good Start!

...because a new set of ACs
can save three times their cost in gasoline!

AC HOT TIP SPARK PLUGS

3

1. Thin-pillar styling made it hard to tell an
Olds Ninety-Eight sedan from the stronger-
selling Holiday hardtop. Sharply slanted
windshield pillars were responsible for
many sore shins. 2. An Olds Ninety-Eight
ragtop cost $4300. Most sheetmetal was
new, but the cars lost their styling continu-
ity. 3. Budget-conscious couples had to cut
corners where they could. Hot-tip AC
plugs promised to save up to one gallon of
gas in every ten. 4. Each series included a
convertible. The Super 88 went for $3529.
5. Boasting a typical look for the times, this
showroom was in Williamstown, New
Jersey.

> 66 There's no sense fishing in a
> swimming pool. 99
>
> *Unidentified* **Seattle new-car
> dealer**, *on his unwillingness to
> undertake elaborate promotions
> in a depressed economic climate;
> February 1958*

Oldsmobile 1958

1. A fleet of Oldsmobile Ninety-Eight convertibles marked the opening of the Mackinac Bridge, linking Michigan's upper and lower peninsulas. 2. A newly optional Trans-Portable Radio slipped out of its slot in the Fashion-Flare dash to run on its own batteries. Note the pull handle and lock. 3. Just $3262 could buy a Super 88 Holiday hardtop, but this coupe is loaded with extras—skirts, outside spare, and J-2 Tri-Power engine. 4. Super 88 Holiday hardtops sold well, with 18,653 built. 5. The 88 series included both a regular four-door sedan—the top Oldsmobile seller—and a pillarless Holiday hardtop. 6. Fiesta wagons came in pillared or hardtop form. 7. The six-millionth Oldsmobile, a Holiday Ninety-Eight four-door hardtop, was built on November 8, 1957.

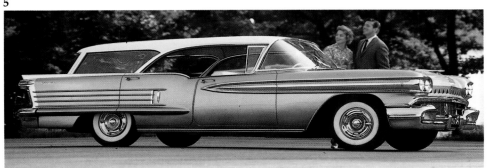

> 66 With one out of every seven American workers dependent directly or indirectly upon the automobile industry for his livelihood, the effect of this decrease in automobile sales in aggravating and deepening the current recession should be obvious. 99
>
> *Tennessee senator*
> **Estes Kefauver**; *March 1958*

1958 Pontiac

1

2

3

4

5

6

1. Pontiac's flagship Bonneville, billed as "America's hot road car," rode the Chieftain's shorter 122-inch wheelbase. 2. An external spare-tire mount and super-hot 330-bhp Tri-Power engine added extra bucks to the $3586 tariff of a Bonneville convertible—Pontiac's costliest model. Just 3096 were built. 3. Dazzling upholstery in a Bonneville ragtop comprised "hand-buffed glove-soft cowhides" to match the body color. This car has the Tri-Power triple carburetion option. 4. Pontiac issued 9144 Bonneville Sport Coupes, starting at $3481. This one has Rochester fuel-injection, a $500 option. Bonneville hardtops had a fake vent above the rear window, like Chevrolet's Impala. 5. Pontiac's Chieftain and Star Chief series included Safari wagons, promising "road-wedded stability." 6. Testing under NASCAR auspices bore out Pontiac's claim to be America's top road car. Sporting a fresh "New Direction" look, Pontiacs measured up to 8.7 inches longer and 4.5 inches lower.

1

2

3

1-3. In Pontiac's entry-level Chieftain series, a Catalina hardtop cost $2707. Though less lavish than upper models, Chieftains were generously chromed. The gas cap hid behind the left backup light. **4.** Leather was a no-cost option on the $3122 Star Chief Custom Catalina hardtop, billed as "Luxury Unlimited." **5.** Only 2905 Star Chief Custom Safaris—Pontiac's top wagon—went on sale at $3350. This one has Tri-Power. **6.** This special Bonneville was upholstered with 11 African leopard pelts. Stylist Sandra Longyear wears a then-fashionable leopard coat for the publicity photo. **7.** A Tri-Power Bonneville convertible, driven by Sam Hanks, paced the Indy 500 race on May 30.

4

5

6

7

> **❝**If all cars were 1958 models, we would be in trouble.**❞**
>
> *Norfolk, Virginia, city traffic engineer* **Fenton G. Jordan**, *on a street-parking crisis caused by 1958 automobiles too long to fit comfortably into prepainted parking spaces; January 1958*

Studebaker-Packard Corporation

Last Packards go on sale exhibiting hasty restyle

Packard Hawk is strange luxury version of Studebaker Golden Hawk, sporting outside armrests and simulated spare tire

Studebaker-Packard announces halt to Packard production in mid-season

Studebaker President and Commander series add hardtop-coupe body style

Each Studebaker series trims its lineup

Studebaker sedans and wagons (except Scotsman) get grafted-on tailfins and quad headlights

Like most '58 makes, Studebakers are longer and lower, with Flight Stream roofline

Fender vent doors are gone, replaced by cowl ventilation

Little-changed no-frills Scotsman series sells well

Studebaker Golden Hawk output skids to 878 cars, far below the total for Silver Hawk

Only 44,759 Studebakers are produced in the U.S., for 14th-place ranking

Packard ranks dead last, far behind Continental, with only 2622 cars built

Studebaker-Packard loses $13 million for the year

1. Chief stylist Duncan McRae designed the '58 Packards swiftly and cheaply—in most eyes, an ignominious end to the once-grand marque. McRae mainly grafted extra pieces—fins and pod-mounted quad headlights—onto the existing body to differentiate it from the so-similar Studebaker.
2. Studebaker's Golden Hawk and the new Packard Hawk were the only supercharged production cars in America. The variable-speed centrifugal blower delivered up to 5-psi boost to the 275-horsepower V-8.
3. Only 588 Packard Hawks were produced, with a $3995 sticker price—$700 higher than the Golden Hawk and $300 above a Corvette. A Hawk could accelerate to 60 mph in about eight seconds.

66 Our job is far from easy and the current recession has made it all the harder. 99

Studebaker-Packard president **Harold E. Churchill**, *addressing S-P stockholders about the corporation's sales woes; April 1958*

1

2

4

3

> 66 In the opinion of your management, without this plan the chance of restoring any real value to your stock is practically nonexistent. 99
>
> *Studebaker-Packard president* **Harold E. Churchill**, *on a refinancing and diversification program intended to bolster S-P's fortunes; September 1958*

5

6

1-2. A 210-horsepower rendition of Studebaker's 289-cid V-8 went into other Packard models, including the new Starlight hardtop. An automatic transmission was standard. Just 675 hardtops rolled off the line, priced at $3262. Note the two-step outward-leaning tailfins—a fin atop a fin. **3.** Packard Hawks stuck with single headlights instead of the trendy four-light setup installed on other models. A low, full-width grille opening gave the Hawk's long, bolt-on fiberglass nose a puzzled grin. **4.** Hawk dashboards held small round gauges on a tooled panel. Based upon the posh '57 Studebaker Golden Hawk 400, Packard Hawks had leather interiors and extra trim—including unique exterior vinyl padding on door tops. **5.** Hawk decklids displayed a simulated spare tire, and tailfins held mylar inserts. **6.** The rarest '58 Packard of all is the $3384 station wagon, with a mere 159 produced. Note the four headlights, stuck into twin pods tacked onto the fenders.

1958 Studebaker

1

2

4

3

1. Studebaker added a hardtop coupe to its President and Commander series. Billed as "scintillating," this Starlight President cost $2695. 2-3. Not much change was evident in the supercharged Golden Hawk, except for 14-inch tires and optional air conditioning. 4. Studebaker promoted the "Hawk-inspired" styling of its full-size models. 5. Presidents got 14-inch wheels and a 225-bhp engine. 6. Part of the Commander series, the Provincial wagon cost $2664 and used a smaller 259-cid, 180-bhp V-8. 7. A Commander hardtop cost $202 less than its President cousin. 8. Commanders came in three body styles, including the $2378 sedan.

5

6

7

8

1

2

3

4

1-3. Studebaker's Champion dropped to a sedan-only lineup. This four-door sold for $2253. The 185.6-cid L-head six-cylinder engine again put out 101 horsepower. Pod-mounted quad headlights were optional on Champions, standard on upper models, but not available at all on the low-budget Scotsman. Flight-O-Matic was optional, but plenty of Champions had stickshift or over-drive. **4.** Champion dashboards had a basic look with small gauges. Flight-Style instrument panels featured a Magna-Dial speedometer and Safety-Cone steering wheel. Studebaker promoted the safety of its cars, interior space, variable-rate front springs, and variable-ratio steering. **5.** A no-trim Scotsman two-door sedan went for just $1795, while the four-door version cost $1874. Scotsman models accounted for 38 percent of total production. **6.** The Scotsman station wagon cost $2055. Ads promised three-way economy: when buying, driving, and reselling.

5

6

1959

f any year serves as the consummate example of Fifties immoderation, it has to be 1959. Cadillac tailfins reached as tall as they ever would, and virtually every other make's stretched only a little shorter. Chevrolet sent its fins soaring outward instead of skyward, but they served the same dubious purpose. Buick also took the sideways route with its new "delta-wing" styling, and each upper GM make adopted a massive rear "picture window." GM also increased the use of shared bodyshells.

Ignoring the troubles GM had experienced with air suspensions, Chrysler launched its own version this year. Studebaker dropped the hot Golden Hawk but issued a more modest Silver Hawk coupe.

After arriving on the market with such promise and potential a year earlier, Edsel was already on the ropes. A handful of 1960 models were issued, built late this year; after which the name survived only as a virtual synonym for mammoth failure. Engines continued to grow in size and strength as the horsepower race wore on. Chrysler abandoned the legendary Hemi V-8 engine but had a selection of wedge-chambered powerhouses to take its place.

Pontiac went "Wide-Track," and Chevrolet added four-door models to the top Impala lineup. Ford launched a Galaxie to rival the Impala, while Chevy turned the tables with an El Camino car-pickup to go against the Ranchero. Checker expanded beyond taxicabs, introducing a Superba passenger car.

At the small end of the scale, American Motors—focusing solely on compacts— built a record number of cars and earned a rewarding profit. Studebaker was in the throes of a comeback, courtesy of the compact Lark, a "new concept in motoring."

Analysts predicted a more stable market, courtesy of the now-required price stickers on new cars. Model-year auto output grew by 30.7 percent to more than 5.5 million. The federal gasoline tax was raised from three to four cents per gallon.

Imports enjoyed record sales, with a 62-percent increase over 1958. Shoppers could get foreign cars priced from $1048 (for a tiny Isetta) to $14,000, as the import boom went full steam ahead.

Nearly 700,000 imports were on the road as the model year began, but the total topped 1.1 million a year later.

Chrysler dealers began to sell Simcas, imported from France. In addition to the expected Volkswagens, Renaults, and Austins, buyers could choose a Berkeley, NSU Prinz, Goggomobil, or Goliath, as well as a Citroën or Hillman—even a Skoda from Czechoslovakia or a Wartburg from East Germany. This year's convention of the National Automobile Dealers Association asked the vital question: "Are imported cars here to stay?"

Unemployment eased a bit, to 5.5 percent, after the great downfall of 1958. Overall inflation actually approached zero, though new cars cost 2.6 percent more as the model year began, and the average price paid for a new automobile rose sharply (to $3150). The average used car went for just over a thousand. Despite the economic downturn, average incomes of employed workers continued to rise, nearing $4600. Physicians topped $22,000. Nearly three-fourths of families had a vehicle, but only 38 percent paid cash for one.

Rawhide and *Bonanza* entered TV screens for the first time, as did Rod Serling's *Twilight Zone*. Movies included *Anatomy of a Murder* with James Stewart, Billy Wilder's *Some Like It Hot*, Alfred Hitchcock's *North by Northwest*, and *On the Beach*.

In cities, at least, Americans saw more foreign films; but *Ben-Hur* would earn the best-picture Oscar. On another level, moviegoers savored such fare as *The Ghost of Dragstrip Hollow* and *Speed Crazy*.

Fidel Castro's troops moved into Havana, sending dictator Fulgencio Batista out of Cuba. Soviet leader Nikita Khrushchev toured the United States, stopping off at Disneyland—where he was denied entry for security reasons. Hawaii was admitted to the Union as the 50th state, and Charles Van Doren admitted having received answers beforehand on the popular quiz show *Twenty-One*.

Bobby Darin won a Grammy for his offbeat recording of "Mack the Knife," Johnny Mathis got "Misty," and Dion and the Belmonts warbled about "A Teenager in Love." Ace rock 'n' roller Buddy Holly was killed in a plane crash along with Ritchie Valens and The Big Bopper.

William Burroughs published *The Naked Lunch*, Norman Mailer delivered *Advertisements for Myself*, and Kurt Vonnegut issued *The Sirens of Titan*. Best-sellers included everything from *Exodus* and *Hawaii* to *The Ugly American*.

Go-carts were popular with kids and teens. Radio disc jockeys were investigated for accepting "payola" (bribes for playing certain recordings). America's first seven astronauts were selected, including John Glenn and Alan Shepard. The average person watched 42 hours' worth of TV a week.

The Automobile Manufacturers Association announced that a crankcase-ventilation device would go on cars sold in California, effective on '61 models. Before long, emissions and safety issues would change the way Americans thought about their cars and the way manufacturers built them.

Compacts would lead the way into the Sixties, followed by a fleet of mid-size models. Goliath full-size cars would not disappear for many years, and the horsepower race would gain in frenzy as "muscle cars" were added to the mix, so Americans were about to face an even wider array of automotive choices.

American Motors Corporation

Rambler earns $60 million profit, building a record 374,000 automobiles

Production almost doubles in model year, as company rises to sixth place in the industry

Ambassador output grows smartly to 23,769 cars

Two-door station wagon joins Rambler American lineup; roof luggage rack is available

More than 90,000 Rambler Americans are sold, despite competition from Studebaker's new Lark series

Rambler American gets self-adjusting brakes

Ramblers use three wheelbases: 100, 108, and 117 inches

New grilles and rearranged side trim give modest facelift to middle-sized Ramblers

Separate front seats available with ten-way headrests

Six-cylinder Ramblers outsell Rebel V-8s by wide margin

Nash Metropolitans add trunk lid and wing vents

More potent Austin engine is available in Metropolitans

Metropolitan sales grow considerably—22,209 are shipped (20,435 of them to U.S.)

Among imports, Metro is second only to Volkswagen in sales—but gulf between the two is vast

1

2

3

1. A Rambler Ambassador Custom Country Club four-door hardtop sold for $2822, but only 1447 were built. The 327-cid V-8 made 270 horsepower. Note the pointed fins.
2. AMC built 4341 Ambassador Custom Cross Country wagons. Super versions lacked the Custom's anodized aluminum trim. 3. AMC president George Romney shows off an Ambassador Custom Country Club hardtop at corporate headquarters. 4. Ambassadors were promoted as sensibly sized, "The Modern Concept of a Luxury Car."

4

> **As a country, we may be in for some tough sledding, based on my survey of the domestic situation.**
> **We have to recognize that since World War II, our enemy has been licking the pants off us.**
>
> *American Motors president* **George Romney**, *on the American work ethic, excess consumerism, and the growth of foreign economies; May 1959*

1. Rambler offered a four-door hardtop with either six-cylinder or V-8 power. Sixes provided 127/138 horsepower; Rebel badges were fitted to models carrying the 215-bhp, 250-cid V-8. **2.** Regular-size Ramblers, here a Rebel Custom four-door sedan, rode a 108-inch wheelbase, versus 100 for the American and 117 for Ambassadors. **3.** A Custom Cross Country wagon cost $2677 as a Six, or $2807 as a Rebel. **4.** Just $2268 bought a Super sedan. **5.** Entrants in this Milk-Bone contest had to compose the best last line of a jingle to win one of eight Rambler station wagons. **6.** DeLuxe Ramblers had two headlamps; other models had four. **7.** Rambler Americans now came in both station wagon and sedan form. **8.** An American sedan cost $1835 with DeLuxe trim, $1920 as a Super. **9.** An American gets its fill of fluids on the assembly line. **10.** Metropolitan sales blossomed. Convertibles cost $1650. **11.** Metro interiors were basic. Note the steering-wheel spinner. **12.** A new Metro engine made 55 horsepower. The 52-bhp version remained an option.

Checker Motors Corporation

Markin Body Corporation merges with Commonwealth Motors in 1921

Checker founded by Morris Markin in 1922

Early cars built in Joliet and Chicago, Illinois

Factory moves to Kalamazoo, Michigan, in 1923

Cars initially use four-cylinder engines; inline sixes and eights are added later

First passenger model, the Checker Utility, offered in 1931-32

Prewar Checkers are changed regularly in design to keep up with contemporary trends

First postwar civilian model, the Superba, released in 1959

Superba based on the A8 taxi introduced in 1956.

Superba gets quad headlights in place of the A8's duals

Power is provided by a 226-cid Continental inline six similar to that used in the Kaiser/Frazer

Engine offered in two versions: L-head with 80 horsepower, overhead-valve model with 122 bhp

Four-door sedan and four-door wagon offered, each in standard or Special trim

Markin promises not to initiate change for the sake of change; indeed, cars continue 1956 styling to the bitter end

1

2

3

1-3. "Taxi tough" Checker sedans rode a 120-inch wheelbase and tipped the scales at around 3400 pounds—about the same as a Chevrolet Biscayne—while wagons weighed nearly 400 pounds more. Sedans started at $2542, wagons at $2896; both about $250 more than the cheapest comparable Chevy. The 80-horsepower Continental L-head six had a 7.3:1 compression ratio that let it run on poor-quality gas, but most cars had the no-cost overhead-valve option with 8.0:1 compression and 122 bhp. Interiors were Spartan with rubber floor mats and cardboard headliners. The model name switched to Marathon in the early '60s and Chevy engines were used after 1964, but the cars changed little otherwise through their final season in 1982. Civilian production rarely exceeded 1000 per year.

Chrysler Corporation

Chrysler budgets $150 million for the '59 models—much of which goes to Plymouth

Swivel semi-bucket front seats are standard on Chrysler 300-E, optional on other makes/models

Chryslers are powered by 383- and 413-cid wedge V-8 engines; legendary Hemis are gone

Chrysler 300-E boasts 380 horsepower from 413-cid V-8; production drops to 690 cars

Chrysler output rises slightly, due largely to Windsor sedans

DeSoto sales continue to sag

Midyear brings Seville editions to mark DeSoto's 30th year

Final year for Dodge/Plymouth L-head six-cylinder engine

Plymouths are sold by Dodge dealers for the last time

New electronic rear-view mirror cuts glare when a headlight beam hits its surface

Rear air suspensions available; speed warnings also optional

Stainless steel roof sections available for Imperial hardtops

Plymouth Plaza gone; Savoy is now the base model

Plymouth finishes third, followed by Pontiac and Olds

Chrysler dealers now sell French Simca

1

2

3

4

1-2. Just 286 open Chrysler New Yorkers went to buyers, at $4890. Taillights were new. So was the 413-cid V-8 developing 350 horsepower. This convertible has the new Autronic Eye headlight dimmer. **3.** Chrysler's '59 facelift included a blunted front with a simpler grille. New Yorker four-door hardtops started at $4533, with 4805 built. Backup lights became standard. Note the distinctive two-toning. **4.** Adding a quart of oil was a regular event, even in a New Yorker. Sunoco stations delivered six grades of fuel from a single pump.

1959 Chrysler

1

2

3

4

6

5

1. Chrysler Windsors got a new Golden Lion 383-cid V-8 promising 305 horses. This hardtop has an optional two-tone roof. Spring action swung the extra-cost swivel seat outward; body motion glided it back. 2. Chrysler's 300-E kept its distinctive grille. Only 550 coupes were produced. 3. Responding to demand for a cheaper convertible, a $3620 ragtop joined the Windsor series. 4. Output of the open 300-E came to just 140 cars. 5. Chief engineer Bob Rodger inspects the new dual-quad 413-cid V-8 in a 300-E. This "wedge" V-8 weighed 101 pounds less than a Hemi and delivered the same 380 horsepower. Hydraulic lifters were new. 6. The Brooks Stevens-designed Scimitar employed a Chrysler chassis and running gear under its aluminum body. Three were built.
7. Restyled "lion-hearted" Chryslers had channeled roofs separated by a stainless-steel band.

7

1

2

3

1. Once again, the Adventurer served as DeSoto's most invigorating model. Only 590 coupes were produced, along with a mere 97 convertibles. **2.** A Firedome four-door sedan started at $3234. Ornate styling was most evident up front, led by a two-section bumper and new grille. **3.** Mid-range Firedome interiors seemed inviting, but the faltering DeSotos looked too much like Chryslers—and cost nearly as much. **4.** A new 383-cid V-8 with dual four-barrel carburetors entered Adventurers, yielding 350 horsepower. **5.** Less-potent renditions of the 383-cid engine powered Firedome (shown) and Fireflite models.

> "DeSoto is looking forward to a rising long-range demand for its cars."
>
> *DeSoto general manager*
> **J. B. Wagstaff**; *March 1959*

4

5

1959 DeSoto

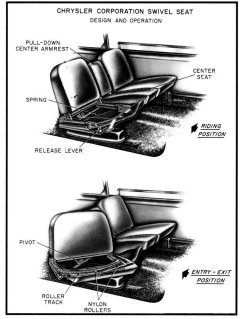

CHRYSLER CORPORATION SWIVEL SEAT
DESIGN AND OPERATION

PULL-DOWN
CENTER ARMREST

CENTER
SEAT

SPRING

RIDING
POSITION

RELEASE LEVER

PIVOT

ENTRY - EXIT
POSITION

ROLLER
TRACK

NYLON
ROLLERS

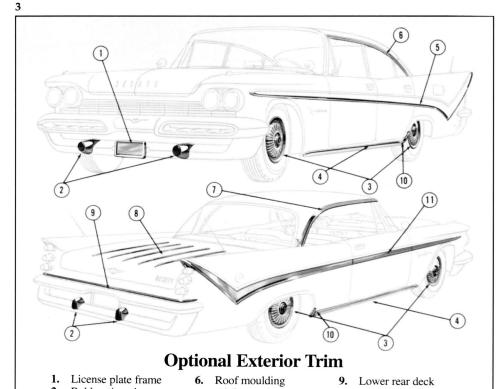

Optional Exterior Trim

1. License plate frame	6. Roof moulding (4 door sedan)	9. Lower rear deck panel moulding
2. Rubber-tipped bumper guards	7. Roof moulding (2 door Sportsman)	10. Stone shield
3. Wheel covers	8. Deck lid accent stripes	11. Anodized aluminum insert
4. Sill mouldings		
5. Color sweep moulding		

1. Nine-passenger Explorer station wagons came in both the Fireflite and Firesweep series, with an $850 price difference.
2. Optional swivel seats rotated outward to a 40-degree angle. 3. The extensive options list allowed a DeSoto to be customized to its owner's taste. 4. Hundreds of towns looked at least a bit like Murphysboro, Illinois, as pictured from the courthouse steps. Note the $2 hotel rooms. Before the advent of major discount chains, small department stores occupied many a downtown corner.

1

2

3

4

5

1-2. A luxurious Dodge Custom Royal Lancer hardtop coupe started at $3201, with 6278 built. This one has the 383-cid D-500 engine, but a Ram-Fire 361 was standard. A comparable Coronet cost $437 less and outsold the Custom Royal Lancer by more than three to one. **3.** Drivers needed to do more than push buttons, but they faced a new elliptical steering wheel and color-coded speedometer, as well as the TorqueFlite control panel. **4.** Six-window styling marked the $3145 Custom Royal four-door sedan, of which 8925 were produced. **5.** This Regal Lancer hardtop might have been the successor to the fancy 1958 Special of that name. Sadly, the proposal was scuttled in April 1958 due to Chrysler's financial ills. The prototype wore unique bodyside moldings with inserts, special roof trim, and other styling deviations.

1

3

2

4

5

1-2. Production of the Dodge Custom Royal Lancer convertible, starting at $3422, dropped a bit to 984 cars. This Canary Yellow ragtop sports twin rear antennas ahead of the tacky-look tailfins, as well as a six-way power seat with swivel operation. Underhood sat Dodge's 383-cid, 345-horse-power Super D-500 dual-quad engine with a high-lift cam. **3.** More than 16,000 Dodge buyers accepted the invitation and paid $70.95 for Swing-Out Swivel Seats. **4.** As you swung your legs into the car, the swivel seat followed and locked into position. **5.** With swivel seating, the center section was fixed in place for three-passenger occupancy—or it folded down as a central armrest. **6.** Some deemed the latest Dodges garish—a virtual caricature of 1957-58 styling, exemplified by the exaggerated fins and Jet-Trail taillights in chrome-bezel tubes. Despite such criticism, shoppers took kindly to the new Dodges. Output rose 13 percent, moving the division up to eighth place in the industry.

6

1. With a fresh front end aiming to impart a sense of motion, the Imperial Crown Southampton hardtop sold about as well as the lower-priced Custom. 2. Base Imperials got a Custom badge. 3. A Custom sedan cost $5016, as did the more popular hardtop sedan. 4. An Imperial Crown sedan brought $5647. 5. Both the LeBaron Southampton hardtop and pillared sedan listed at $6103. 6. Imperial styling had never been more distinct from other Chrysler makes. 7. Imperials adopted a 413-cid V-8, belting out 350 horsepower. 8-9. Ghia continued to issue Crown Imperial Limousines—seven this year—with a $15,075 price tag and 149.5-inch wheelbase. Weighing almost three tons, the luxury boat stuck with the Hemi V-8. Each had a division window, jump seats, and padded rear roof. 10. Britain's Queen Elizabeth II and Prince Philip greeted crowds from a special Imperial.

> **"**Had it not been for the steel scarcity, we would have had the best fourth quarter in Imperial history. **"**
>
> *Chrysler and Imperial general manager* **C. E. Briggs**; *December 1959*

1959 Plymouth

1

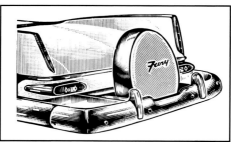

2

5

3

4

6

1-2. Intended as a glamorous rival to Chevrolet's initial Impala, the Plymouth Sport Fury convertible started at $3125. Note the Sport Deck simulated spare tire between the tall fins. The Belvedere series also included a ragtop. **3.** Sport Fury moldings held a textured aluminum insert. Owners got a "Made Expressly For . . ." dash plaque. **4.** A new grille and front end, with wrapover windshield, led Plymouth's facelift. **5.** J. C. Whitney's catalog offered this Continental kit. **6.** Fury models had a standard 230-bhp, 318-cid V-8, an engine destined to appear in many future Plymouths.

1-2. A 260-bhp, 318-cid V-8 was standard under Sport Fury hoods, but many got a Golden Commando 361-cid V-8 that produced 305 horsepower. Hardtops began at $2927. Swivel buckets were standard.
3. George J. Huebner Jr. (*left*), executive engineer in charge of research, and engineering vice president Paul C. Ackerman, examine the experimental Turbine Special at Chrysler's Engineering Building. Running on diesel fuel in this Fury, the engine achieved 19.39 mpg on a 576-mile run from Toledo, Ohio, to Woodbridge, New Jersey. 4. Top-selling Plymouth was the $2283 Savoy sedan, with 84,272 going to buyers. 5. Sport Suburban wagons served in the 'burbs and the great outdoors, hauling six or nine passengers. 6. Disappearing rear windows in station wagons could be controlled from the driver's seat.

1959 Edsel

Ford Motor Company

Wrapover windshields offer greater glass area

Edsel line includes only Ranger, Corsair, and Villager wagon

All-new engines go into Edsels, including six-cylinder; big 410-cid V-8 is deleted

Edsel now aims at lowest segment of medium-priced field

Edsel drops to 14th in industry

Edsel ceases production in November 1959

Conservative, squared-off Ford design wins styling award at Brussels World's Fair

Ford choices include 332- and 352-cid V-8s with up to 300 bhp—or even a rare 430-cid engine

Luxury Galaxie series with Thunderbird-style roof joins Ford in mid-season, and accounts for 27 percent of production

Ford output rises 47 percent—almost ties Chevrolet for Number One in sales

Ford Thunderbirds can have huge 430-cid Lincoln V-8

Continental is no longer a separate marque from Lincoln

Continental Mark IV line includes Town Car and limousine

Mercury is longer and more sculpted; Turnpike Cruiser gone

1

2

3

4

1-2. Edsel's sole convertible came in the Corsair series. Only 1343 were produced. Corsairs got a new 225-horsepower, 332-cid V-8, but $58 more bought a 303-horse, 361-cid V-8. **3.** Buying an Edsel seemed to make very *good* sense to some shoppers, but the die was cast for the car's quick demise. Essentially reskinned Fords, all Edsels now rode a 120-inch wheelbase. **4.** Shorter dimensions allowed Edsel to advertise easier parking. **5.** Evening wear in an Edsel? Why not? This Corsair four-door hardtop listed at $2885.

5

1

2

3

4

The Last Rites

Jim Barnett Lincoln-Mercury in Savannah, GA, ran this ad in the *Savannah News*. Barnett also placed a black pine coffin in front of his dealership to mark the demise of the Edsel. "Here Lies the Edsel!" was painted in white letters on the coffin, which was flanked by two Edsels. Prices of the dealer's remaining Edsels were slashed in line with the "funeral services."

5

1. Edsel Rangers, including this $2691 hardtop, carried a new 292-cid V-8 that made 200 horsepower; a 145-bhp six could be installed instead. Just 5474 were produced. 2. Top Edsel seller was the $2684 Ranger four-door sedan, with 12,814 rolling off the line. 3. This Ranger two-door sedan's top claim to fame is the name of its owner: Edsel Ford—not related to the Ford Motor Company family. Edsel output totaled 44,891 cars. 4. Nine-passenger Villager station wagons easily outsold their six-seat companions. 5. A Villager wagon and Corsair hardtop matched dimensions at the Ford Proving Grounds.

1

2

3

5

4

6

1. Until the new Galaxie series arrived at midyear, Fairlane 500 was the top model. Ford issued 23,892 Victoria two-door hardtops, at $2537. Ford called its '59s "the world's most beautifully proportioned cars." 2-3. Galaxie Club Sedans started at $2528 and sold well. Ford's outer body panels were new, and much of the inner structure revised, on a 118-inch wheelbase. Taillights reverted to round shape. 4. Economy got a big push in ads, along with roominess—big enough for a man wearing a fedora and his daughter wielding a hula-hoop. 5. Almost 46,000 Ford fans got their hands on a Galaxie Sunliner, which started at $2839. 6. Convertible dashboards matched the body. Windshields curved at the top, for 29-percent more glass area. 7. Workers guide a sedan body onto its chassis. 8. Naturally, Fairlanes could get a Continental kit from J. C. Whitney catalog.

7

8

1. Wearing a fresh horizontal-themed grille, Thunderbird convertibles listed for $3979. Output soared past the 10,000 mark. The automatic top was stowed completely out of sight. **2.** T-Bird hardtops were near-duplicates of '58, but volume rose to 57,195 cars. Buyers could now order Lincoln's 350-horsepower, 430-cid V-8 instead of the 300-bhp, 352-cid engine. **3.** Ranchero car-pickups were based on big Fords for the last time. Interiors compared to a Country Sedan's. **4.** Optional air suspension helped keep a Country Sedan on an even keel, regardless of the load inside. **5.** Campers could survive almost indefinitely with all that gear packed in—and on—this wood-grain-trimmed Country Squire wagon. **6.** The Skokie, Illinois, fire department employed Ford Country Sedan station wagons—and Mack fire trucks.

> 66 We have tried to learn the business and have learned one thing the hard way: It was our business and no one gave a tinker's dam whether we won or lost. 99
>
> *Houston, Mississippi, Ford dealer* **Harry J. Vickery**, *on small dealers' struggles with manufacturers and political legislation; May 1959*

1959 Lincoln

1

2

3

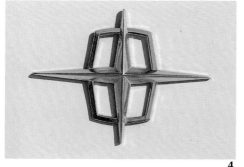

4

1-2. Lincoln's Continental Mark IV series included this $6845 four-door hardtop, plus a hardtop coupe, pillared sedan, and convertible. Defying recent trends, Lincoln's 430-cid V-8 dropped to 350 bhp. 3. All instruments sat ahead of the Continental driver, who faced an upright-looking dash. Upholstery conveyed subtle elegance.
4. Billed as the "world's most admired car," Continentals featured a reverse-sloped, retractable back window.

1

1. Hess & Eisenhardt, an Ohio specialty coachbuilder, turned the Continental Mark IV into a divider-window Limousine with a $10,230 sticker. The company also issued a $9208 Town Car, with the same padded landau-style roof and tiny rear privacy windows. Stately interiors in leather and gray broadcloth imparted a conservative demeanor, but held plenty of amenities. Finished only in Presidential Black, these formal machines were built in small numbers: 49 limos and 78 Town Cars. 2. A Lincoln Capri four-door hardtop cost $5090, as did the slower-selling pillared sedan. Premieres came in the same body styles. Lincoln had its own grille texture, but shared front-end changes with Continental. Ads pushed classic beauty, craftsmanship, prestige—plus "sheer elegance." 3. Ford car/truck chief Robert S. McNamara (center) looks pleased with the corporation's full '59 line: Ford, Thunderbird, Edsel, Lincoln, and Mercury.

2

3

1959 Mercury

1

3

Makes you feel good just looking at it, or sitting in it

'59 MERCURY
Planned for People

2

1. Wrapover windshields gave Mercury 60-percent more glass area. Each model displayed a fresh grille and restyled trim. Mercury issued 6713 Montclair four-door hardtops, starting at $3437 with a 322-horsepower, 383-cid V-8 engine. 2. Economy got more emphasis, though Mercury ads focused mainly on the joys of driving a spacious convertible. The monstrous 400-horsepower engine option was gone. 3. A Colony Park station wagon seated six and started at $3932, with 5929 built. Note the woodgrain trim. Transmission tunnels shrunk in size for more legroom, accomplished by moving the engine and wheels forward. 4. Toll booths weren't yet common, but appeared here and there. This one stood along the Turner Turnpike between Oklahoma City and Tulsa.

4

1

2

3

AMERICA'S LIVELIEST LUXURY CAR

1. Top-of-the-line Mercury was once again the Park Lane, its 430-cid V-8 engine detuned to 345 horsepower. Convertibles cost $4206—1254 were built. **2.** A Park Lane two-door hardtop went for $3955, with 4060 produced. **3.** Longer and roomier this year, with a lowered hood, Mercs weren't quite as lively as before but managed to exude luxury for a moderate entry fee. **4.** Drive-in movies had existed since 1933 and continued to draw crowds—both whole families and just teens, most often in couples and groups. Cartoons and coming attractions typically preceded the feature movies, as at this Gary, Indiana, outdoor theater.

4

> 66 The factory just ain't building many lower-priced units. 99
>
> **Unidentified California new-car dealer**, *lamenting the paucity of American "economy" models desired by recession-scarred buyers; February 1959*

1959 Buick

General Motors Corporation

Four-door hardtops get flat roofs and "picture window" wraparound back glass

Buick line is renamed: LeSabre, Invicta, Electra, Electra 225

Buicks wear "delta-wing" canted fins, which are reflected in front-end shape

Buicks offer new 401-cid V-8

Buick drops from fifth to seventh in production race

Cadillacs carry new 390-cid V-8 and wear towering fins

Eldorados no longer display unique tail treatment

Bigger Chevrolet body flaunts "batwing" rear deck—far more radical than this year's Ford

Chevrolet's 119-inch wheelbase is the longest yet

Impala is now a full top-of-the-line Chevrolet series, sending Bel Air down a notch; Pontiac's Bonneville series also expands

Chevrolets can have close-ratio four-speed manual

Chevrolet finishes first again, with output up 28 percent—but Ford nips at its heels . . . both makes top 1.4 million cars

Oldsmobiles have Air-Scoop flanged brake drums for quicker cooling and less fade

Pontiac introduces split-grille design and Wide-Track stance

1

2

3

4

1. Electra 225 designated Buick's new posh series, displacing the Roadmaster. Canted headlights flanked yet another chromed-square grille. 2. Electra 225 convertibles sold well, with 5493 built carrying a $4192 sticker. The "225" stood for the length of the stretched body. 3. Sharply curved back glass gave a four-door Electra 225 hardtop good visibility. 4. Folks in '59 evidently got a lot more than a car when they bought a Buick. According to ads, at any rate, ownership of a LeSabre, Invicta, or Electra "proclaims your good judgment, your good taste [and] says wonderful things about you." This year's Buick was "so new," said General Manager Edward T. Ragsdale, that "it had to have new series names."

1

2

3

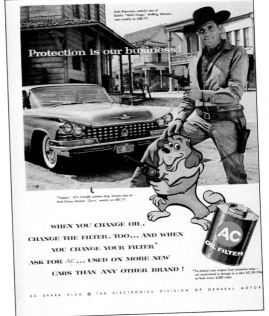

Protection is our business!

WHEN YOU CHANGE OIL,
CHANGE THE FILTER, TOO... AND WHEN
YOU CHANGE YOUR FILTER'
ASK FOR AC... USED ON MORE NEW
CARS THAN ANY OTHER BRAND!

AC SPARK PLUG ⊕ THE ELECTRONICS DIVISION OF GENERAL MOTORS

5

4

BUICK
OFFICIAL
PACE CAR

MAY 30,1959
APOLIS 500 MILE RACE

6

1. LeSabre was billed as "the thriftiest Buick," Invicta "the most spirited." This LeSabre hardtop cost $2849. 2. LeSabres got a 364-cid V-8, rated 250 bhp. Buick issued 10,489 LeSabre convertibles, at $3129. 3. This LeSabre hardtop sedan shows off its wraparound rear window. 4. Buick's bread-and-butter model was the LeSabre sedan, with 51,379 produced. 5. AC advised an oil-filter change every 5000 miles. TV gunslinger Dale Robertson starred in the Buick-sponsored *Wells Fargo* series. 6. An Electra 225 paced the Indy 500 race, won by Rodger Ward.

1

2

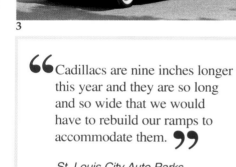

3

> **"**Cadillacs are nine inches longer this year and they are so long and so wide that we would have to rebuild our ramps to accommodate them. **"**
>
> *St. Louis City Auto Parks vice-president* **Wayne Stedelin**, *on his firm's instruction to its attendants not to accept 1959 Cadillacs for parking; October 1958*

4

5

1-2. Eldorados lost their unique tail treatment and wheels. Both the Biarritz convertible and Seville hardtop cost $7401. Output totaled 1320 and 975 cars, respectively. 3. Both Eldos wore wider upper-body chrome moldings, plus block lettering on front fenders. Air suspensions proved to be leak-prone. The enlarged 390-cid V-8 delivered 345 horsepower under Eldorado hoods—an all-time peak for rear-drive Eldos. 4-5. An Eldorado Brougham four-door hardtop wore different fins than other models—a design that would go on all 1960 Cadillacs. Just 99 were built this year, priced at $13,075. Broughams were the first Cadillacs to oust the Panoramic windshield. Dashboards held less chrome, and interiors were a little less lavish, lacking the prior perfume bottles and silver cups. With a 130-inch wheelbase, like most Cadillacs, space was roomy in the rear. Broughams now were built at the Pinin Farina plant in Turin, Italy.

1

2

3

4

6

5

> " Big cars will stay in the fore-front. "
>
> *Cadillac general manager* **James M. Roche**, *on increasing buyer interest in small cars; March 1959*

1. Critics faulted Cadillac's wild fins, but the public liked them. Rear side windows were fixed on hardtop sedans. **2.** To most people, Cadillac still stood for quality. **3.** A Series 62 hardtop went for $4892, but the fancier Coupe de Ville cost $5252. **4.** In addition to the six-window Sedan de Ville, Cadillac offered a four-window model. **5.** More than 11,000 buyers paid $5455 for a Series 62 ragtop. **6.** Doors on the Cyclone show car slid to the rear as the dome opened. Nose cones contained radar.

1959 Chevrolet

1

2

1-2. Impala Sport hardtops and ragtops commanded attention, but Impala was now a full series. With a V-8, the coupe listed at $2717, but a six-cylinder version saved $118. 3. Impala interiors exhibited their top-of-the-line status. 4. Base V-8, for an Impala or any model, was the carryover 283-cid version with 185 horsepower. Ratings up to 290 bhp were available—or a 348-cid V-8 could be installed with as many as 315 horses. 5. An Impala convertible cost $2967 with V-8 power. 6. Fender skirts and a Continental kit might come from the factory—or the J. C. Whitney catalog.

3

4

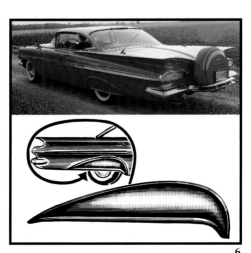

6

5

1

2

3

4

5

1. Corvette production hit 9670 cars. The standard 283-cid V-8 made 230 bhp with options to 290. New trailing radius rods helped during hard acceleration. **2.** A new El Camino car-pickup carried an 1150-pound load. **3.** With a V-8, a Parkwood wagon cost $2867. Chevrolet also had Brookwood, Kingswood, and Nomad wagons. **4.** Plenty of Bel Air sedans held the 235-cid six. **5.** Not everyone called Chevy's deck "saucy" or its grille "elegant." **6.** Danger! Hanging onto a Chevrolet to pick up speed was not a wise move. **7.** A front end takes shape as its fenders and grille drop into position. **8.** That Chevy's driver could have stopped at the Orange Julius stand while awaiting a $1.25 wash.

6

7

8

407

1959 Oldsmobile

1. Super 88 and Ninety-Eight Oldsmobiles earned a bored-out 394-cid V-8 making 315 bhp. This low-slung Ninety-Eight Scenic hardtop cost $4086. Lengths grew ten inches as part of the "Linear Look." 2-3. Top-selling Olds Ninety-Eight was the Holiday hardtop sedan. Note the huge expanse of back glass. 4. Occupants gained four inches of shoulder room. Options included a Safety Sentinel and Autronic Eye. 5. An Olds Ninety-Eight sedan went for $3890. Lower-body sheetmetal was fuller, atop a stronger, wider Guard-Beam chassis. 6. Visibility improved via the new Vista-Panoramic windshield.

First Daytona 500— February 22, 1959

In the final lap of this historic event (*upper left*) at the new Daytona International Speedway, Lee Petty in Oldsmobile number 42 vies for the lead with Johnny Beauchamp. After a photo finish, Beauchamp and his Thunderbird went to Victory Circle. However, four days later (*above*), judges changed their minds and NASCAR head Bill France, Sr., awarded a trophy to Petty.

1

2

3

4

5

6

1. A thin-section roofline is evident in the $3328 Super 88 Scenicoupe. Oldsmobile called its '59s "the most distinctively different models in our 61-year history." 2. Dynamic 88 models got a 371-cid V-8 engine with 270 or 300 horsepower. 3. A sectioned panel made the Super 88 dash look immense. 4. A roll-down rear window eased access to the cargo area of a Super 88 Fiesta wagon. 5. Print ads promoted coming TV programs, such as Bing Crosby's golf tournament sponsored by Oldsmobile. 6. Shoppers in Louisville, Kentucky, might have bought an Olds at this dealership.

1959 Pontiac

1

1-2. One of four Bonneville body styles, the $3257 two-door hardtop was outsold by the Vista hardtop sedan. **3.** New Wide-Track engineering increased tread width by nearly five inches, greatly improving stability. Pontiac's claim to have "broken all bonds of traditional styling and engineering" turned out to be valid. **4.** Bonnevilles contained plenty of dashboard brightwork, along with colorful upholstery. **5.** Crisply styled on all-new bodies and introducing the split-grille theme that would become its trademark, the '59s established the pattern for Pontiac performance in the Sixties. Wide-Track Pontiacs really did rank among the most roadable American cars. **6.** Bonneville production included 11,426 convertibles, which listed for $3478. Seats were trimmed with leather and jewel-tone Morrokide, with buckets optional.

2

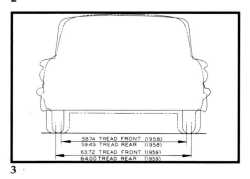

58.74 TREAD FRONT (1958)	
59.43 TREAD REAR (1958)	
63.72 TREAD FRONT (1959)	
64.00 TREAD REAR (1959)	

3

4

5

6

1

2

3

1. Pontiac Catalinas rode a 122-inch wheelbase, two inches shorter than the Star Chief and Bonneville. **2.** Catalina models included a two-door hardtop. **3.** Top seller was the Catalina sedan. This year's V-8 made 245 to 345 horsepower, though a 215-bhp economy engine was also available. **4.** Dealers issued promotional postcards. This Pontiac store served the Camden, New Jersey, area. **5.** Superior Coach Corp. marketed this Cargo Cruiser on a Pontiac chassis, with a stretched 148-inch wheelbase. Priced at $7775, it promised 50 percent more cargo space than a wagon.

5

4

Studebaker-Packard Corporation

Compact Lark introduced—with perfect timing

Lark two-doors and four-doors are built on 108.5-inch wheelbase; wagons ride a 113-inch wheelbase

Body styles include four-door sedan, two-door sedan and wagon, and two-door hardtop

"Standard" Studebakers and the Golden Hawk hardtop coupe are dropped; only the Silver Hawk pillared coupe carries on from '58

Despite fewer model offerings, Studebaker sales skyrocket

Production increases by over 150 percent thanks to new Lark compact—and, oddly, the nation's economic recession

Larks carry dual headlights while most cars have quad headlights

Larks boast large, square grille similar to Hawks

Packards are history, though the name remains in the corporate title

All six-cylinder Larks and Hawks are powered by de-stroked 169.6-cid engine making 90 horsepower; Larks so equipped are designated Lark VI

Eight-cylinder Larks (designated Lark VIII) and Hawks get a 259.2-cid V-8 making 180 or 195 horsepower

Larger 289-cid V-8 from '58 is dropped

1

2

3

> **"** It's the only passenger car I have ever driven that has the feel and handling of a sports car. It's very stabilized, very solid. **"**
>
> *Laguna Beach, California, Studebaker dealer* **Frank M. Darling**, *on Studebaker's "Model X" small car, which debuted for 1959 as the Lark; August 1958*

1. Released during an economic recession, the compact Lark replaced Studebaker's standard line—and more than doubled the company's sales. Six-cylinder models, called Lark VI, brought back the smaller 169.6-cid L-head six last used in '54, now making 90 horsepower. Prices started at $1925 for a DeLuxe two-door sedan. This upscale Regal hardtop coupe sold for $2275 as a six, $2411 with a V-8. **2-3.** Eight-cylinder Larks carried a Lark VIII designation, signifying a 259-cid V-8 with 180 standard horsepower or 195 with the Power Pack. Opting for the V-8 added only about $135 to a Lark's price, but it was available only with Regal trim. In these economy-conscious times, sixes outsold eights by a wide margin.

1

2

3

4

5

6

7

> 66 The year 1959 will have sent production of cars and trucks about 50 percent above the break-even point. 99
>
> *Studebaker-Packard Corp. president* **Harold E. Churchill**, *on S-P's $20 million profit for the model year; September 1959*

1-3. Lark wagons came only in two-door versions for '59. Offered in DeLuxe or Regal trim with six-cylinder or V-8 power, they rode a longer wheelbase than other Larks, 113 inches versus 108.5. 4. These '59 Larks are nearing the end of Studebaker's assembly line in South Bend, Indiana. 5. Leo Newman and Nathan Altman, partners in this South Bend dealership, later went on to buy the rights to build Studebaker's Avanti coupe . 6. The state of Indiana bought 35 Studebakers for government service. 7. Silver Hawks offered the same engine choices as Larks, but Hawk V-8s outsold six-cylinder counterparts. 8-9. Hawk interiors looked sporty with rolled upholstery and tooled metal trim.

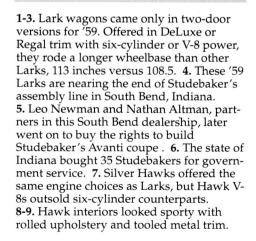

8

9

INDEX

INDEX